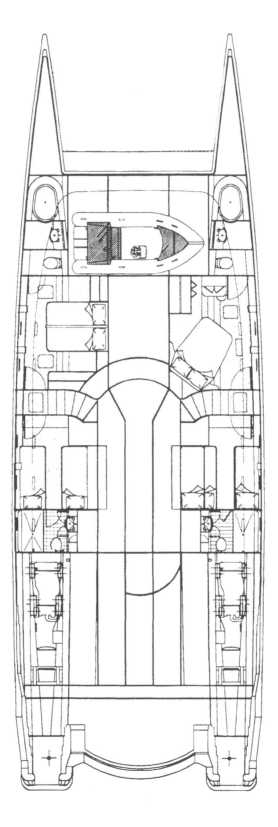

MOANA

118,000 mile odyssey to the world's most remote places

LEW MAURER

Compass Rose Press
2726 Shelter Island Drive, Ste. 151
San Diego, CA 92106
CompassRosePressUSA.com

Book Cover and Interior Design by Monkey C Media
Copyediting by All My Best
Front cover photo by Lew Maurer
Interior photos from the author's personal collection or courtesy of the Marchandise family

First Edition
Printed in South Korea

ISBN: 978-1-7335150-0-9 (hardcover)
ISBN: 978-1-7335150-1-6 (eBook)

Library of Congress Control Number: 2019940013

For Lucyn and Tiara,
My "Two Rascals"

CONTENTS

WORLD MAP

Arctic Circle

Bering

Tropic of Cancer

PACIFIC
OCEAN

Equator

INDIAN
OCEAN

Tropic of Capricorn

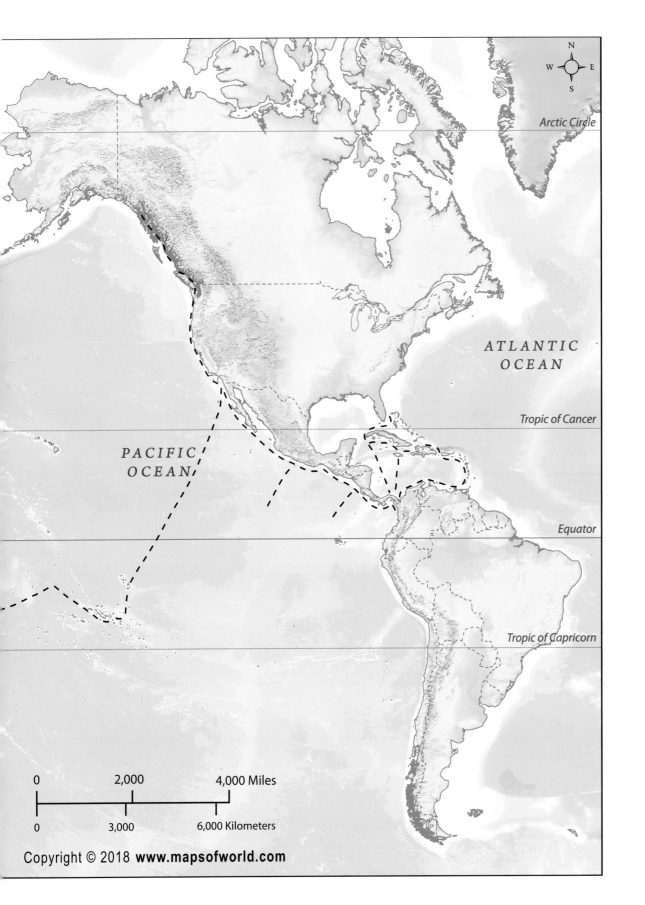

N
W · E
S

Arctic Circle

ATLANTIC
OCEAN

Tropic of Cancer

PACIFIC
OCEAN

Equator

Tropic of Capricorn

| 0 | 2,000 | 4,000 Miles |
| 0 | 3,000 | 6,000 Kilometers |

FOREWORD

I first saw *Moana* and met Lew Maurer in an anchorage in Honiara, the capital of the Solomon Islands. The Solomons were a stop that my wife, Pierrette, and I were making on our sail around the world in our aging 32-foot sailboat.

There were not many boats in the anchorage and the standout among them was a beautiful, 80-foot white, power catamaran: *Moana*. She stood out like a diamond among the raggedy old boats that inhabited the rest of the fleet in the anchorage.

We weren't there long before Lew and his ship's cook, a Frenchwoman, Pascale, came over in their dinghy to introduce themselves. Pierrette was a French-speaking Canadian from Quebec, and she and Pascale formed an immediate friendship. Their friendship led to my friendship with Lew. From him, I learned of the fantastic adventures that had drawn *Moana* to the most remote places on the planet. The boat was owned by a wealthy European who had decided to expose his four young children to a world that few had ever seen, and to do so without sacrificing their educations. The trips were all timed to take advantage of their school vacations. No fancy hotels and yacht clubs for them. The family visited outposts so primitive that most of the natives would never own a pair of shoes nor make a phone call. They visited isolated islands from some of the lesser-known ones off the Cuban coast to those belonging to India in the Bay of Bengal. For fifteen years, they traveled to these places and more: as far north as Alaska and as far south as the South Island of New Zealand. Over the decade and a half they spent exploring, the young children grew into adulthood having experienced adventures and seen places others could only dream of.

Under Lew's experienced and careful stewardship, *Moana* logged a total of 118,000 miles, the equivalent of sailing around the world five times.

Otto J. Lehrack, III
Lieutenant Colonel, United States Marine Corps, retd.
Author, *Road of 10,000 Pains*

INTRODUCTION

"When you meet him, you will do it."

Many times I had reflected on this statement from the lawyers that July day in 1998. Long before 118,100 nautical miles of many oceans passed under the double hulls of the long range, power catamaran *Moana*. Long before the seemingly endless adventures of a fifteen-year odyssey to some of the most remote, wild, and beautiful places on our planet.

They were right.

After many years of dealing with lawyers, I well knew the difference between facts and conjecture, but the man I was to meet was no ordinary man. Michel was a man with an extraordinary dream—and the resources to make it happen. He could well afford to travel the world, visiting all the high-end tourist destinations, and always in the finest accommodations, but his dream was different; it was a dream that would take him and his young family far from the safe and trendy tourist world, to a world experienced by very few.

But first, he needed the boat. A very special boat that could safely take him and his young family across oceans for extended periods, visiting those little specks on the pages of a world atlas, those developing countries and uninhabited or sparsely populated islands where native peoples still paddled out in canoes to greet the rare visitors to their remote villages.

Challenging weather and limited or nonexistent support services would often be the norm, so the boat would need to represent the very best of current design and construction specifications to produce an ultra-reliable, safe, yet sophisticated vessel. A beautiful yacht, with all the features of a five-star hotel, and reflecting his personality, would be finished with understated class and luxury. He and his family would go in style.

I never imagined on that first day when I met his lawyers, that I would be a key player on the team that would make his dream happen. The high-powered law office was on one of the top floors of a modern high rise in downtown San Diego. It occupied an entire floor, and as the elevator doors opened, the entire staff of lawyers was standing in formation, right in front of me. Dressed alike in their expensive suits, they looked to me like a flock of penguins. Serious penguins, however, who looked me up and down with nary a smile.

The smile was mine. I was dressed nicely in my professional "waterfront look," with khaki shorts, my collared "Compass Rose" tee shirt, and white deck shoes; and with a nice, leather briefcase in hand, I was not intimidated. After all, my small surveying and consulting business

Finished galley and salon

enjoyed an excellent reputation on the waterfront. They knew who I was, and they knew they needed me, which was exactly why I was there. With the dress inspection over, we got down to business. And the business at hand was to find someone who could save a boatbuilding project that, just started, was in serious trouble. My first task was to visit the boat yard where the project had started and give them a report on the state of construction and quality of the work.

This set in motion the story of how my company came to build a unique and successful boat, how I came to be the captain, and how three people from different lands and cultures came together to begin an epic and wonderful adventure. While an inseparable part of our story, I have decided to get on with the adventures and place the making of *Moana* at the end of this book, where my fellow captains, boat builders, and waterfront people will enjoy the details of a difficult endeavor.

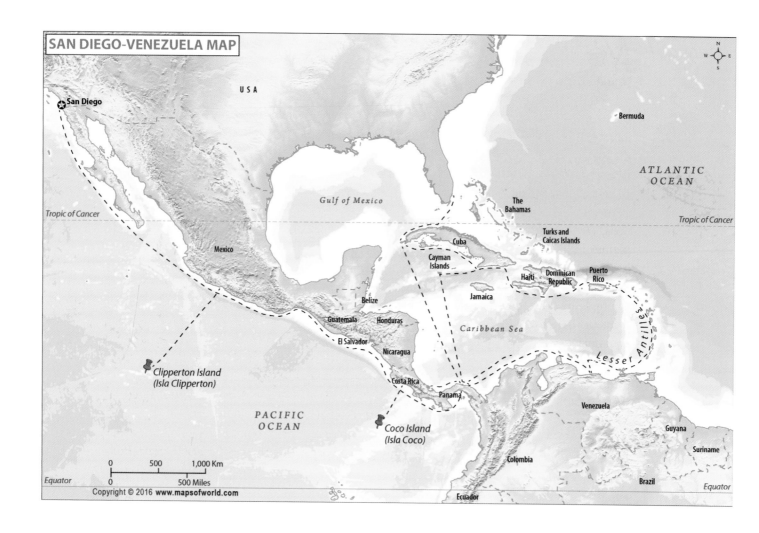

SAN DIEGO-VENEZUELA MAP

USA

San Diego

Bermuda

ATLANTIC
OCEAN

Gulf of Mexico

Tropic of Cancer

Tropic of Cancer

Mexico

Cuba

The
Bahamas

Turks and
Caicas Islands

Cayman
Islands

Haiti

Dominican
Republic

Puerto
Rico

Belize

Jamaica

Guatemala

Honduras

Caribbean Sea

El Salvador

Nicaragua

Lesser Antilles

Clipperton Island
(Isla Clipperton)

Costa Rica

Panama

Venezuela

PACIFIC
OCEAN

Coco Island
(Isla Coco)

Guyana

Suriname

Colombia

Brazil

Equator

0   500   1,000 Km

0   500 Miles

Ecuador

Equator

Copyright © 2016 www.mapsofworld.com

2000
MAIDEN VOYAGE

Michel and his family were from Belgium, and after another cold and rainy winter they were ready for the warm weather of the tropics. For our very first trip, our destination would be Panama and the offshore islands, over 3,000 nautical miles distant.

I found his decision interesting. Yacht harbors are full of boats that never go anywhere, owned by people who talk year after year about going on trips but seldom leave the harbor, and never for a long-range voyage. Michel, on the other hand, seemed to see the world quite differently. He had an amazing dream for his family and had the resources and will to make it happen. They would spend all the children's school vacations and summer vacations aboard the boat, no matter how difficult their journey to the wild, faraway places he wanted to visit.

Long flights from Europe, multiple connections, charter planes, dirt landing strips, pickup-truck taxis, etc., were only part of the complicated challenges he accepted. He researched and planned all the destinations, over a year in advance, in professional detail. As the years went by, I would often tease him about how he could know so much about a country we had yet to visit. "You have a special secretary, just for planning our trips, Michel?" He was unafraid of the significant challenges, danger, and uncertainty that would deter others.

Fuel, oils, spare parts, maintenance supplies, tools, food, dry goods, first aid supplies, safety equipment, fishing and diving gear, electronic and paper charts, navigation supplies, ship's documents, legal needs and insurance, satellite communication accounts, ship's agents for countries to be visited, crew visas, crew personnel and clothes, etc.—the list was daunting, but we somehow got through it, and on March 25, 2000, *Moana* was finally underway. The run to Panama would certainly prove the quality of the boat and crew!

Stories abound of maiden trip disasters such as *Titanic's*, and our maiden voyage was to be longer than hers, over 3,000 nautical miles on a boat with only one day of sea trials. But *Moana* was no ordinary boat. To stack the deck in our favor, we took three of my men from the construction project, and it was a wise decision. We did have some surprises, but with the expertise aboard, we kept everything up and running and pushed hard to reach Panama on schedule. Some tough spots on our course were almost guaranteed, however, and the notorious Gulf of Tehuantepec was at the top of the list.

Captain's log, April 4

1716 position abeam Bahia Grande in 44ft, offshore breeze @ 35kts, gusting higher. Steering difficult, on various courses to transit gulf as close to shore as possible.

2200 position 16°10.8' N, 95°W. Running in 30ft, .5 mi off, in screaming full gale winds. Classic Tehuantepec! Gusts over 60kts heeling boat over, screaming thru upper station mast and pipework. A hand steering nightmare.

The violent gusts of a classic "Tehuantepecker" are an amazing force of nature to behold, and they gave us a lasting memory as *Moana* slowly passed abeam Salina Cruz, on the central Mexico coast. The intense winds, coming all the way from the Caribbean, create nasty, dangerous seas in the offshore waters of the gulf, so running close to the land was common strategy. Only 100 yards off our port side, headlights of cars and our deck lights on blowing sand created an eerie glow in the darkness. As tight to the beach as I dared, in only twenty to thirty feet of water, the gusts hammered us, over and over, heeling the boat at amazing angles. It was then we noticed the port side engine hatch was open, and we realized the wind was so strong that it entered the large air scoop on the cabin side and created so much pressure in the engine room, it blew the hatch open from the inside out! And it was at this time I heard the long, ominous, moaning noise created by extremely high winds through a boat's upper rig. My commercial fishing days were behind me, but some memories are never forgotten.

Captain's log, April 10

1503 pos secured to mooring buoy, Balboa Yacht Club, Panama

A difficult but successful maiden voyage was behind us. Peter, Mike, and John departed that evening. Joubert, our extraordinary engineer and I, and Kari, our young cook, scrambled to get the boat ready for our first trip with the family who were already in Panama and would board the very next morning.

2000

CENTRAL AMERICA, CARIBBEAN

Our first trip with the family aboard was to visit some of the interesting islands off-shore the Pacific coast of Panama, for exploring, fishing, and diving. After the building project, I knew Michel well, but the dynamics of a family, all together in a small space, are definitely an unknown until actually experienced. We had the boat, and we had a great crew, so I was optimistic.

We had arrived only the day before, so getting the boat cleaned up and provisioned was an all-out effort, long into the night. By the time the yacht club fuel dock opened in the morning, we were ready to go, and we idled over to pick up our fuel and the family. It was a beautiful, calm morning in Balboa, and after our 3,200-nautical-mile "sea trial," pushing hard to arrive in time, I was pleased with the boat and my crew. I was confident we had discovered and resolved any major issues with all the equipment and expected a good trip with the family. *Moana* was sparkling clean, and I felt a measure of pride when it was obvious the locals were impressed with our big power catamaran as we came alongside the fuel dock.

My happy dance was suddenly interrupted when, just as we were tying up the boat, the steering system failed completely, confirmed by all the hydraulic oil in the bilge. At that very moment, I counted ten people coming down the dock, instead of the family of six we expected. Now, we had a hydraulic steering problem to fix and another trip to the markets for my cook, before the trip could even begin. What a start!

The hydraulic oil leak turned out to be an easy fix, and it was repaired quickly. The fuel dock sold compatible oil, so we had the system up and running fine in less than two hours. The additional food provisioning, however, required several hours of taxis and markets. Kari, our young cook, was unhappy with the last-minute shopping challenge, made hectic by the lunatic driving habits and streets of Balboa. She was further discouraged because I had told her she would be cooking for the family, plus crew, nine total. Now it would be thirteen, a big number for one cook on a new boat. I felt for Kari.

I was unhappy with Michel. We had discussed how he planned to use the boat from the very start of the project. "We will have only family aboard," was how he described using the boat. His family was six, total, and that is what we had planned for. He was as frustrated as

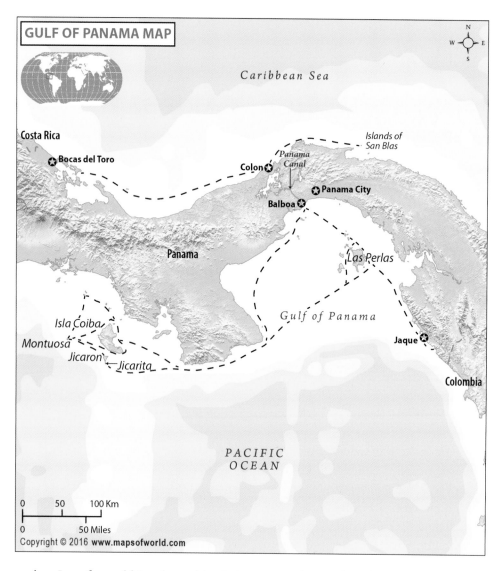

I was when I confronted him about this obvious misunderstanding. "Family," to Michel, was simply that. Sons, daughter, nieces, nephews, brothers, sisters, etc. Except it was far from simple for the crew and the equipment. More people meant more food, more cooking, more load on generators, fresh water pumps, watermakers, clothes washers and dryers, air conditioning, etc. And load equals horsepower equals fuel, so we took on more fuel. Our innocent misunderstanding was luckily and quickly forgotten in the excitement and anticipation of his wife, Martine, and their children. Thomas, Rachel, Louis, and Donald knew only that they were leaving on a wonderful adventure, far from the world of video games and cell phones.

Captain's log, April 11

1643, depart Balboa Yacht Club fuel dock, idling out on various courses, dodging thick commercial ship traffic

The number of ships anchored off Balboa, on the Pacific side of the Panama Canal, is an impressive sight to see. Over one hundred ships of every possible kind—fishing vessel, ferry, or strange commercial vessel—are there. Many of them are in terrible condition and probably will never again make any money for their owners. Many of them fly flags of convenience and are crewed with people from faraway lands, so it is easy to imagine strange cargoes, third-world bank accounts, and phantom owners. Modern, operational ships, inbound or outbound the canal and passing through the crowded anchorage, make it necessary to pay close attention, especially in the dark. Over the years I have found this place fascinating, observing some vessels never moving, and unlit small boats visiting them in the night.

Our first destination was Las Perlas, a group of islands in the Gulf of Panama, southwest of the canal, from thirty-five to fifty miles offshore. Beautiful little islands, many of them uninhabited, they are popular cruising destinations for yachts in Panama. We spent four days there, visiting the islands of Contadora, Galera, and San José.

Thomas (17), Rachel (14), Louis (10), and Donald (8)

Isla Montuosa

Captain's log, April 14

1347, anchor down in 26ft, sand, N side of Isla Galera, in beautiful weather, calm sea

Not long after the above entry, I made another entry in my log:

Galera Island: A beautiful, tropical island, complete with wild sugar cane, palms, a small "lighthouse," and big sandy beach facing to the north. With a big tidal range, dramatic change comes to the island in the form of dangerous surf, very suddenly. Fast current and surrounding rock reefs belie the tranquil appearance of this beautiful island.

As captain, I have the responsibility of keeping everyone aboard safe, at the top of my list. When everyone is off in the dinghy, there is a limit to what I can do, but one of those things is to be vigilant, to watch everyone I can see, for as long as I can. When our anchor went down off Galera Island, Michel and the family all piled into the dinghy. Michel dropped Martine and Donald off on the island, and Michel and the kids went to a nearby reef for snorkeling. When they first arrived on the beach, the sea was calm, and Martine and Donald began exploring and walking around the sand perimeter of the small island. From the pilothouse, I could see the surf on the beach change as the tide rose, and by the time I saw Martine and Donald return to the beach that was very serene only an hour before, I could see a set of large waves on the horizon, bearing down on the island. Martine and Donald were at the bottom of the steep beach, in the worst spot, when the swell hit the island and the big shore break crashed over them. Martine was knocked to her knees, but poor Donald, only eight years old, was pounded into the sand and tumbled over and over, up the beach. Watching helplessly through the binoculars, I was relieved to see he was not seriously hurt.

Aboard the boat, we had a "walkie talkie" locker, where we kept four VHF hand-held radios on their chargers. I tried hard to insist that everyone going ashore, whether in remote islands or just in foreign ports, take a radio. But sometimes in the excitement to explore the remote and beautiful places we visited, not everyone listened to the captain. Had Martine taken a radio with her, I could have warned her of the approaching waves. She never shared their experience on Galera that day, and she did not know I had seen what happened, so we missed a chance to discuss how important the radios were. Far from civilization, paradise can hide tremendous danger.

From Las Perlas, we ran west and north to islands far more wild, and most of them uninhabited. I had visited Islas Jicarita, Jicaron, Coiba, and Montuosa in years past, while passing through on long-range deliveries. On those trips, the crew and I stopped to enjoy a calm anchorage, or to catch a fish for dinner. Now, I would be able to spend some time and really explore these rarely visited islands.

Our first stop was Isla Jicarita, where we anchored in a small bight on the east side of the island. On a previous visit to this very anchorage, my deckhand, while trying to spear a fish for dinner, was chased from the water by very territorial gray reef sharks. This time, uncomfortable swells from the southwest rolled through the anchorage, so after just an overnight stay we departed the next morning for Isla Montuosa.

Over forty nautical miles offshore mainland Panama, Isla Montuosa was just the type of island *Moana* was built to visit. A remote, uninhabited, mysterious place, it was visited only occasionally by fishermen. Poorly charted, with big tides and strong currents and encircled by rock reefs, it was a dangerous island. We found a good spot on the southeast corner of the island and dropped anchor in twenty-seven feet, sand bottom. Immediately we felt the wildness of the island as the current ripped through our anchorage, and we heard an amazing sound come out of the dense, impenetrable vegetation covering the entire island. Although we never found the source of the noise, we suspected the high-volume turbine-like "hum" was probably from thousands and thousands of insects. Combined with the steam rising off the tropical forest and hundreds of seabirds soaring above the single high mountain, Montuosa was indeed wild!

As soon as the anchor went down, standard procedure on *Moana* was to launch the dinghy for exploring, diving, or fishing, and in some cases all of the above. Within minutes of our first day there, a spearfishing group departed for an offshore rock we observed while approaching the island. The rock turned out to be a pinnacle, rising up from 80- to 100-foot depths, to just above the sea surface, with lots of ledges and caves, and swarming with thick schools of jacks, snappers, barracuda, and all manner of reef fish. The water visibility was exceptional, with just enough surge to make it exciting. Thomas was first in the water and, with one look down, let out a yell in his snorkel tube. On his very first dive, he came up with a big cubera snapper and pushed it over the tube and into the dinghy. Two days of diving the rock provided us with plenty of snapper fillets in the deck freezer.

"Standard procedure" with the kids was interesting. The kids, especially Louis and Donald, spent every moment possible in the cockpit fishing and, when it got dark, catching small tropical fish attracted by our underwater fishing lights. As dinnertime approached, Martine

Thomas: Serious waterman, deadly spearfisherman

made the boys come in, take a shower, and get ready for dinner. With dinner over, dressed in their pajamas, the boys would immediately return and continue catching pet fish for the bait tank. We had a big TV aboard and many video cassettes of current movies, but when Martine would finally tell the boys it was bedtime, they begged to catch "just a few more," instead of "The movie's almost over." These were very different kids, with different parents. I was impressed.

We did not see another boat at Isla Montuosa, for good reason. It was poorly charted, and the big tides and ripping current were a real challenge when anchoring. The other reason Isla Montuosa was difficult to visit was because of the nightly offshore breeze. The strong offshore breeze, coming all the way from the mainland, created close, steep, wind-driven seas. The seas were not large, but they were very close together and rolled right through our anchorage. This was not a problem initially because *Moana* simply swung around and came up into the wind and seas, very stable as big catamarans can be. Unfortunately, the breeze went down around 0400 in the morning, the boat swung in the current, parallel to the island, and the wind seas that continued to roll through caught us on the beam and rolled us so much I was forced to raise the anchor and find a temporary anchorage on the other side of the island. Every other boat owner I had worked for would have given up and simply moved, but not Michel. He and his family loved the wildness of Isla Montuosa and the excitement of visiting such a place. The crew and I, with our quarters in the high pilothouse, suffered the most when an anchorage was rolly, so I had to come up with a solution, and a unique double-anchoring system was born.

Moana had an anchor and electric windlass on both port and starboard bows, always ready to go, so we came up with a double-anchoring technique that took advantage of our catamaran configuration. This maneuver was not easy in actual practice, but after a few tries we became very good at it and, most importantly, fast. I sometimes miscalculated drift or did not set up the anchors in the right position, requiring a second attempt, but once we had the anchors down and the bows into the seas, we could change a miserable anchorage into paradise, with quiet, slowly rising and falling seas. Sleeping like babies! Over the years, we used this technique many times, often laughing when boats would sometimes come into our anchorage, only to leave after immediately rolling badly. From another boat, it was usually impossible to see our stern line, so I am sure some people wonder to this day how *Moana* could defy the forces of nature and lay at anchor so calmly.

First yellowfin tuna for Louis

Captain's log, April 18

1545 to 1635, fishing tuna in big dolphin school

Underway for Isla Coiba, we came upon a big school of spinner dolphins, accompanied with petrels, a sea bird known to follow feeding dolphins. As a former commercial fisherman, I knew immediately the chances would be good that yellowfin tuna would also be with this species of dolphins, following below. We began trolling tuna lures and immediately caught several in the twenty- to thirty-pound range. I will always remember this day because, as I was bringing a tuna aboard by grabbing the line and swinging the fish aboard, it slammed into Donald, who had quietly come behind me and had no idea what was coming. Poor Donald was down again, fish blood and scales flying, but he never lost his nerve or sense of humor.

Next, we visited Isla Coiba, a large island with an unusual history. It was a prison island for many years and at the time of our visit housed over 100 inmates. The government recently declared the island a national park, but it was still a penal colony with murderers and rapists freely wandering around. Only the ranger station was safe to visit, so our stay was only an overnight anchorage. We were told the government was going to relocate all the prisoners and develop the island for tourism, so we marked the island for future trips and moved on.

We finished our first trip with the family aboard with visits to Isla Brincanco and Isla Jicaron. Brincanco was too close to the mainland and the water was not clear, so we ran offshore again to Isla Jicaron, where we enjoyed the beautiful, uninhabited island in perfect weather, with white sand beaches, blue water, and great fishing and diving.

Captain's log, April 21

0756 position abeam Punta Mala, .5 mi in stiff breeze 25+ kts, and steep, 4–6ft seas on bow, A/C to 030°

We fought our way around "Bad Point" again and by 1513 arrived in Balboa and picked up a mooring at the Balboa Yacht Club. As I shook Michel's hand and wished him a safe trip home, he smiled and said, "You know, Lew, it was a very good trip, and not just because it was the first trip." The crew and I agreed, and we were very appreciative of his heartfelt thanks. It was indeed, a very good trip. We had learned a lot about Michel and the family, and it was very positive. It seemed the entire family shared a fantastic thirst for adventure.

It was my first glimpse of the man with the extraordinary dream.

2000
PANAMA CANAL

After our first trip, we moved *Moana* to a small marina behind the Miramar Hotel in downtown Panama City. The hotel was new and beautiful, but the marina was a great example of the terrible engineering and planning often found in developing-world countries. At low tide all the water ran out, and the marina became a huge mud flat, with all the boats lying on their bottoms. A huge dredge was brought in to remove all the mud, but it was discovered the mud was only a thin layer covering a rock bottom. Before the hotel was built, the rocks could have been broken up with dynamite and heavy equipment and removed, but now it was too late. What could have been a beautiful downtown marina was forever doomed to be a classic engineering failure. The hotel hired a small dredge to suck out the mud around a dozen boats on their dock, so we were floating most of the time, but we could come and go only at high tide.

Preparing for a transit through the Panama Canal caused me to look up an old friend, Pete Stevens. Pete was a legend, and unquestionably the best ship's agent in Panama. I had first used his services in the mid-'70s, when I was delivering commercial shrimp boats from the Gulf states to an emerging shrimp fishery in the Pacific Northwest. I continued to use Delfino, his company, over the years, while passing through on yachts. This included a historic trip in January of 1990 on a yacht named *Tango Amour,* which arrived in Cristobal on the Caribbean side of the canal at the very time US forces invaded Panama to oust Manuel Noriega, the very unpopular dictator of the country. *"Piña"* (Spanish for pineapple, a description of his acne-scarred face) was holed up in the Nunciatura, or Vatican Embassy, and bullets were flying in the streets. Boats had been stuck on both sides of the canal, anchored while waiting for hostilities to end. I assumed we would be waiting as well, but Pete had connections and informed me we would transit the very next day. "Connections" was an understatement. I later learned Pete had modified our papers, identifying the boat as a CIA vessel, with top military clearance, and even requesting a military escort. It was almost hilarious the next day, to be cruising across Gatun Lake with high speed gunboats on each side, and a helicopter gunship hovering over us. Even while inside the locks, young Marines with wild looking weapons stood guard on the wall tops and made sure we had no problems. To my knowledge, *Tango Amour* was the only yacht to transit the canal during the fighting.

Marina mud bath at low tide

It was great to catch up on old times and to get the latest info on life in Panama. This included getting the name of the best taxi driver in the city. "Taxi Billy" became our driver and a good friend. He was as honest and dependable as he was colorful, and considering his flashy dress and personality, that meant a lot! Billy could find anything and everything we needed, and he knew every back-street shortcut to get it done quickly. And like taxi drivers worldwide, he was a great source of information on just about everything going on in the country. One of his first questions was, "What was your President Carter thinking about when he gave the canal back to Panama?" Billy explained it ruined the Panamanian economy when the US shut down all the military bases, sending thousands of US servicemen and millions of dollars home. For Billy, the good times taking all the military from one nightclub to another were gone. His business, and the local economy in general, was in the tank. Without US expertise, maintenance of the canal spiraled down, accidents began to happen, and the future of the Panama Canal looked questionable.

Our first transit with *Moana* included the *Ocean Master,* a high-end twenty-seven-foot sport fisher Michel wanted to tow behind *Moana.* The concept was to have the ability to fish offshore spots while most of the family remained aboard *Moana*, anchored inshore for diving and exploring. Pete had to grease some palms, but he got us permission to tow the small boat through the canal. With the current problems in the canal, he thought it would be the last time a yacht would be allowed to take a small boat alongside or on tow. As it turned out, we got a great pilot, and the forty-seven-mile transit was uneventful.

Captain's log, June 17

Anchor aboard, dep "The Flats," Panama Canal, 0715. Idling outbound, NNW courses, with Ocean Master *on long tow astern*

Venezuela, with its beautiful offshore islands, was to be our next trip. After several thousand miles on the boat and equipment, we were confident surprises were behind us, and we looked forward to a good trip. We were very wrong, and the trip from hell awaited.

Nina, our new cook, had problems with motion sickness, so with 800 miles of what I knew would be a tough slog, I hired a second deckhand to help with the run to Venezuela. José was a young Costa Rican surfer and born waterman. He was strong as a bull, smart, and a real team player.

The run from Panama to Venezuela, going east along the coasts of Panama and Columbia, is a well-known ass-kicker. The strong northeast trade winds and the South Equatorial Current are compressed as they reach the northeast coast of South America, and they combine to create brutal head seas for anyone trying to fight their way south along the east coast of South America. In winter months, passing cold fronts from the north shut off the strong trade winds for brief periods, permitting the transit we were contemplating; but this was mid-June, and my weather routing experts said there would be no chance for calm weather for months to come. In fact, they predicted the best we could expect would be head seas of eight feet and strong trades at twenty-five knots, with far worse possible with the coming summer months. And we would be towing a twenty-seven-foot sport fisher.

In years before on different boats, I had towed small boats on many occasions, for short runs in moderate weather. Depending on conditions, it was sometimes okay, but my personal experiences taught me it was not a good idea, a view shared with all of my captain friends. But Michel had purchased a very impressive, high-tech, and fast sport fisher he knew would be great to fish in the wild places we would visit. I expressed doubt about it, but Michel wanted to try, so we set up *Moana* with a very professional approach to the situation. Heavy duty towing tangs, high tensile shackles, and very long tow lines on a bridle kept the assembly underwater, providing a smooth towing force that worked well in moderate sea conditions. *Moderate.*

Captain's log, June 18, 2000

1300 pos 9° 50' N, 78° 31.3' W. SOG 10kts in 6–8ft seas, occasionally 10ft. Variable breezes, now picking up from N, 6–8kts. Ocean Master *towing OK, but bouncing on big sets.*

Captain's log, June 19

Underway in Caribbean Sea, offshore Panama/Columbia border in miserable, pounding seas, zero visibility and intense rain squalls. Gusting winds in squalls to 40 kts. 0000 pos 10° 50.9' N, 77° 16.8 W', drop RPM to 915, SOG only 7.3kts. Strobe on Ocean Master *out 0800 pos 11° 25.1' N, 76° 34.4' W, in miserable, dangerous traveling weather. Seas to 15ft, boat bucking and pitching, very hard to move about. Engine room inspections dangerous 1100 pos 11° 34.6' N, 76° 22.4' W. Seas now breaking, spindrift starting to run down faces of waves. 40kts! Miserable.*

* * *

Captain's log, written June 23, 2000, at anchor in Cayos Holandes, San Blas Islands, Panama:

As night fell on the 19th, the breeze came down on us like a hammer, but I felt we were ready. Years of experience told us how to prepare, and we checked and rechecked everything. We were a floating fortress, ready for the onslaught, which came with east-northeast winds steady at forty to forty-five knots on northeast seas fifteen to twenty feet. Gusts at the breaking crests were blowing spindrift airborne, with some swells over twenty feet. SOG (speed over ground) was reduced to 2.7 knots to reduce impact after going over swell crests and crashing at the bottom, and to reduce the tendency of our sharp bows to penetrate the next wave, which put too much heavy water on deck. The Ocean Master *was not visible during most of this period, occasionally bursting through the crests, completely airborne. Framed with spray, and surreal in our deck lights, it appeared and disappeared, ghostlike, far astern.*

On the 20th, at 0623, we drove through a towering swell. At the time, our speed over the bottom was only 4.7 knots, but the impact, which almost stopped the boat, was shocking. The top eight feet of the swell engulfed the entire forward area of the boat, slamming against the cabin, cascading up and exploding over the pilothouse, and landing in the wake astern. With the engines immediately at idle, we checked to see if everything was okay, and at that time, realized the Ocean Master *had broken free of the towline and was not in sight. Idling downwind, with breaking seas and white water all around, it was very difficult to find the white boat, and the extreme sea clutter prevented the radar from "seeing" her radar reflector. After backtracking more than two miles, it was José, with the eyesight of an eagle, who spotted her. She had broken free from the towline when the safety wire failed and the pin in the high tensile shackle backed out.*

José being thrown around like a rag doll

With the terrible conditions at hand, we knew reconnecting the towline would be extremely difficult. After approaching close, José donned a ski jacket, swam to the boat, and pulled himself into the cockpit. I swung the stern of Moana *very close, and Joubert threw a ¾ line to José, who tied it off on a forward cleat. Now, we had a line to the* Ocean Master, *but it was just to capture her. Both the line and the cleat were far too weak for towing. We needed to reconnect the heavy towline to the special towing ring, located on the stem, just above the waterline. It could not be reached from above, so it would have to be reconnected from the water.*

Wrestling the heavy line, with huge thimble and shackle into place, long enough to install and start the threads on a pin, proved to be difficult and dangerous to the extreme. Unfazed by the conditions, José again swam to the boat, pulling the towline behind. Strong as a bull and fearless in his natural environment, he tried over and over to get the shackle connected, but the fury of the elements was too much. We watched in fear and awe as he was thrown around like a rag doll but continued to attempt the impossible. After more than two hours, he found enough strength to once again pull himself into the cockpit of the boat, and rested. Too tired to make the return swim, he rested for a very long time.

Hours later, and with slightly less fearful weather, Joubert came up with Plan B. A window maintenance harness with snap shackle and a large adjustable wrench were attached over José's ski jacket, and with no hesitation, he swam back to the Ocean Master. José was able to connect the snap shackle to a small ring above the towing ring, and was then held in position, with both hands free to make the connection. With José hanging like a puppet on the maintenance harness, we held our breath as the wildly swinging boat snapped José around with deadly force. Somehow he held on, got the pin in the shackle, and tightened it as best he could. It was a show of strength, courage, and determination we would never forget.

It was a long and miserable day. We never had a chance to eat, and now we were soaked to the skin and exhausted. With the wild boat motion, Nina was seasick beyond any hope of food preparation, and glued to her berth. This was probably just as well, because in all likelihood, she would have been thrown off her feet and badly hurt. The proof of this was immediately apparent when we shuffled in, off the deck, like beaten soldiers, and saw the condition of the boat interior. In spite of our efforts to secure every last item, it was a mess. A million shards of glass were all that remained of the (latched and taped) tempered glass door to our main electrical panel, the TV had exploded inside its (latched) cabinet, and the coffee machine had somehow vaulted out of the sink and self-destructed in pieces all over the galley floor.

At idle, we coasted down swell, making the boat stable, and giving the crew time to clean up and find a way to get something to eat. It was at this time I discovered my engine controls were not working properly. The engines were going in and out of gear, and at the same time my pilothouse electronics were all failing, one by one. The electrical panel confirmed the DC batteries that powered the electronics and many other systems were slowly dying. I stared at the instruments, not believing this could be possible. With huge alternators on each main engine, and two battery chargers, we had four individual units, each powerful enough to maintain heavy loads on the batteries, and each backing up the others in a fail-safe electrical system.

The image of a dead boat drifting helplessly at sea competed at laser speed with logic. Although sleep deprived, exhausted, cold, and hungry, the facts of our situation went around and around in my head: My company built the boat. I was involved with the engineering of all the systems, and I knew them down to the smallest parts. How could I not know why all of the charging components failed, and all at the same time?

And now we were drifting beam-to the seas, taking a beating from the breaking crests, hanging on at all times, and tormented by the horrific, continuous, and nerve-wracking noise inside. The impact of the seas against the composite hulls and under the wing deck sounded like one explosion after another. Beaten down and desperate for sleep, we had the solution for at least this situation. For just this type of emergency, we had aboard a sea anchor, the same type I had used many times while commercial fishing, years before. Essentially a huge, heavy-duty parachute, it was fabricated specifically for use at sea in severe conditions. In the strong winds, it was tough to get it in the water without its being blown back, over the boat, but we were careful and managed to shoot it successfully.

In the clear, blue-purple water of the Caribbean, we could see the parachute open underwater, like a huge, lovely flower, but the situation allowed only a moment of distraction before the heavy-duty line came taught with intense force. Moana swung hard into the seas and breeze, the long line stretching and groaning under the force of holding fifty tons into the elements. From the 'chute, the heavy-duty line came back to a long bridle, attached to the bows, which split the load and kept the boat into the wind; but as the very next crest broke over us, the extreme pressure on everything made us question how long it would last. But last, it did, and my crew collapsed in their berths and fell instantly asleep. For me, there were too many things, even in my completely exhausted state, running wild in my head, forcing me to go to the engine rooms, battery lockers, electrical panel, and on and on. In the pilothouse, at almost midnight, both the smoke alarms and the equipment alarm system suddenly shrieked, weakened, and then went silent, signaling a loss of power to the point of total failure. I shook my head, and thought, "Like a death rattle."

In the pilothouse, isolated from the rest of the electrical system, we had two batteries, making up an emergency bank that would provide power to our communication electronics. These batteries were intentionally high in the boat, in the pilothouse, where they would continue to function, even on a sinking vessel; a feature found on many of the fishing boats I grew up on. I called Debbie on our satellite phone and let her know our situation, shut down the emergency batteries, and slept the sleep of the dead for four hours.

At 0915 the next morning, we found the problem. When we impacted the huge swell the morning before, the batteries shifted in their box with such force, a solid copper bar that connected the batteries in series, broke in half. We had looked for this problem but previously did not see the break, which separated the bar by only a fraction of an inch. Four hours of sleep, several cups of coffee, and renewed determination caused a close inspection of the batteries that revealed the "simple" cause of our torment. The break in the copper connector, in effect, disconnected the batteries from all our charging equipment. All of our equipment was fine; they simply could not "see" the batteries. We fabricated and installed a short cable to replace the copper bar, and problem solved.

By 1000, our situation had changed completely, and we were underway once again, but after crashing over the very first swell at only four knots, I had enough. Enough, enough, enough! The safety of my crew, and the integrity of the boat, along with knowing the shackle on the towline, *in all likelihood, would fail again, made for an easy decision. Hot showers, clean clothes, hot food, and precious sleep were the order of the day, as we slowly ran downhill, back to Panama. The* Ocean Master *towed poorly, catching the momentum of the big swells, running down the wave faces, and almost capsizing at the bottoms before the towline came taught again. It was hard to watch, as the wild episode was repeated, over and over. In these large, steep, and close seas, towing was a big mistake.*

The next day, we anchored again at Kayos Hollands, in the San Blas Islands of Panama. In the calm water of the beautiful anchorage, we did a thorough inspection of the boat and all her systems. We had endured a terrible beating and some damage was possible, especially to the underside of the structure we call the wing. The wing connects the hulls of a catamaran, and bears the brunt of heavy weather, especially head seas. To our relief, the damage to this area was minor. The cowling that housed the lower unit and propeller of the dinghy outboard had been torn off completely, and docking lights were blown out of their housings, but there was no structural damage. The electrical panel door, the TV, and the coffee machine were destroyed, but the boat had survived well and emerged almost unscathed.

Sadly, the same could not be said for the Ocean Master. *Crashing through the seas, into the full gale winds, had driven salt water into every imaginable crack and crevice, every electrical connection, and filling the bilges over and over again. Such was the power of the wind and water, it somehow found its way inside the exhaust system, and ultimately into the intake manifold of the engine. The next time we tried to start the engine, it was severely damaged.*

* * *

Captain's log, June 24, 2000
1220 pos 9° 40.04' N, 79° 26.7' W, off Escribanos Shoals, A/C to 266° in good traveling weather. High speed, aluminum gunboat with Panama flag approaching on port bow. Crew is armed, 50 caliber machine gun at bow is manned. We are ordered to follow the gunboat to Isla Grande.

In the lee of Isla Grande, we were amazed to find a secret, completely camouflaged command post and small fleet of heavily armed, high-speed gunboats all around us. It was like a Hollywood action movie, but in real life! This was a serious anti-smuggling operation. After a thorough inspection and surrendering our passports, armed and very serious officers ordered us to proceed directly to Panama. I was nervous about surrendering our passports, but they were returned to us the following day in Panama.

The trip from hell was finally, mercifully, over.

Venezuela, from Panama, was simply not a good idea, especially at this time of year, so Michel came up with Plan B. We would visit the interesting and beautiful islands of San Blas and Boca del Toro, offshore Panama. We left the *Ocean Master* with a trusted mechanic and waited for the family and guests to arrive.

Captain's log, July 19, 2000

Dep Panama Canal Yacht Club, 1025, idling outbound in hot sunshine, cloudy sky, heavy ship traffic. CC 300°, clear with Cristobal Signal to enter outbound lane.

With the family aboard, we ran down the coast of Panama to the "Comarca de San Blas," the land and offshore islands of the Kuna Indians. No one knows for sure where the Kuna came from, but they have lived in Eastern Panama for at least two centuries; and since the 1920s, after an uprising that killed Panamanian policemen and Kuna alike, they were granted self-rule. We found the Kuna to be very interesting.

Prior to arriving at any of the remote lands and islands we visited, we always did our homework and researched everything important for us to know about the land, people, culture, and customs, and especially how to interact in a positive way with the people, so we would be accepted and welcome to return. This included learning what local people needed to improve their lives. Usually, these were very basic things, so we always had aboard items like rice, sugar, flour, tinned beef, clothes, and magazines for the families. For the men, who were almost always fishermen, we had flashlight batteries, fishing line, lures, and hooks. For the kids we had school supplies, lesson books, toys, and candy, and we even had fingernail polish (a favorite) for a chief's wife.

In all our travels over the years and miles, only once did a group of natives demand something of us without offering something in return. Normally, as soon as our anchor went down, someone in a canoe would come out to greet us and we would ask permission to visit the area. Often it was a local woman, who would have some vegetables in the bow of her canoe and shyly ask if we wanted to trade. Sometimes it would be a village elder, or even a chief, and it gave us the opportunity to present a generous gift of the things we felt that particular village would want. This simple exchange of goods and smiles transcended language and cultural barriers, opened the door into the personal lives of fascinating people, and was a source of priceless memories.

Physically small, with distinctive features, we found the Kuna a proud people, struggling to hold onto to their independence and distinctive traditions, typical of island people whose lives are so linked to the physical environment and geographical limits of their territory. The men are strong, excellent seamen, totally at ease and confident in the water, and are good craftsmen, known for building strong canoes from the giant trees in the highlands. The women make and wear some of the most colorful clothes in the world and are famous for handmade molas, a multi-layer cloth art form. When the women would come in their canoes to sell

Kuna bride for Captain Lew

them, I noticed they were very different looking than the natives of the Panama mainland, having an exotic and sometimes beautiful look about them. Their main sources of income are the women's molas and harvesting coconuts on the more than 400 islands. In fact, each and every coconut is so valuable to the Kuna, it is considered disrespectful and a serious offense if a visiting boat takes even one. We knew of this and other customs and religious beliefs, so we had no problems during our cruise in San Blas.

The main islands, close to the mainland, were intensely overcrowded. Yet some of the outlying islands had not even a single hut among the coconut palms and dazzling white sand beaches, so most of our time in San Blas was spent on the postcard-beautiful outer islands and cayos, many of them uninhabited. This was a puzzle to me, but after establishing good relations with our Kuna landlords, we learned a lot about these mysterious people. And the first thing we learned was that years and years of dealing with powerful neighbors (Columbia and Panama) who could crush them at any time has made them clever in business. To survive, the Kuna learned to charge a fee for everything imaginable, and even after closing the deal, they would sometimes change the rules. For instance, they would charge a fee for anchoring next to an island for a day or two, and then a different man would show up a day later, claiming to be the "real" owner of the island, and asking for another fee. Or, a group would ask a fee for allowing photos; but after a few were taken, an individual would declare the fee did not include him, so he had to ask for another fee.

A first-time visitor might be offended by this behavior, but after many years of visiting remote villages in Mexico, I learned to see this as comical, borne of necessity, and rarely motivated by greed. Besides, the "fees" were very small. In fact, a big smile while a fee was being asked almost always resulted in another smile from the man who could see you were onto his game. I enjoyed this kind of interaction with our hosts to the point I was "honored" one day with a very unusual visit.

A canoe arrived with what appeared to be a family on their way to a special event, based on their clothes, which were obviously their very best. They were very friendly, and the man, who could speak Spanish, asked if they could come aboard. For me, this looked like just the kind of opportunity to learn about the locals that I loved, so I agreed immediately. As the man began to explain the reason for their visit, the grandmother noticed I was about to take their picture, and hurried to move away. I had just gotten the photo of the entire "family" when I noticed Joubert almost running to the bow. The strange behavior of both the grandmother and Joubert added to the reason for the visit. The man, who was only a friend, explained they were there to see if I would be interested in marrying the daughter and becoming father to the three young children! He went into great detail what would be required of me, which was mostly a description of the clothes the young mother wanted. It was hilarious, but I maintained my composure, not wanting to offend the mother or grandmother, who were smiling but quite serious. It was not difficult to explain that although I was honored by their request, and impressed by the beauty of the young mother and her children, I was a boat captain and could not accept such a wonderful opportunity. They did not seem to be too disappointed; they returned to the canoe and paddled off. Joubert reappeared and seemed to know exactly what had happened, even though he was on the other end of the boat and could not have possibly heard anything: "Hocus pocus," and the reason she did not want her picture taken, he explained. Joubert was from Indonesia, saw the "power" in the eyes of the grandmother, and wanted nothing to do with her!

It was the rainy season in San Blas, but we had to take a chance on the weather, due to our aborted trip to Venezuela. Luck was with us: Sunny, hot weather was the norm for almost the entire time, which was fine with me because the outer islands and reefs are poorly charted, requiring "eyeball navigation" when moving from one place to another. Our normally accurate electronic charts were so far off that we laughed to see our system had us anchored in the coconut palms most of the time. This meant, in spite of modern technology, safe travel through the reefs and islands depended on the sun overhead, clear water, and good visibility. Rain was unwelcome.

Begging for food, pelican style

But the beautiful, clear water held little life. Overfishing had stripped San Blas of the resident marine life we expected to find. The young Kuna fishermen were free diving to almost 100 feet, a testament to their skill in the water, for lobsters that were normally prolific in less than fifty. The lobsters were going to luxury hotels in Panama, for cash. There was no season or quota. The lobsters would exist until the last one was sold.

But Michel continued to snorkel and explore, simply enjoying the beautiful coral reefs, and quite by accident found a small, underwater canyon he called "the pool." There were no land features to hint of this place, and we never saw the Kuna fishing or diving there, so it seemed Michel had found his own personal fishing hole. And what made it special was every afternoon, just before sunset, large pelagic fish streamed through a narrow, underwater entrance into the pool to feed on small baitfish that also entered, to feed on plankton. It was like spearfishing in a fish bowl, and Michel did not miss.

From San Blas, we ran north to Bocas del Toro, on the Panama-Nicaragua border, and explored some of the offshore islands where we found some beautiful anchorages and long sandy beaches, but poor fishing. Like San Blas, the islands and reefs were overfished. And when man disturbs the balance of nature, strange things can result. While anchored close offshore Isla Escudo de Veraguas, a pelican landed in the water close astern *Moana*, paddled up to the stern, and hopped aboard. He was obviously very hungry, as he waddled over to the bait tank and eyed the small fish he could see through the glass. This behavior surprised me because he was a young pelican. Old pelicans sometimes get cataracts or have other eye problems from years of high-diving impact with the water, and they resort to begging for food from fishermen when they can no longer catch their food. But this never occurred with young birds that could see and feed normally.

Our guest was obviously a young bird and appeared to be in good condition. Normally, he could catch fish and not need to beg from humans, so probably his food source was so depleted he was starving. We had no way to know for sure, but after feeding him all he could eat, which was a lot, for three days, he became the house guest who would not leave! Like a stray, cute puppy, he was adopted and spoiled rotten by the kids, who delighted in his silly expression and goofy behavior, and became tame to the point he would waddle around behind everyone. For me, his silliness reached Academy-Award material when he hopped up on the aft seating, waddled over and looked over my shoulder as I was reading a book.

Captain's log, September 1
   Dep Panama Canal "Yacht Club," 0734, idling outbound, CC 300° in calm weather, gray sky

From Panama, we ran north and had a good run through the Caribbean in fair to good traveling weather, non-stop to Miami, Florida. After routine and some specific boatyard maintenance, we were ready to go, and on December 18, we were underway for Havana, Cuba.

We arrived in Havana the next day, first securing the boat at the Customs and Immigration dock. Flying a US flag in Havana, Cuba, in 2000 was not common, but as we found a few other US boats there, it was not that unusual. The unusual part was the customs inspection, which featured not one, but two sniffer dogs. The dogs and their very serious handlers inspected every space on the boat, a process that took several hours before we were allowed to move to Canal #3, in Marina Hemingway. And there, it took less than an hour before a man approached with a deal. Glancing around, he casually offered USD 8,000 per head, to smuggle people out of Cuba.

This was the danger of visiting Cuba in those days. Police and security forces were everywhere, and while a taxi driver or individual would freely answer any question from an obviously American boat captain, the conversation would stop immediately if another person approached. Personally, I found the Cuban people to be the friendliest people on earth, something that was truly amazing as I slowly learned about the country and the lives of average Cubans.

Havana was crumbling. Buildings were literally falling down from neglect and lack of materials for repairs. The locals even had a gallows-humor word to describe the noise of a

Cuban transportation: Origin, age, future unknown

building falling down at night, tragically for the occupants. There was no paint. The entire city was gray, looking to me like an old black and white television documentary of bombed-out, WWII Europe—except for the cars, trucks, and buses that appeared to be locked in some weird kind of 1950s time warp. It was fascinating and humorous to see the old Buicks, Oldsmobiles, and others, bouncing along the streets, belching black smoke, and sounding strange because some had Russian or Chinese engines under the hood.

Crappy weather set in, with constant rain and high winds. WRI, my weather gurus, said to stay put for a few days, so Michel and guests did the tourist thing in the city while the crew and I tried to relax. We did wander around the marina a bit, wondering what the locals really thought about the big Che Guevara billboards. We did not need any fuel or food, so when the weather finally gave us a break, we were off. We were bound for the offshore islands and reefs on the south side of Cuba, and as we passed the various points it was very clear the authorities kept track of our daily movements.

We had a great trip with the family and guests, but as is sometimes the case, the first trip was largely exploratory. We found great diving and fishing, and beautiful sand beaches near the island of Cayo Largo, but the most important thing we found was Pire. Pire was a ship's

Havana: Once beautiful, now crumbling

agent, helping foreign yachts with all the regulations, details, and information impossible to find in tourist publications in the year 2000. He was well educated and well connected, and at one time had been Fidel Castro's personal interpreter. We were immediate friends, sharing sea stories along with all the interesting politics of the day. I had no idea this friendship would one day keep me out of big trouble.

Cayo Largo was like a best-kept secret. While Havana was crumbling and the total government control over everything was suffocating, Cayo Largo had developed into a jet-set destination for rich tourists from Europe. Jumbo jets were coming and going on a giant airstrip, and sparkling new Mercedes Benz buses were shuttling their customers in air-conditioned comfort to five-star hotels located on dazzling white sand beaches. All things imported and expensive, including liquor, designer clothes, jewelry, and beautiful women, were in abundance. Cuban cigars also, amigo! Capitalism was alive and thriving in Communist Cuba, and the rumor on the street was Fidel Castro was the richest man in the Caribbean!

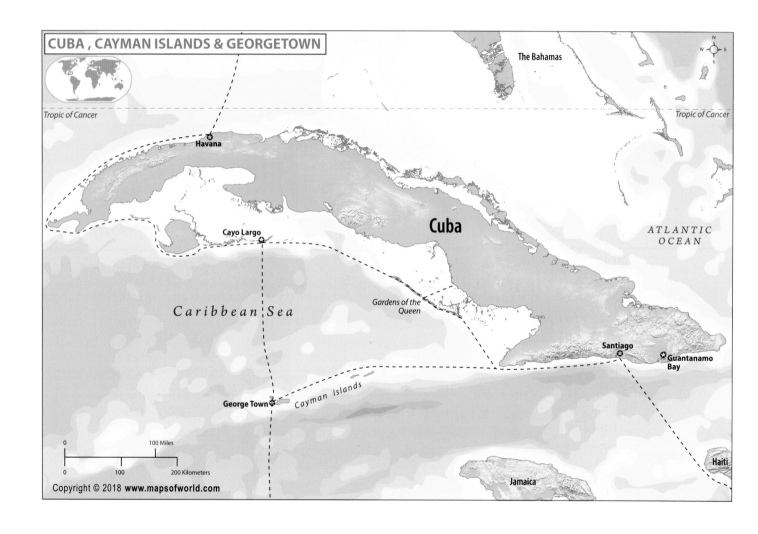

CUBA , CAYMAN ISLANDS & GEORGETOWN

The Bahamas

Tropic of Cancer

Havana

Cuba

ATLANTIC OCEAN

Cayo Largo

Caribbean Sea

Gardens of the Queen

Santiago

Guantanamo Bay

George Town

Cayman Islands

Haiti

Jamaica

Tropic of Cancer

0   100 Miles

0   100   200 Kilometers

Copyright © 2018 www.mapsofworld.com

2001

CARIBBEAN, NORTH AMERICA

Captain's log, January 6

1002 pos clear Cayo Largo entrance buoy, A/C to 180°, up rpm to 1600. Clear sky, warm temps.

We were underway for the Cayman Islands for resupply and brief maintenance. Michel had done his homework and with Pire's help, knew exactly where we would go on our next trip. We would return to Cuba and visit Jardines de la Reina, the Gardens of the Queen. Like a long string of pearls in the blue-purple waters of the Caribbean, the reefs, cayos, and islands offshore the southeast coast were the most untouched and pristine in all of Cuba. Uninhabited and difficult to reach, with poorly charted, shallow, and dangerous reefs and with no water or any supplies available, the gardens were not on the cruising itinerary of deep-draft power yachts. They were also patrolled by Cuban military, enforcing strict conservation laws. Beachcombing, snorkeling, and non-commercial photography were permitted, but scuba diving, fishing, and touching or taking any form of marine life was out. Just our kind of place!

Actually, there was fishing in the gardens. Avalon, an Italian company, had somehow curried favor with Fidel and was granted the only license to operate a sportfishing business there. They had an impressive operation that included a barge/hotel, supply boats, and a fleet of small, very fast fishing boats. The fishing for their European customers was fantastic and commanded top prices in the world of charter fishing. After a photo or two, all the fish were released. Naturally, the owners of this gold mine were very protective of their lucrative operation and worked with the authorities to discourage any visitors from so much as dropping an anchor in the gardens.

Pepe, the manager of the fishing operation, understood immediately that *Moana* was not the average yacht. With our shallow draft and running gear that could not be damaged, we had the ability to go where few boats would dare. When we began showing up in cayos where no power boats had ever been seen, his captains were impressed, but he began to watch us like a hawk. We were not commercial fishermen, but we did enjoy catching or spearing fish for dinner, so the game was on, and it was not hard to get a nice grouper or snapper whenever we wanted.

In a wild place like the gardens, finding a calm anchorage at night is often a serious challenge. Many places on the nautical charts that looked great were inaccessible due to coral reefs or shallow sand bars blocking entrance to calm lees and beautiful lagoons. The charts were not accurate, especially with depths, so we had to be very careful when approaching any anchorages. In some cases we found tall sticks driven into the bottom by fishermen, marking very small channels into the lagoons. The sticks had no flags or anything attached, and many times they were difficult to see. But with a person on the bow, looking down into the clear water, we were sometimes able to find our way into some of the most secluded, idyllic lagoons imaginable. This included Cinco Balas, or Five Bullets, where we met Elvis. His real name was Rey, but when our cook admired his good looks, warm personality, and resemblance to the famous singer, we simply called him Elvis. With a personality that matched, and speaking perfect English, he enjoyed his new nickname. He worked for Pepe, running one of their supply boats that was also set up for fishing. When he came into the lagoon and was very surprised to see us anchored there, he came over to give us a typical Cuban welcome. We gave him a tour of the boat and a cold beer, and we asked a hundred questions about the gardens, which he answered quite candidly. This included his instructions from Pepe to report our whereabouts and activities whenever he saw us. We really enjoyed his company—even more so, when he located the best anchorages and the access channels on my charts.

The next morning was memorable. There were two channels into Cinco Balas, and the one I used to enter was so difficult, I decided to use the other for leaving. It was marked with sticks pretty well at first, but then it became very hard to see the channel, and I slid into the bottom on one hull or the other, over and over, stopping the boat. With her protected running gear, this was not dangerous for *Moana*, but it was embarrassing for me. I felt like a Sunday drunk who could not find his way home. Elvis suddenly appeared in a small boat, hopped aboard, and came to my pilothouse, which was now full of people wondering what was going on. With a smile worthy of his namesake, he took the controls, lined up his run, dropped the engines in and out of gear, and, while the boat slowly slid through the narrow spot in the channel, raised his hands in the air and sang out, "Don't worry, be happy!" Laughter and applause was instant, while I could not help but notice a wading bird less than one foot from the starboard side, and was sure it was the same to port! It was an amazing display of local knowledge and boat handling skill.

Thanks to Elvis, we found and enjoyed the Gardens of the Queen as if in the company of the queen herself. Fishing, diving, and exploring pristine reefs and beaches by day, and night after night anchored alone in one or another beautiful, calm lagoon or island lee, it was an epic trip. But epic trips to wild places are never without some unexpected drama.

We discovered a really beautiful anchorage one afternoon, inside the lagoon of Boca de Juan Grin. We anchored in very shallow water, as we often did, especially with the notes of Elvis on our charts. It was a spectacular spot, with sand and turtle-grass bottom, surrounded by white sand beaches and a few mangroves, and with just enough room for the boat to swing with the change of tide and current. The water was perfectly clear, and after anchoring we could see our big "Bruce" anchor resting on the bottom, just off the bow of the boat. There was little current, so the anchor was on its side, with one "arm" sticking straight up.

Without a lot of current or wind, this was normal, and I went to bed that night confident everything was okay. In the middle of the night, Gerard, one of our guests, gently shook my arm and told me he could hear something strange. And it was very strange, indeed, to see the anchor chain rubbing against the line cutter on the port bow, due to an extreme angle on the chain. The tide had fallen, as I knew it would, leaving only one foot of water under the boat, but the breeze had come up in the opposite direction of the current, pushing us to the side of the lagoon. This crazy combination made the anchor chain run off from the starboard bow at the extreme angle I could see in the light of my flashlight.

We needed to spin the boat around so the anchor chain would run out straight ahead, instead of under the hull or against the cutter on the port bow. In daylight, with deeper water and more room, this would have been a simple maneuver; but as I tried to power the bow around, I realized the elements would not allow it. In the dark, everything was difficult to see, and the radar did not show a well-defined lagoon. As I tried to envision the forces working against us, I noticed the chain angle was slowly changing with a change in the current, and the boat was slowly starting to drift sideways, toward the anchor. In a normal situation, the boat would have coasted past the anchor, the chain would come up tight, and the boat would have aligned itself normally, into the current. But this night, nothing was normal and our boat was a double hulled catamaran. In a matter of minutes, the boat was going to drift over the big Bruce anchor, and its steel "arm" was going to slice us open like a knife through soft butter!

The last thing I wanted to do was raise the anchor, drift down current, and wind up aground, but I had no choice. I used both engines and serious power to get the bow around, and as we quickly approached the spot where I was sure the anchor lay, Joubert hauled the chain. The moment the anchor came out of the water, I spun the boat in her own length, we dumped the anchor again, and in the darkness, held our breath. Moments later, tragedy was only a word. With the current and breeze now from the same direction, *Moana* once again rested quietly in the center of the small lagoon, and no one would ever know the anxiety and fear felt that night in "paradise."

Two days later, while leaving Pasa Cachiboca, we encountered a small commercial fishing boat, with its two-man crew. It was rare to see such a boat in the gardens, where everything was protected, so I brought *Moana* alongside to learn what they were doing there. Debbie had some scrambled eggs leftover from breakfast, so we passed over a plastic bag and used it as an excuse to say "hello." At that moment, and without a word, the crewman began scooping lobsters from a hidden compartment in the deck, throwing them into our cockpit. At the same time, we saw an adult turtle with her flippers tied up, lying on her back on the deck.

Cuban commercial fishing boat

The silence of the captain and deckhand confirmed they were fishing illegally, and they were worried about what we might do. I understood their fear, and tried to gain their trust by telling them about my younger years in the commercial fishing business, and that I would never report them to the authorities, but they refused to say a word. Then, I told them the women aboard our boat were very sad to see the turtle, and lectured them a bit about taking turtles and their eggs (I assumed they had caught her when she was laying her eggs), which was a little ridiculous, given the plight of Cuban fishermen. It was an odd "standoff." The fishermen clearly understood my words, but they simply stared at me in silence, as if waiting permission to leave.

Michel ended the strange standoff by suggesting we simply buy the turtle, which is what we did. The fishermen seemed relieved, passed over the poor animal, and immediately got underway. We ran outside the pass and released the turtle offshore the reef. She was apparently unharmed by her brief captivity and swam off fast, while I wondered if our short encounter with the fishermen was good or bad for them. We received a dozen lobsters and rescued a turtle, but I wondered how they would be able to spend the money ($ US) we gave them. Quite possibly, they could not spend the money for years to come, or ever.

Luis and Donald with pet jutía

One day, a very old and worn commercial fishing boat anchored nearby, launched its small boat, and came alongside. The captain, one of the largest and most muscular men I have ever seen, was very friendly and eager to learn about us. I was especially interested in how and what they fished for, and in general, what their lives were like in Cuba, so we had an interesting exchange. We learned they fished primarily for lobsters, which were in abundance in certain areas of the gardens and were the property of the government. The fishermen could not sell them to anyone else, and they told us how many they caught in an average year. We were astounded! Their usual catch was worth nearly US $250,000, but the total the entire crew received was less than US $8,000. Viva Fidel!

Before leaving, the captain asked if we could give them some beer, a precious cargo they could never afford. It was near the end of our trip, and we did not have much aboard, but I gave them a case we could spare. They smiled broadly and rowed back to their boat. And the next day, we saw the warm hearts and generosity of the Cuban people. They returned with two five-gallon buckets containing an amazing assortment of beautiful tropical reef fish. On their previous visit, they noticed our bait tank held not just bait fish, but "pets," so they brought us a nice, thoughtful gift. But that was not all. They also brought us a baby jutía, on a little leash for the three-year-old son of one of our guests. They also brought two adult animals, skinned, dressed out, and ready for the barbecue. When the fishermen left port they only had aboard some rice, so to augment the crew stores, they immediately went to the mangroves and caught jutías for fresh meat. They were giant tree rats! When the captain divulged this and saw the reaction of the women aboard, he told us to roast them and give a small piece to the little boy. He promised the boy's reaction would prove how delicious they tasted, and that evening, we saw the proof. Little Luis ate the jutía with gusto, as did all the men and crew. To this day, I have to say the meat of those tree rats was absolutely delicious.

Two days later, at sunset, a different but equally old and beat-up fishing boat came alongside. They immediately gave us a large bucket of live lobsters. We had no more beer, so we put together a huge care package of food and clothes. We offered money also, but they did not want any kind of money. They explained that being caught with any kind of money other than Cuban pesos would land them in jail, so they were very happy trading for food and clothes. They said they were headed back to port, and quickly departed. The trap was set.

Minutes later, as darkness fell, we turned on our bright deck lights, which blinded us from seeing the Cuban military patrol boat that was suddenly alongside. Six armed soldiers burst into our cockpit and immediately found the bucket of illegal lobsters. The commanding officer slowly came aboard, his eyes fixed on mine. He knew I was the captain and, with his short, direct Spanish, made sure I knew he was in charge.

"Now, you will raise your anchor and follow us to port. Your boat is now the property of the Republic, and you and your crew are going to jail."

"I don't think so."

"Start your engines, and do as I say."

I met his stare, and with a slight smile bordering on arrogance, silently turned and went to the pilothouse. I was more than a little nervous as I retrieved a letter from Pire. The letter was simply an invitation to come back to Cuba and visit the Gardens of the Queen, describing the beauty of the area, listing all the services his company offered, and thanking us for coming to Cuba and using his agency. But it had lots of "scrambled eggs," and official looking stamps and insignia of a government document. At the bottom was Pire's signature, bold and impressive, and his title of ship's agent. And most importantly, it was in English.

When I returned to the aft cockpit, the officer's posture and attitude was unchanged. His men stood around us in a semicircle, waiting, I was sure, for their commander to show his power over the stupid American. I held up Pire's letter, pointed to his signature, and in my best Spanish, demanded, "Do you know who this is? This letter is permission to visit the Jardines de la Reina and enjoy the wonders of this paradise. And it is from the personal representative and official interpreter of El Commandante" (Fidel Castro). As I said this, I stroked my chin, letting him know I knew the meaning of this act. (Castro had a beard, and whenever a Cuban wanted to convey that the subject being talked about was Fidel, he simply stroked his chin.)

In this case, I wanted to suggest I was no mere tourist and, in fact, could have connections all the way up the chain. Connections that could make things uncomfortable for the officer who continued to coldly stare at me.

He reached for the letter, but I held it back, saying, "You can read it, but you cannot have it."

"We will see about your letter," he said.

And with that, he barked orders to his men, returned to his boat, (with the lobsters, of course), and leaving one of his men to wait for his return, disappeared into the night. He was out of radio range and would have to return all the way to port to confer with his superiors. I knew this, and knew it would be a very long night for him if he returned. What I did not know for sure was if he could read English.

When I held up the letter in front of him, he scrutinized it as if he wanted to know every detail. I had seen this act before, in several developing-world countries, and immediately surmised he could not read it. Now the game had changed. Now, the most important thing to my Cuban "general" was to show his men that he was smart and educated and was the man in charge. And to go home to his warm bed and forget about bothersome boat captains. Several hours later, a small boat arrived to pick up the last soldier.

This, our second trip to Cuba was spectacular. The weather was good almost every day, and the fishing, diving, and exploring were unbelievable. With a boat like *Moana*, we sometimes joked about living in a five-star hotel, but when the weather was good, in a place like the Gardens of the Queen, even the best hotels in the world could not match the combination of luxury, locale, and ambiance we enjoyed. Sunrises to sunsets were filled with lifetime memories. We lacked for nothing. With our big generators supplying electricity to commercial grade equipment and sophisticated systems, the family and their guests enjoyed the luxury and elegance that defined our operation. Our feet never saw shoes. We enjoyed gourmet seafood cuisine in laughter and tee shirts. It was paradise.

With our second Cuba trip behind us, Michel and the family flew home, unbelievably beginning with a flight to Havana in an old Russian biplane. Viva Fidel! With the freezer full of fish and lobster, we ran south to Grand Cayman, and on to Panama. It was a mix of fair to sloppy weather, with only the bad fuel we purchased in Georgetown being a surprise. With a system designed to clean and remove water from a bad load of fuel, we did not miss a beat, and we arrived in Cristobal on February 20. Two days later, we picked up our pilot in the morning and idled to Gatun Locks.

For me, the Panama Canal is a historical and unbelievable marvel of engineering, and for years I loved taking boats through. The procedure of putting a boat inside a chamber, filling it with millions of gallons of water to raise the boat to another level, crossing a lake, and reversing the procedure to take a boat to the sea level on the other side of the canal, all the while surrounded by dense, tropical forest, is simply a fantastic experience. The pilots were very knowledgeable, and it seemed I always learned some new and interesting facts about the

Panama Canal, locking down

history or current events regarding the operation. In those years, the pilots were American or foreign captains, and very professional. But there was tangible animosity in those days between the pilots and the line handlers who worked on top of the lock walls to secure the lines from the boats to the chamber walls. The line handlers were Panamanian, and on my very first transit many years before, I saw just how much they resented the foreign pilots.

When transiting the canal locks "center chamber," a boat uses four lines, two on each side, that are made fast to cleats on the top of the lock walls. This procedure keeps the vessel in the center of the lock chamber, which is very important due to the intense and dangerous current that could otherwise slam a boat against the concrete walls of the chamber. To get a heavy line from a boat, the line handlers throw a light line with a "monkey fist" (weighted end) to the boat, and a person on the boat ties it to a heavy line that is then pulled back to the top of the wall and tied to a cleat. This is a simple operation, carried out many times every day, and the line handlers are extremely accurate with where the monkey fist lands on the boat in transit. In fact, to this day, they have a contest every year in which the line handlers demonstrate impressive skill.

Any boat was fair game for a monkey fist into a glass window, or very close to the head of anyone on deck. But that was not the most dangerous thing the line handlers could inflict on a pilot they did not like. When a boat moved from one lock chamber to the next, in the procedure to "lock up," or raise to the next level, the explosive current created by millions of gallons of water rushing into the chamber made it very difficult for a captain to control his vessel. Every second it took to get the lines attached to the wall tops were a white-knuckle eternity for even the best captains, so a slow line handler could mean a vessel suffered serious damage. This was the payback vindictive line handlers could exact on an innocent vessel, her captain, and the hated foreign pilot.

In 1999, the US operation of the canal was given back to Panama by President Jimmy Carter, and there was big change. The Panamanians took over everything, and from my limited view the first years were a disaster. The foreign pilots were sent packing, and all vessels, including giant ships, were piloted by Panamanians. This also included all the scheduling and maintenance of all of the equipment special to the canal. As time passed, things improved, but animosity toward boats flying the US flag sometimes endured. This attitude was quickly made clear to me by our pilot on the morning of February 22, 2001.

My first clue was when our young Panamanian pilot asked about the food he would be served at lunch time. And the second clue was when he informed me he would allow two sailboats, one on each side, to be rafted (tied alongside) to *Moana*. With our big beam, and no bow thrusters, maintaining control inside the lock chambers was very difficult, and to compound the danger by rafting another boat on each side was inviting a serious accident. I reminded our pilot that our assigned schedule did not include the sailboats and that I was very concerned about the safety of the boats and everyone aboard.

"Do you want to transit today, or next week? If you refuse my request, I will take the sailboats through, and you will have to wait in The Flats for another yacht opening."

"You and I know this is a bad idea."

From there, the conversation became heated, with me letting him know he was behaving like an amateur, and he reminding me Americans were no longer telling him or anyone else how to run the canal. It was a bad start to a bad day.

My fear factor ramped up considerably when the sailboats came alongside, and I discussed the situation with the owners and their crews. Neither had ever been through the canal before, and they had no idea what was going to happen. Because all vessels transiting the canal must have a pilot, each sailboat had a young Panamanian pilot aboard, and both were inexperienced, stupid, or willing to be part of the coming game. I shook my head in disbelief when I noticed the sailboats had only a few yacht-duty fenders on their outboard sides, where they could be ravaged by the rough concrete walls of the lock chambers.

It was calm in the first lock, and I was able to slowly coast in and hold position while the line handlers did their jobs. But we were tied behind a large commercial ship, and I knew what that meant. As the giant gate doors opened, the ship powered out of the lock, and the surge of current produced by its propellers was a frightening sight. As soon as our pilot saw the dangerous, swirling water, his panic and lack of experience was clear for all to see.

"Power, power! Go forward with power!" he commanded. "Take control of your vessel, captain!"

"You, sir, are a fool. Even the line handlers know to hold a few moments more."

Just as we became engulfed in the swirling, but diminishing current, I came on with just enough power to control a living nightmare. Even so, one of our deck cleats was ripped out of the boat, and the stern of one of the sailboats missed the chamber wall by inches. Our completely distressed and angry pilot was speechless. He knew at this point his decision to raft the sailboats against *Moana* was a very big mistake, but we had one more chamber to enter. Very fortunately, we were the only vessels entering the third chamber, and I had just enough room to keep the boat in the center of the chamber long enough to allow the current to subside and get the lines to the walls. Even so, we lost a second cleat to the overwhelming power of the current, and one of the sailboats lost several deck-railing stanchions to the unforgiving chamber walls. It was my worst-ever experience in the canal. As I powered out of the third and last of the Gatun locks, I was relieved to find no counter-current just beyond the gates and was able to maintain my center course into the calm waters of Lake Gatun. Here, while the shocked crews of the sailboats untied their boats (they, being much slower than *Moana*, would transit the lake without our company), I noticed a strange sight.

When a ship transits the canal, the "lines" are steel cables, attached to small, specially designed locomotives that control the ships as they pass from one lock chamber to the next. They are necessarily very powerful units, operated by a single engineer, and they run back and forth on rails alongside the lock chambers. On this day, I noticed two locomotives off the rails, sitting on the ground at the edge of the jungle. They had obviously been destroyed by fire. My adrenalin from the lock chamber nightmare was still on overload, so I did not hesitate to take a shot at our now silent pilot and pointed to the burned-out locomotives.

"Looks like a good example of Panamanian maintenance and expertise. I also heard one of the locomotives fell into a lock chamber recently. Never saw any of that when the Americans were running the show."

"You Americans had plenty of problems you covered up over the years!" he exploded.

The run across beautiful Lake Gatun was in silence. I knew the route well, even using the short cut without any assistance from our fuming pilot. Locking down from the lake to sea level on the Balboa, or Pacific side, is very easy, like a rubber duck going down in a bathtub when the plug is removed. But of course, our angry pilot was not finished with me.

The last locks, approaching Panama City, are at Miraflores. As we approached the lock gates, our pilot went outside, on the aft deck, while talking on his hand-held radio. The pilots must be in constant contact with their supervisors and the ships they are to share lock

Container ship prop wash

chambers with, so I thought nothing of his leaving the pilothouse. In this, our last lock, we were to share the chamber with a huge container ship, which was slowly coming up astern.

We entered the chamber and went to the far end, just behind the last gates. I watched warily as the line handlers made our lines fast to the cleats with no drama. And the big ship kept coming. And coming. The cables to the locomotives were on, but it was not slowing down at the normal rate I had seen many times. Suddenly, line handlers began scrambling away from the lock walls as chaos erupted. Black smoke appeared over the ship and we could feel the rumbling of her engines in full reverse. Alarms shrieked, bells sounded, line handlers and ship crew were in panic, and the cables to the locomotives were spraying rust and singing the song of wire taut to the point of snapping as the locomotives were dragged down their rails by the overwhelming tonnage and inertia of the massive ship.

Our ashen-faced pilot was screaming into his radio. His stunt had turned deadly serious.

As in slow motion, the ship kept coming, consuming the last space in the lock chamber like the mindless behemoth it was, heartbeats away from crushing us like a tiny grape. I could see every scar in the paint, every streak of rust, as the bow loomed above *Moana*, and the air was filled with the sound and smell of steel on steel. For us, there was no escape.

Joubert and I stood frozen, looking straight up, as rust rained down from the bow of the rumbling ship onto our cockpit deck.

And the giant stopped.

For me in those moments, time stood still. Miraculously, a catastrophic accident did not occur, and would not be recounted in history. People's lives were not changed, but our shaken and silent pilot would certainly remember this day. An hour later, when he disembarked our boat, he refused to meet my stare.

Captain's log, April 2

1508 pos abeam Taboguilla Island, 1 mile, in great weather. Light breeze from NNE 8–10kts on long swell from SE, 2–3ft. Hot, muggy air temp, smoky sky. Ocean Master towing very well, 13kts SOG, line staying in water and boat tracking straight.

After all the hard miles and damage in the Caribbean, we towed the completely repaired *Ocean Master* sport fisher to our favorite islands offshore the Pacific side of Panama. Jicarita, Jicaron, Montuosa, Hannibal Bank, and Ladrones—all were revisited and wonderful memories added to previous ones. This time, Michel finally had his "hot rod" *Ocean Master* sport fisher to add to our already great operation. The marlin, sailfish, and tuna fishing on the Hannibal Bank was very good, and Michel and Louis had wonderful father-son trips while the rest of us enjoyed beautiful Isla Montuosa, at anchor on *Moana*.

With Michel and Louis off in the *Ocean Master*, the activity aboard "the big boat" changed a lot. The relaxed, quiet atmosphere was quite different from the constant excitement and enthusiasm Michel created around the clock. Martine and Rachel were content to lie in the sun on the big bow cushion while Donald and I fished off the stern. It was at this time I came to know Rachel and Donald a little better. Rachel, a beautiful sixteen-year-old girl, was the quiet, thoughtful type around me, and had I not noticed how adventurous she was. I would have thought her to be boring. The truth was quite the opposite, and as time went by, I was quite impressed by this young lady who was surrounded but never intimidated by male siblings, or even by her parents.

Donald, now ten years old, was quite the observer. He never missed a thing. He was the quiet one but was never far from the action. This was due in part to his age and the fact he was yet to speak English. I could tell he was eager to share his feelings with me, and he looked forward to when his schooling would allow it. He was also "the reader." My lasting memory of Donald went back to the first morning on the first trip with the family aboard. It was very early, just breaking day, and everyone was still asleep while the crew and I were going about our routine. Well, everyone except Donald, who was lying on the salon settee, silently reading a book. From that day to this, it was obvious our "observer/reader" had a lot going on in his

Louis and Dad: A day to remember

little head. An avid reader myself at that age, I was impressed by his love of reading and the number and speed of books he consumed.

It was also on this, the "Easter trip," that I was very impressed with Martine. On a sunny, hot day, boys being boys, they were running top speed around the deck and squirting each other with huge water guns. It was easy to imagine a seriously injured boy, and I asked Martine to have a word with them. Her answer was a surprise.

"That's how they learn."

"Do you know how far we are from a hospital?" I replied.

"That's how they learn."

Although I would have liked a different response, I totally agreed with Martine. No one got hurt, and I got a preview of how Michel and Martine would raise their children.

Los Sueños: Future fisherman's dream marina

Captain's log, May 26

2120 pos abeam Punta Mala, .7 mi, in miserable, confused seas, on various courses to hug coast, run for anchorage

Next on the agenda was a trip to Isla Coco, the famous "pirate island," where fabulous stories of buried treasure had lured treasure hunters there for many years. We ran north to Costa Rica and on June 4 arrived at Los Sueños, a beautiful marina that was under construction in the hook of Herradura Bay.

Captain's log, July 18

Underway offshore central Costa Rica coast, en route to Isla Coco. Poor traveling weather, no sleep. 0000 pos 7° 28' N, 85°57.6' W. Drop RPM to 1100.

To visit Isla Coco, 342 nautical miles offshore Costa Rica, requires a good boat and crew, which eliminates the Sunday sailors and their weekend boats. The sea state can make it a real slog, and without any fuel or supplies at the island, a boat must have the range to get there,

Boobies returning

operate for at least a week, and make it back. Add to that a tough anchorage, almost daily rain, and regulations that discourage many, and you have a remote island visited by very few. Just our kind of place!

After grinding out some very poor weather on our thirty-six-hour run, we could see the mist-covered island, and ten miles off we found huge schools of yellowfin tuna feeding on acres of bait fish. Thousands of leaping, boiling tuna were spread out over a huge area in almost calm seas. Marlin were feeding on the perimeter, and countless sea birds were diving everywhere on the hapless bait fish. It was a feeding frenzy every fisherman dreams about, but few see on such a scale. We slowed to trolling speed, put the jigs in the water, and instantly caught several tuna in the twenty-to-thirty-pound size. It was a nice reward for a tough slog out, and a great start to a great trip.

We arrived at Chatham anchorage on the north end of the island and got the anchor down just as it was getting dark. And what a greeting on our first night at Coco! We turned on our big deck lights, finished filleting and putting away the fish, and began washing the stern of the boat when the first fish fell from the sky. Followed by another, and another, and within moments, small fish, scales, blood and crap were raining from the sky!

Rare sight: A wet frigate bird

Many, perhaps a hundred boobies were in a tight circle over *Moana*, flying around and around, all the while squawking, throwing up fish, and crapping. The falling bait fish were landing on the boat, but most of them were actually falling into the water, next to the boat. This feast of small fish brought snapper, grouper and others to the surface and added to an already amazing sight. As the boobies became tired, they tried to land on the water, but the boiling predator fish were in a frenzy and were attacking anything the instant it touched the water. As soon as a booby would try to land, a fish would snap at its feet, and the poor bird would take off again. This chaotic scene went on for quite a while before I finally figured out what was going on.

The boobies were returning to the island after their day of fishing offshore. They don't like to fly in the dark and typically time their arrival to their home island just as it becomes dark. This strategy is because frigate birds, hovering near the island, will attack boobies that have a freshly caught fish in their belly, forcing them to throw up the fish, which the frigates then catch and eat. By arriving at the same moment the frigate birds return to their favorite tree on the island, the boobies avoid most of the frigates. Our big deck and cabin lights blinded the boobies as they tried to fly past. Suddenly, they could not see the island, so the confused birds circled above *Moana*, terrified to be lost in the darkness; and in their panic, they were throwing up their precious food and defecating. As soon as we turned off all our lights, silence

Isla Coco waterfall

reigned and the magic show ended. But when the sun came up the next morning, boobies were definitely not on Joubert's "favorite bird" list!

The next morning, we were visited by Freddie. Isla Coco is a Costa Rica National Park, and Freddie was their senior park ranger. Only park rangers are allowed to live on the island, at two small stations on the north end. A "serious" park ranger, Freddie watched over the island like a mother hen with her chicks. Other than swimming in the water, he made sure we understood we were not allowed to do anything. We could not touch anything underwater or on the land; and if we wanted to fish, we had to be at least eight miles offshore. We were not a commercial boat and had no desire to cause any kind of damage to the ecosystem or the fish

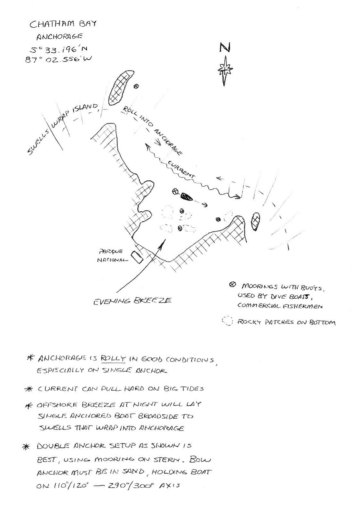

CHATHAM BAY
ANCHORAGE
5° 33.196' N
87° 02.556' W

N

SWELLS WRAP ISLAND

ROLL INTO ANCHORAGE

CURRENT

PARQUE NACIONAL

EVENING BREEZE

⊗ MOORINGS WITH BUOYS,
USED BY DIVE BOATS,
COMMERCIAL FISHERMEN

◌ ROCKY PATCHES ON BOTTOM

✳ ANCHORAGE IS ROLLY IN GOOD CONDITIONS,
ESPECIALLY ON SINGLE ANCHOR

✳ CURRENT CAN PULL HARD ON BIG TIDES

✳ OFFSHORE BREEZE AT NIGHT WILL LAY
SINGLE ANCHORED BOAT BROADSIDE TO
SWELLS THAT WRAP INTO ANCHORAGE

✳ DOUBLE ANCHOR SETUP AS SHOWN IS
BEST, USING MOORING ON STERN. BOW
ANCHOR MUST BE IN SAND, HOLDING BOAT
ON 110°/120° — 290°/300° AXIS

Hand-drawn map of Chatham Bay

population, but we did not pay serious money for all the permits and come all that way to eat frozen hamburgers. Fresh fish and lobster were on the menu, so the game was on.

During construction of the marina in Los Sueños, the steel pipe dock pilings were cut off at the desired height, and the scrap pieces of pipe were laying all over the bottom. This provided ideal habitat for lobsters, which we caught easily with our trap. This was prohibited, of course, but along with my Tico friends, it was all part of the game. When we arrived at Isla Coco and Freddie made his visit, he saw many of these lobsters in our bait tank but said nothing, as he knew we had just arrived from the mainland, without enough time to prey upon "his" lobsters.

Isla Coco is a unique island. It was never attached to the mainland, so most of the different species of plant and animal life are endemic. Far offshore, in very deep water, it is in the stream of several powerful ocean currents, providing the nutrients to support an unbelievable variety of fish and marine animals. A mountainous, densely forested island, it is almost always shrouded in rain clouds that cast dark shadows and give the appearance of a cold island typically found in far northern latitudes, instead of the tropics. With the almost constant rainfall and the vertical cliffs at the edge of the sea, beautiful waterfalls crash down directly into the sea; they were a source of fresh water for seafarers for centuries.

We were certainly not pirates, but in this wild setting it was easy to imagine one of their sailing frigates anchored in our very same anchorage. We went ashore and walked on the same beaches, and visited the same waterfalls where they no doubt filled their water casks. This was a truly wild island, almost untouched by man.

To visit such wild places, one must be ready to accept the things that go with it, and the anchorage in Chatham Bay was one of them. After our first night of rolling around miserably in the ocean swells that wrap around the island, Joubert and I used our double anchor setup that changed sleepless nights and flying food to sleeping like babies and happy family mealtimes. As I sometimes do in such places, I made a sketch and glued it into my log book, hopefully to use again one day.

Rain or shine, we enjoyed fantastic scuba diving, snorkeling, beachcombing, and hiking. Offshore, the fishing was fantastic, as the acres of baitfish seemed self-sustaining, holding huge schools of tuna. I love to free dive and found an unbelievable quantity and variety of marine life while swimming very close to the anchorage. This included the world's largest population of hammerhead sharks, fascinating creatures. These big sharks were curious and had a heart-stopping habit of suddenly surprising me underwater by silently appearing alongside, only an arm's length away from the big eye on the end of the "hammer." On one occasion, I was completely surrounded by at least twenty to thirty beautiful scalloped hammerheads. Twenty feet down and gliding along, as quietly as I could, I was the center of attraction, as they jockeyed for position to look me over closely. Breathtaking!

Freddie watched us like a hawk. He viewed us as modern day predators and was sure we were breaking his strict rules. Of course, he was right, which made the game even more fun. He came to the boat almost every day, looking around for anything that would indicate forbidden activities. On one occasion, he found an interesting tree leaf Rachel had brought back from a hike, and he lectured me on what a serious issue this was. It was hard not to laugh because Freddie was a bit of a hypocrite, bending the rules for himself and his buddies. Hunting of any animals was strictly prohibited, but he was the number-one land predator on the island. He did not know that I knew the captain who gave him a crossbow and bolts. Freddie kept all the rangers in fresh meat with his silent weapon. Had he shared his secret with me, I would have actually admired his hunting skills, but he did not. Over the years, man had introduced deer, pigs, cats, and rats, and all were detrimental to the ecological health of the island, so I had no problem with Freddie's activities. But I did not try to discuss it with him.

We soon discovered lobsters in unbelievable numbers at a nearby island. It was in clear view of one of the rangers' camps, so we knew Freddie's boys were watching our every move as we free dove and gathered a few. When we explored the many reefs and small islands, we used our dinghy, talking occasionally on the VHF radio with *Moana*. Freddie spoke to me in Spanish, but I knew he spoke very good English, so we were sure he was listening to our every word. As I came to the surface with a dive bag and a dozen lobsters, his boat was headed our way at full throttle. Rachel, our observer aboard *Moana*, instantly radioed Donald, who was sitting in our dinghy.

"Ils arrivent." (They are coming!)

Poor Freddie's high-speed approach was foiled by Rachel's message, in French, the first language of the family. This gave me just enough time to dive down and hide the dive bag in a small cave. At the same moment I came back to the surface, Freddie was there, sure he had made a bust. It was hard not to laugh at the look on his face. I held up my underwater camera and remarked at what a great time we were having. I even mentioned how amazed we were to see lobsters crawling around in daylight. He was not amused and followed us back to *Moana*, certain to solve the mystery of disappearing lobsters. Later, Michel and Thomas paddled over to the island in the kayak and, using my marks, found and retrieved the bag of lobsters. All of this was even more amusing when, a few days later, Freddie looked down into the bait tank. Our recent lobster additions to the tank replenished the ones we had eaten a few days before, so we still had about the same number in the tank as the first day we arrived.

"How come you are not eating those lobsters?"

"I don't know, Freddie. Sometimes the family does not want them."

Poor Freddie was frustrated. Had he taken a good look into the bait tank, he would have noticed there were now two different species of lobsters in the bottom of the tank. The Isla Coco lobsters were really beautiful creatures with vibrant accent colors of blue, red, and purple, whereas the mainland lobsters were slightly different, with an overall greenish body hue.

"Le gusta una cerveza, Freddie?" (Would you like a beer?)

It really was funny, so I tried to win him over with a cold beer, something in very short supply at his little camps. But he knew his men were watching in their binoculars and he had to maintain his "serious" status, so the poor guy could not even get a cold beer from the *Moana* pirates!

Captain's log, July 26
2100 pos 8° 28.4' N, 85° 21.9' W in scattered showers, good downhill traveling weather. A/C to 030°. Aircraft with no lights, on radar, flying low, in big circle around boat.

After an epic trip to Isla Coco, we were underway for mainland Costa Rica, when out of the darkness came a reminder we lived in a very different time than the pirates of old. On my radar, a target was coming in very fast. Flying low, a blacked-out helicopter suddenly shone a massive blue-white strobe light on us. Aboard the boat, we were stunned and completely blinded by the intensity and huge footprint of the light. Flying very low, the chopper's strobe penetrated every window, illuminating the boat inside like a hundred flash bulbs. Thoughts of seized yachts and murderous drug runners flashed through my mind as I called out on VHF, channel 16. The swish-swish-swish of the rotor blades on the chopper were the only answer as it continued to fly low, large circles around us. After more than an hour, three warships appeared, and a voice finally identified them as US, and asked for my personal identification. After another hour of silence, the voice thanked us for our cooperation, and the drug enforcement ships disappeared into the night.

Back in Los Sueños, we reprovisioned, picked up a few more guests, and got underway for "Islas Murcielagos," or Bat Islands, on the northwest coast of Costa Rica. The islands and part of the nearby Guanacaste coast are a national park and a truly beautiful stretch of Pacific coastline. Our timing was not great, however, and we experienced several days of the strong Papagayo Wind that can blow offshore hard for days on end. Michel and the family were never slowed by much, and the wind made little difference to them. We found very good anchorages in protected bays, with long, white-sand beaches, and even a hidden lagoon that we could access from a mangrove-lined stream that emptied into the ocean. A variety of crocodile lived in the lagoon, which confirmed the "wildness factor" and added to our excitement when paddling in the kayak, very low to the water!

At night, we found the Bat Islands were named such for good reason. It was here we saw the only fishing bats in all our travels. These large, orange bats used our bright bait lights, which brought small fish to the surface, where the lightning fast bats would catch them in their feet. It took many attempts by each bat to catch a single fish, due to the need for perfect timing and speed. It was also one of those times I could not capture a unique event with a camera. For hours, I tried every combination of settings on my camera, but the darkness above, bright light from below, glare, and speed of the bats defeated my every effort. I went to bed totally frustrated on more than one night.

At the head of another bay was "Ollies," a surf spot named for Oliver North, who was involved years before with gun-running into nearby Nicaragua during the so-called Contra conflict. A small river mouth formed the sand bottom just right, and on a good tide the waves were a surfer's dream. We had two surfboards aboard, so I took Louis for his first lesson and was very impressed with his natural ability. After only a few waves, he was standing and having a great time!

But by far, Michel had the biggest challenge of everyone on the trip. He had torn a tendon in his calf and came to the boat with his lower leg in a strange, pneumatic "cast." Determined to not let such a trivial problem affect his diving, he put a weight belt over the cast to offset the buoyancy, and with a fin on the other foot, hit the water. All in all, another great trip with the family.

Captain's log, September 11, 2001

0736 pos abeam Cabo Corso, 1.5 mi in poor, uphill traveling weather with W breeze @ 15kts on mixed, confused seas and swells from SW, to 6ft

We were homeward bound for San Diego and had no idea the United States was under attack by radical terrorists. Satellite communication was far from perfect, so I did not suspect anything when I discovered I could not send or receive data (email) that evening, or the next day. On the evening of the 12th, I decided to anchor up in the small, fisherman's anchorage at Islas San Benito, get a good night's sleep, and give the weather a chance to calm down. With my email not working, I called Debbie, our ever-vigilant secretary, on the satphone and got the news. My email was not working because our satellite data provider was in the Twin Towers. People I had personally talked with from time to time were all gone.

Captain's log, September 14

2010, Coast Guard inspection team aboard, idling off ship channel buoy #5

San Diego, being a major US Navy port, was under strict Coast Guard control, and all vessels entering the port had to undergo a thorough inspection. We were directed to stand off a ship channel buoy. As soon as *Moana* stopped, a military patrol boat was alongside, and camouflage-clad Marines came over the rail. Never in my life had I experienced armed and deadly serious US Marines aboard any boat I was operating. We were impressed by their professionalism, but all the while I wondered if this could possibly be the beginning of something very big.

2002

NORTH AMERICA, CARIBBEAN

Captain's log, December 5, 2001

1300 pos 31° 54.3' N, 117° 05.7' W. Breeze picking up from WNW, 12–15kts on swells 6–8ft from W. Clear sky, beautiful downhill traveling weather.

South of San Diego, we were underway non-stop for Panama, over 3,000 nautical miles distant. Few motor yachts can lay claim to such range, especially at twelve to thirteen knots, but we built *Moana* to cross oceans; the distance was not a big deal for us. Weather, other boats, and floating debris are the real issues on a long, coastal run. In modern times, the emergence of very accurate weather routing services and satellite communication has taken much of the uncertainty out of the weather issue.

Small fishing boats are a much bigger issue. They often do not display any lights, their low profile does not give a good radar return at longer ranges, and the crew is sometimes sleeping as the boat drifts along in the night. Fishermen are well aware of the shipping lanes traveled by commercial traffic and are rarely found that far offshore at night. Unfortunately, this often places them directly in the path of smaller commercial boats and yachts traveling closer to the coastline. Many small boats and fishermen have been tragically lost in nighttime collisions, and I have personally had close encounters that could have ended badly had I not made a last-minute course change.

Floating debris, which includes lost or discarded fishing gear, logs or entire trees, miscellaneous trash, or even commercial shipping containers, are an ever-increasing danger, particularly at night. Lost or discarded polypropylene (plastic) fishing gear or nets float on the surface and are a common problem.

When fouled in a boat's propellers, these melt into a tight mass that can stop a vessel's engine, or at the least, cause tremendous vibration. This becomes a dangerous situation when it is necessary to dive under the boat to cut it off, when the boat is rising and falling in a large swell. For this run, my biggest concern was trees, washed down rivers and streams during periods of heavy rainfall, typical of this time of year off the coast of Mexico.

Fishing gear cut off propeller. Bald head to support my friend's son, undergoing chemotherapy for cancer

As it turned out, we did have to stop once. Offshore Acapulco, a Mexican navy patrol boat ordered us to stop for an inspection. The inspection took a bit longer than usual when it was discovered we had no papers from ports where motor yachts normally stopped for fuel and supplies. My explanation, that we were traveling non-stop to Panama from San Diego, was met with instant disbelief by the officer in charge. Fortunately, he understood the speed-equals-horsepower-equals-fuel formula; and after I showed him my logbook and fuel gauges, he smiled and admitted he had never before boarded a motor yacht with such long-range capability.

Eleven days around the clock was a long trip; but, since luck was with us, it turned out to be a good one. We had a lot of rain, which meant running a little farther offshore the central Mexican coast to avoid floating debris and trees, and the usual mix of calm to breezy weather. We never needed to slow down, and even had decent weather in the notorious Gulf of Tehuantepec, which means we had a very good trip, all the way to Panama.

Our next trip with the family was our "Christmas trip," and a rerun of the previous year, to the islands offshore Panama. We again visited the islands of Las Perlas, Jicarita, Jicaron, Coiba, and Montuosa, and again fished the Hannibal Bank. The weather and water temperatures were a little different from last time, so we caught different species of fish, but in general it was another great trip.

Back in Panama, we welcomed the arrival of a new cook. The cook's job on *Moana* was a real challenge, confirmed by the fact we had gone through five already. Gourmet cuisine, with seafood the specialty, was expected. Provisioning and supplies management, a big job in any modern city, was far more difficult in strange countries and developing island nations. Interior cleaning and laundry were also on the list, and when all that was combined with the isolation of living on a boat in remote places and long, rough passages, the job was too tough for most young women. But Pascale would prove to be unlike all before her. She was a lovely French woman that Michel and Martine interviewed and sent to the boat, assuring me she was energetic and enthusiastic, but "has limited English." They should have told me she could not read, write, or speak English! When I picked her up at the airport in Panama, she blushed slightly and was so quiet I was sure she was shy to the extreme. I could not have been more wrong!

On the boat, Pascale took over the galley and her cooking with confidence. She never used a cookbook (they were all in English, anyway) or measured anything (all tools were in imperial units, not metric), or said a word. But everything she made was great, so Joubert and I were very happy with our "shy" cook. Unable to say more than "hello," Pascale was so clever, she was able to convince us she was quiet because she was shy, not because she could not speak English. And with her impressive recipes, all in her head, she did not even need to use cookbooks or measuring tools. It was almost a month before I realized she could not speak English.

Cuba was to be our next trip with the family, so we again transited the Panama Canal from the Pacific to the Caribbean. Our pilot was a young Panamanian who proved to be one of the best we ever had aboard. Highly educated, well trained, and from a family of professionals, he was a classy guy and a fantastic pilot. Our transit was uneventful and enjoyable, and on March 15 we were underway for the Cayman Islands.

Captain's log, March 15

1600 pos 10° 35.2' N, 80° 09.8' W. Drop RPM to 1170 in miserable, pounding, crashing weather. Breeze, ocean swells, and wind driven residual seas all coming from different directions. Nasty, "vagrant" seas sweeping across beam, making boat snap roll beam-to-beam.

It was one of those very tough slogs in the Caribbean, all the way north to Georgetown, on Grand Cayman Island. We were exhausted on arrival and happy to clear in with customs and find a quiet moorage at the yacht club in Governor's Cut. Over the years, clearing in with the senior customs officer in Georgetown was always "interesting," depending on one's sense of humor. He was a tall, pale, and very English-looking man, and I never knew his name. But he had been there forever and never failed to give me his little speech decrying any behavior in life he deemed offensive. His parting words were always, "Not a drop has ever passed these lips" (index finger tapping lips), as he described his disdain for alcohol.

Santiago, Cuba

Georgetown was a great place to resupply, especially with the fresh and very expensive food flown in daily, and on March 24, we were underway for Cuba again. This time, the family would join us in Santiago, on the southeast end of the island, so we ran for the Windward Passage in mixed and sometimes uncomfortable weather. We passed under "El Morro," the Colonial Era fort overlooking the bay, and then followed our government escort vessel to the marina in Santiago.

Santiago was a classic city of the Colonial Era, with a huge and beautiful church flanked by other tall buildings around a traditional city square, complete with fountains, tiled walks, and lovely landscaping.

Beyond the square and the encircling buildings, however, the rest of the city was in desperate need of repair, and everything and everybody appeared poor. As in Havana, the mix of old cars and trucks was amazing, and all of them belched black smoke as they bounced along on worn-out springs and rough stone streets. The oldest house in the Americas was here long before Fidel Castro started his revolution from this same area. Perhaps knowing it could happen again, the government security, or "watchers," were everywhere. And although Santiago and Cayo Largo were tourist destinations, the people here were far more fearful.

My first visit to the marina manager's office underscored the reality of that fear. The marina docks and office buildings were old but apparently justified some maintenance, as they were in much better shape than other buildings or homes in the area. The docks were raised concrete and actually well done, except the water pipes and electricity were nonfunctional. This did not matter much. Only three or four sailboats shared the small marina with us, so we just ran our generators. As I walked into the manager's office, I was surprised to see eight to ten men pounding away on old typewriters. With so few boats in the marina, I did not expect to see such a large office staff. Then came a big surprise. On a big, dirty, video screen, mounted high on the wall, a 1950s-era black-and-white film flickered to the sound of a tired marching band, and a troop of flag waving, military-uniformed children marched down a street, singing loudly the praises of the revolution.

Being an American, and probably a bit naïve, I smiled and blurted out, "Viva Fidel!" In most places in Cuba, this was met with smiles from the people who shared the joke and understood my sense of humor, but not here. The manager's eyes went wide, the typewriters fell silent for a moment, and the office staff kept their heads down. After a very quick sign-in with the manager, I had to be interviewed by two different officials in small offices. One insisted we speak in Spanish, the other spoke absolutely perfect "American English," and I had no idea the purpose of the interviews. At that point, the crew and I were officially cleared to come ashore and travel wherever, and I walked outside the offices where I found the marina manager was waiting for me.

"Luís, you must be very careful here. Never make jokes about the government, especially in offices or any places where they are working with other government workers. You are probably smart enough to see the people watching you, but you must understand security people are being watched by others, and you will never know who they are."

The seriousness of his tone and the look in his eyes was naked truth. And he then revealed another truth when he asked me if we could give him some basic school supplies for his young daughter. Pencils, paper, erasers! I was surprised with his request, as it was "well known" that the government provided a free, quality education to all Cubans. I offered to go to the boat immediately, but he gave me yet another surprise.

"Luís, all those other men in the office would like to have my job. They watch everything I do, and if I am seen receiving anything from you, no matter what it is, I will lose my job. Tomorrow morning at 0835 I will walk down the enclosed stairwell next to the office. You will walk up the stairwell at the same time, with the school supplies inside your shirt. We will meet at the middle landing, where no one can see us, and you can give me the supplies. You will continue up the stairwell and visit one of the little shops at the upper level before returning to your boat. My daughter has only a little stub left of her pencil, and has no paper at all. Luís, all the people here are very poor. We have nothing."

And while pointing at *Moana*, as if conducting business, "I will understand if you do not want to help me."

As a father of two girls, I never considered declining to help another father who was trying desperately to help his daughter. The transfer in the stairwell was uneventful, a measure of trust was established, but friendship was always guarded. He and I had several small talks after, but he was always so nervous, I was never able to learn the answers to many of my endless questions. This was the reality of life in Santiago, Cuba, in 2002. A year later, I found a way to smuggle in some kerosene lantern mantles that were difficult to get, even on the flourishing black market.

Out of curiosity, we visited a couple of government stores and, after seeing the terrible quality and very limited quantity of everything, it was easy to see why the black market was the only game in town. The black market was survival for the local people. A huge embarrassment to the government, it was also one of Cuba's best kept secrets. When Pascale needed some fresh eggs, we took a ten-minute taxi ride and found everything she wanted at a farmer's house. This area was far from any that might be visited by tourists, and it held an interesting secret. A football-field distance off the dirt road, amongst some trees, our driver pointed out a rusting, abandoned Russian rocket. Dirty green, with a still visible red star, it was on its launcher and pointed in the direction of Florida. Viva Fidel!

Captain's log, April 1

Underway off SE coast of Cuba in very good, downhill traveling weather. Swell rolling through Windward Passage, to 6ft, no wind. 0000 pos 19° 47.7' N, 77° 41.3' W, A/C to 294°.

At 0612, we dropped anchor off Cayo Caguama, and our third trip to the Gardens of the Queen began. We were very excited to return because there would be no guesswork. Thanks in large part to "Elvis," we returned only to the very best spots we had found before, and each night anchored in calm, safe anchorages. The constant laughter and endless energy of the children created a wonderful ambiance to long, full days. Cachiboca Canal, Punta Caballones, Boca Grande, Alcatracito, all names of postcard-beautiful places we swam and fished in warm, transparent water, explored on white sand beaches, and anchored all alone.

It was our eighth trip with the family aboard. The crew and I were now very comfortable and efficient with our usual routines in "family mode," which was simply to do whatever it took, to get as much fun and excitement into every hour for everyone aboard. Michel, the "leader of the pack," would choose the water activities for the morning, based on our location and conditions at hand. Snorkeling, spearfishing, scuba diving, or fishing was on the menu, and everyone up for that activity piled into our small boat and was off early (sometimes in the dark). Martine, Rachel, and female guests quite often, but not always, took a more relaxed approach to the day. With *Moana* anchored close offshore, it was usually a short swim to beautiful white-sand beaches that encircled dense rain forests on uninhabited islands. From the pilothouse, I could often see wildlife and birds surprised by humans on their island, and wondered how many footprints were ever seen on those remote, pristine beaches.

Donald's big lobster

At 1300, the small boat always returned and our adventurers replayed the morning over a nice lunch and then decided on the afternoon activities. Sometimes they would be worn out from the morning trip and elect to stay aboard in the afternoon, but given the incredible conditions we often found in remote places, they could not resist a second trip. This routine kept our deck freezer stocked with fish, lobster, and, in the case of Cuba, jutías, the giant tree rats! It also resulted in early bedtimes and a seldom-used TV, for everyone.

With the arrival of Pascale, a trained French chef, the stern of the boat soon became the center of pre-dinnertime activity. She was thrilled to find that Joubert and I could barbecue all manner of seafood, so what was previously a once-a-week activity became an almost nightly event. She planned her menu around barbecued seafood and coordinated the cooking time to coincide with her other dishes. In beautiful anchorages, with warm, tropical breezes, the sight and smell of fresh fish cooking on the barbecue was an irresistible magnet for the entire family and guests alike. Combined with our special underwater lights, attracting everything from sharks to tiny, unknown creatures, every evening at the stern of the boat was an exciting,

Bait tank pets

unpredictable, and sometimes unforgettable event. And after only a few days, the kids would have an amazing variety of the most interesting and beautiful tropical fish and other "pets" in the bait tank.

We did keep live bait fish in the tank for catching large fish, but the kids' real interest in the tank was to use it as a big aquarium. By the end of a trip, it usually held many species of fish and marine creatures never to be seen in a saltwater aquarium store. This, our third trip to Cuba, was spectacular. The weather was good almost every day, and everyone agreed it was the stuff of dreams.

Captain's log, April 15
2300 pos 9.7 miles abeam Cap Tiburon, Haiti

Next on the adventure list was Venezuela, via Dominican Republic, Puerto Rico, and the Windward Isles. Puerto Rico was US territory, which meant questions might be asked of a boat and crew coming from that dastardly, enemy country of Cuba, so we made a stop in the Dominican Republic. By clearing in and out there, our passports showed us to have

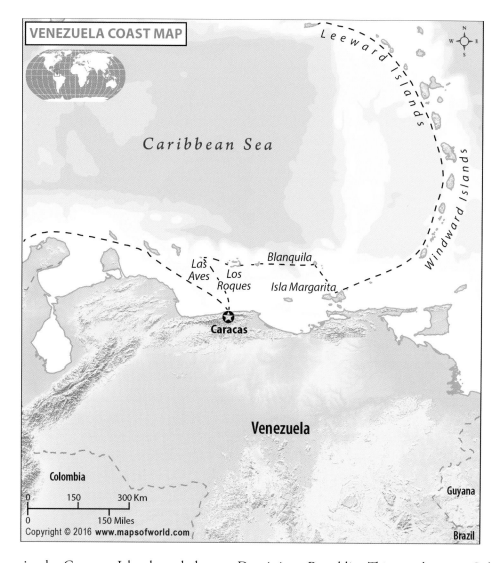

been in the Cayman Islands and then to Dominican Republic. This was because Cuban Customs did not stamp our passports. They simply inserted a small, stamped paper inside the passports, which was removed when we left Cuba. Of course, there was a one-month time gap between when we left the Caymans and arrived in Dominican Republic, but some boats take forever getting from one place to another, so on paper we were not unusual. This was how it was done.

I had been in San Juan, Puerto Rico, on another boat, a few years before, so I knew my way around and figured our pit stop would be easy and brief. Of course, wrong again! Maintenance and provisioning went well, but that was not the case at the Venezuelan Consulate.

To visit Venezuela, we had to have an unbelievable quantity of documents, and the detail required to receive the documents was beyond anything I had ever been subjected to, in any country. After five trips to the Consulate, I looked across the desk at the agent, who did not hide his delight in tormenting me, day after day.

"In my life as a boat captain, I have to tell you, this has been the most difficult, frustrating, and maddening experience I have ever had to obtain permission to visit another country."

"Really?" (Big smile)

Unbelievably, my statement was this agent's personal requirement to get final approval. In his small mind, being sure I had been properly antagonized was a necessary part of the process, and my admission demonstrated respect for his authority (power), which sealed the deal. This should have been my first clue of what was coming in Venezuela.

Captain's log, June 16

Underway in Eastern Caribbean in windy, nasty traveling weather. 0000 pos 17° 43.9' N, 63° 34.1' W. Slamming, banging, and hanging on.

We had typical, twenty-knot Trade Winds from the east and east-southeast all the way south, on the run from Puerto Rico to Venezuela. Running close, in the lee of the many islands in the chain, we found good traveling weather, but we got roughed up in the passages between. This was expected, so we anchored up for the night at several beautiful islands, got a good night's sleep, and continued on in the mornings.

On the afternoon of the 18th, we anchored in Peter's Hope Bay, in the lee of Saint Vincent Island. A calm, lovely anchorage, with rainforest right down to the water's edge, we were alone and enjoyed the tranquility as we prepared for dinner. Off the point of the bay, a man furiously rowing in a small boat caught my eye. He was rowing straight out to sea, as if his life depended on it, stopping for a while, and then rowing as fast as he could, back toward the island. This went on, over and over until I saw him stop and pull in a fish. It was not only a fish, it was a tuna! He was trolling for tuna, from a rowboat, propelled only by oars and muscle. Considering we typically trolled at eight knots for tuna, it was an impressive show of strength, technique, and endurance.

Captain's log, June 20

0600 pos 11° N, 63° 37.8' W. Approaching Isla de Margarita.

Pre-trip research painted an interesting picture of Venezuela in 2002. The offshore islands we planned to visit were reported to be exactly the type we loved; remote and pristine.

The mainland, however, was in political and economic turmoil, with the emergence of Hugo Chavez and his "Bolivarian Revolution." The US State Department issued a travel warning to

Aves Sotavento

all US citizens, advising against travel to Venezuela. Captain friends in Florida who had been to Venezuela a year prior reported good fishing but said, "Be careful." They did not plan to return.

In our case, though, we had a fantastic summer trip. The small, low, offshore islands were the most remote and seldom visited in the Caribbean and were everything we hoped for. Powder white-sand beaches meeting beautiful coral reefs in clear, aquamarine water provided excellent beachcombing, birdwatching, and photo opportunities.

We had some breezy days but for the most part found good, sheltered anchorages. Huge populations of seabirds nested on Aves Sotavento ("birds of the leeward"), including three different species of boobies. Being a lover of seabirds, I was always watching for behavior I had not seen before, and I was in for a funny show at Aves Sotavento.

On the first morning we were there, red-footed boobies were flying in a circle around us, and most of them with a small twig from a mangrove tree in their beaks. Suddenly, one of the boobies was attacked by the others, and I noticed the twig he had in his beak had two leaves attached. Boobies are fast, powerful birds; seeing this behavior so close, I was amazed to see how aerobatic they could be. Like children playing a schoolyard game, the booby with the "special" twig would fly around at top speed, making every maneuver imaginable to prevent his buddies

Los Roques: The only islands where we saw other boats

from stealing the twig. If none succeeded, this would go on for several minutes, until he tired and dropped the twig, when one of the others would catch it in midair. Then, the new "keeper of the twig" would be pursued by the others, and on and on, until the twig fell into the water.

At that point, the game would stop, with most of them again flying around and around with a bare twig in their beaks, but not doing anything special, until suddenly, one would appear with a twig that had two or three leaves on it, and the game would instantly be on again. This comical game would start every morning at the same time and end about the same time when they would suddenly fly off to their fishing grounds. Both the red-footed and blue-footed boobies would do this, but not the brown boobies. It was interesting to me that a twig with a leaf or two could be plucked from the nearby mangrove trees at any time, by any one of the birds. I tried to figure it out, but it was not obvious why one would suddenly start the game. All I knew for sure was it made my morning coffee time a lot of fun!

The roots of dense mangrove forests around some of the islands provided giant nurseries for countless numbers of fish, including tarpon, known worldwide for their spectacular jumping displays when hooked. When conditions were great and lots of fish were around, which was usually the case, a friendly spearfishing competition would often break out between all the boys and men aboard. Sometimes I would post a "tournament scorecard," complete with colorful names for the competitors, and listing points for sizes and species caught. In the beginning, Michel dominated these contests, but the boys were nipping at his heels and pushed him hard to maintain "Top Gun" status. When Louis won one of these competitions in a very flashy style, I began to call him 007, after the famous James Bond character. Like some nicknames, it seemed to fit, and we called him that for years.

We saw a few sailboats, but most of the time we had one beautiful anchorage after another all to ourselves. An exception was Isla Blanquilla, where we shared a nice anchorage with a small commercial fishing boat. Anchored just off our bow, I could not help noticing the three-man crew continuously bailing buckets of water overboard the old fishing boat. In the binoculars, I could see the fishermen sweating heavily in the hot, tropical sun. My lifelong bond with fishermen, forged by several very hard years in that business, prompted an easy decision, and armed with four cold beers, I approached the small boat in our dinghy.

The look on their faces was pretty funny when I handed over the beers. This was exactly the kind of thing I loved to do, and while drinking mine, enjoyed the camaraderie of my fellow fishermen. While exchanging the usual fishing stories, the bailing water continued and it was obvious their bilge pump had failed, and their boat was taking on water continuously. Another easy decision: After a quick trip to *Moana*, I gave my new friends an electric pump from our extensive spare parts inventory. Cold beers, and a new bilge pump! From an American! The fishermen were stunned, and as the new pump began a steady stream of water overboard, we all began to laugh.

It is funny how a small thing can become a great memory and have lasting effects. As I started my engine and got ready to leave, the very appreciative fishermen gave me the only thing they had of value. It was an ugly, very pungent, dried egg sack from a large fish! They explained that while looking and smelling revolting, when the dried eggs were mixed with oil and spread on a cracker, it was really delicious. I hid my doubt the family would endure the smell of the truly disgusting egg sacks, thanked them back, and returned to *Moana*. To my surprise, Thomas immediately took the eggs into the galley, and in minutes we sampled the most delicious pâté imaginable! Thus, a small electric bilge pump was traded for what became a *Moana* tradition of dried and exquisite fish-egg pâté. Thomas, always up for anything new, different, or even a bit dangerous, developed a technique that would make the finest gourmet chef jealous. A nice glass of Chardonnay, fish-egg pâté on homemade bread thins, and the nightly fish-catching activities under the underwater lights were my best memories of being the barbecue man.

The family and guests departed from a small marina in Puerto Viejo, on the mainland. The marina was directly behind a big, luxury hotel, and was well done by Venezuela standards. We were the only US boat in the almost empty marina. Ringed with razor wire and patrolled day and night by security guards toting sawed off shotguns, it was the most dangerous and filthy of all marinas we had yet visited. Alongside the marina, a small river slowly flowed into the sea. This river was absolutely choked with every kind of waste, including dead animals, creating a putrid river of floating debris and black filth. Immediately carried off by the northerly current, and stretching as far as the eye could see, I wondered how our poor ocean could digest the never-ending onslaught. The surrounding neighborhood was similar. Poor and dirty, home to seedy karaoke bars, it was definitely unsafe at night, when gunfire could sometimes be heard.

With our maintenance done, food and fuel (diesel cost less than bottled water) aboard, we were ready to get underway for Panama. We had a little time to spare, so Joubert, Pascale, and I planned a day trip into Caracas to visit the famous museums. When our agent came to the boat to deliver our outward clearance papers, I told him of our plans and asked if the museums were indeed worth the long taxi ride. In that microsecond of time that he understood we would all be off the boat, I saw a flash in his eyes. The next morning, Joubert and Pascale took a taxi to Caracas, and I stayed aboard, inside the boat.

When clearing in previously, our ship's agent introduced himself as a lawyer who worked part time as an agent. Given the fact that many ship's agents in remote locales were not to be trusted, and he was wearing a pager on each hip, like six-guns in a Hollywood movie, I was not impressed. Now I knew what I had seen in his eyes, so giving up the trip into Caracas was not a difficult decision. And shortly after Joubert and Pascale departed in a taxi, the marina security guards were not to be seen. The dark glass of *Moana* allowed me, unseen, to watch the five strange men approach. We were the only boat on that dock, so their intentions were obvious when they stopped alongside and looked around. At that moment, I stepped out on the upper aft deck, hand-held VHF radio in hand, and silently stared down at them.

I saw surprise, anger, and then, fear. They did not run, but they did not linger. The marina security guards did not return, and by 1330 we were underway for Panama.

Captain's log, September 5

Underway in SW Caribbean, in lee of Curacao, in clear, hot weather. 0000 pos 11° 58.2' N, 68° 41' W

Traveling in drug- and arms-smuggling territory at night provokes interest from those who would protect you, as well at those who would do you harm. Not long after the preceding entry, an unlit vessel appeared on my radar and in the darkness just beyond our big deck lights, matched our speed, and silently followed. A long hour later, a Curacao Coast Guard patrol vessel turned on his navigation lights, identified himself on the radio, and escorted us into Willemstad. Thorough and professional, the two-hour inspection was complete and a small boat guided us out of the harbor, and we were underway for Panama again.

Donald and Louis, doing what brothers do

Captain's log, September 8

0945, pilot aboard, anchor aboard, dep "Flats" for transit through Panama Canal. Idling southbound.

Two hours after arriving, Pete had our pilot aboard; and ten hours later we exited Mira Flores, the last Panama Canal lock. It was a beautiful day and an uneventful transit.

The 3,000+ nautical miles' run back to San Diego was tough. Off Costa Rica, Nicaragua, and El Salvador, we had intense rainsqualls and the worst lightning storms I had ever experienced. Two nights in a row, we had lightning so intense and constant that the sky was as bright as high noon for hours at a time. As the lightning crashed down all around us, the noise and concussion rocked the boat with terrifying power. With all electronics off except the auto pilot, and with our tall VHF antenna disconnected, Joubert and I endured four-hour wheel watches by standing against the wood bulkhead at the aft end of the pilothouse,

Rachel and Elisabeth

as far as possible from any metal. Those four-hour watches were an eternity, and it was a miracle we were not struck.

Beginning off Guatemala, a strong west swell caught us on a poor angle and kept us from having a single good day, all the way to Cabo San Lucas. Two inspections by the Mexican Navy and screaming wind in the Gulf of Tehuantepec added to our torment, but all the equipment ran fine, and like the faithful, dependable companion she was, *Moana* powered through the miles, arriving in San Diego on September 25.

Donald's big rooster fish

Swimming with humpback whales

Captain's log, December 14

1000 pos 24° 48.9' N, 112° 26.6' W. Beautiful morning off Baja with clear skies, bright sunshine, very light breeze and chop from NE. Swells WSW @ 4–6ft.

On a flat-topped mountainside, overlooking the picturesque little river and marina of Ixtapa, was a small settlement known by the locals as "Las Mesas." It was home to the poorest of the poor, who lived in small dwellings built from tree branches and plastic trash bags. The taxi driver who took me there asked, "Are you sure? No one goes there."

For years and years, I took old clothes, toys, school supplies, household goods, etc., to Mexico, giving them out to local people in need. It was a great way to share with people who simply had less, and to make new friends. I was not prepared for what I saw at Las Mesas. Children growing up in that place brought tears to my eyes, but for them, it was their normal. Like children everywhere, they were running around and laughing, without a thought of their surroundings or futures. All they knew was a strange man who introduced himself as "Santa Claus" was there, giving out wonderful things. The men, if they were there, did not come out, but the women did, and shyly accepted my gifts as well. Debbie had gift wrapped all the toys and things for the children, so it really was Christmas for them. I will forever remember a young girl screaming out in delight, and holding her little Barbie doll high, leapt, ran, and bounded amongst the trees. At the bottom of the mountain, the taxi driver stopped his worn out little taxi. Staring straight ahead, and nodding his head, he finally looked over at me. "You know, what you did was very nice."

We enjoyed very good weather all the way down the coast of Baja California and the mainland coast of Mexico en route the marina at Ixtapa, where our next trip with the family began. It was a very good Christmas trip. The weather was sunny and calm every day, and because we were close offshore the long, beautiful beaches of Zihuatanejo, the family enjoyed a lot of beachcombing by paddling through the surf in our kayak. The surf was not huge, but some of the larger sets were powerful. A lifelong surfer, I could see the boys would have trouble getting to the beach safely, and I volunteered to take them in the first time with the kayak. I chose a spot where strong tide rips (powerful, outgoing current) created a calm area between the breakers, and we had little difficulty paddling right up onto the beach. I left Donald and Louis to enjoy the beach and paddled back to the boat, where I related "landing strategy" to Michel.

Unfortunately, Rachel and her friend Elisabeth were sunning on the bow and did not hear any of my important comments. Several hours later, the tide had changed, and with the largest waves of the day pounding the beach, they set off in the kayak without saying a word to anyone. It was a hot, sunny afternoon, with the long, beautiful sand beach calling. They had heard all about it from the boys, and had no idea of the danger awaiting. Surf, from the seaward side looking shoreward, is difficult to judge for the average person, but it is instantly understood by experienced surfers. Rachel was a powerful swimmer, and perhaps her confidence minimized any thoughts of danger as she and Elisabeth paddled directly toward the beach. Already too far to warn when I saw them approaching the surf line, I could only watch and hold my breath as they paddled directly into a very big set of powerful waves. The very first wave overwhelmed the kayak, and "pitch-poled" them, end over end. Thrown out of the capsized kayak, they were then pounded by wave after wave. From the pilothouse, the height of the waves obscured my line of sight, so I could not see how terrified the girls were. Elisabeth had caught her hand in the short bowline of the kayak and could not free herself. Tethered to the kayak, she was pulled underwater by successive waves before finally being dragged onto the beach. In my binoculars, I could see they were shocked by the experience. It was a hard lesson learned. More than an hour later, and after carefully waiting for a lull in the waves, they were able to paddle out and return to *Moana*. Fortunately, Elisabeth's hand was uninjured, and after they related how scared they had been, I knew they would never again fail to tell me they were going off in the kayak.

So close inshore, we did not do much diving, but we had sensational fishing for yellowtail and roosterfish. Just beyond the breakers, as the sun began to slide beneath a glassy calm sea, I shared a wonderful memory of fishing with Donald in the small boat. We were slow trolling with live bait when he had a powerful strike. Our observer/reader was also an excellent student who set the hook and for a long, hard hour battled the big roosterfish like a professional. I'm not sure who had the biggest smile when we returned, but it was definitely Donald's day to shine!

We also used the small boat for a new activity: swimming with humpback whales! At anchor, close to the beach, I noticed a group of whales nearby, repeatedly diving in what I considered shallow water for whales. I could not figure out what they were doing, but I noticed they were not moving away. When I pointed this out to Michel, he and Louis, along with Joubert and Pascale, leapt into the dinghy and approached the whales. From the pilothouse, it looked like lunatics were jumping onto the backs of the whales as they slowly swam along, unaffected and tolerant of the curious humans. When they returned, a wide-eyed Joubert told me he was initially very afraid to be so close to the huge animals and was amazed the whales allowed Michel and Louis to swim so close, at times almost touching them.

Captain's log, January 4, 2003
1000 pos 17° 48.3' N, 102° 09.2' W, abeam Lazaro Cardenas, 6.2 mi in beautiful traveling weather. Long, low swell from W, very light breeze from SE. Hazy, partly cloudy sky, nice air temp.

We were homeward bound after a long and exciting 2002. Luck was with us, and we had a great trip all the way home. *Moana* had proven to be all we hoped her to be.

It was time to cross the Pacific and follow the dream.

Red-tailed tropic bird stowaway

2003

ACROSS THE PACIFIC

Halfway across the Pacific Ocean, we had a visitor. In the fishing cockpit, sitting on the deck in a regal pose, was a red-tailed tropic bird.

I had seen these birds many times when far offshore, commercial fishing for tuna, but I had never seen one up close, so I was surprised to see she was larger than I had previously thought and was stunned by the beauty and elegant behavior of our guest. Her body was flat to the deck, with her feathers ruffled out, seemingly content to catch a ride and a little rest in her daily life at sea. There was just the slightest glow of rose color to her silky white feathers, splashed with black wing accents, and highlighted with a black "comma" at her eye. A bright red beak and two, long, red tail streamers were unique to these members of the Phaethon family of tropicbirds.

Some species of seabirds like to land on boats to rest or catch an easy ride, but this behavior was not normal for a red-tailed tropic bird. I suspected she might be sick, so looked her over closely. She was unafraid and allowed me to come very close, all the while maintaining a still, elegant pose. Her plumage was not quite fully adult, so I guessed she was less than four years old. I took some photos, said "Thank you for the visit," and returned to the pilothouse, sure she would be gone soon.

When I found her in the same spot the following morning, I sensed something wrong. She was alert and did not seem to be in distress, but there had to be a reason she did not take off and fly away. I opened one of my books, and there it was: "Phaethon rubricauda," evolved such that the legs were set back on the body so far, the bird could not stand up. When nesting, the only time they came to land, they had to push themselves along, inches at a time, over the ground.

Our poor guest could not stand up to extend and flap her wings. She was stranded, marooned on our fancy yacht, for which she had no appreciation and from which she had no way to escape. I will always remember how she remained so quiet and elegant, never once protesting, never once making a fuss. In my mind, she was patiently waiting for me to help her. I slid a bait net under her breast, she quietly struggled onto it, and I gently launched her into the air.

Stowaway aloft again

I like to think she looked back. I hoped she would circle the boat in some kind of "good-bye," but it was not the case. She simply returned to her world with the unique wing beats known to her species.

I watched until she disappeared into the morning sun, beyond the towering trade winds swells and cascading whitecaps astern. This was the mid-Pacific, a vast, hostile, and nearly lifeless expanse of water, where only this bird called home.

The ancient Polynesians, the world's finest seamen and navigators, had a deep respect for these birds they saw on their epic, open-ocean voyages of thousands of miles. They well knew every kind of seabird and how far from land each could be found. They were among the very few who have ever seen these birds feed, diving very deep into the sea at twilight to catch small squid. With special feathers to absorb the high diving impact and legs set far back for efficient, powerful swimming, red-tailed tropic birds have superbly evolved to survive where no others can. *How fitting,* I thought to myself. She had come aboard while we were crossing the Pacific on a catamaran. And especially one named *Moana*, the legendary name in the Polynesian language for their "endless, beautiful ocean." Like stars in the night sky, we were a little dot on that endless ocean, following in the footsteps of the ancient Polynesians on their double-hulled canoes.

A year later, on the French island of New Caledonia, I celebrated our voyage across the Pacific and my love of this beautiful bird, with her tattoo inside my left ankle. I see her every day.

Captain's log, March 28
1000 position 4° 47.4' N, 132° 24.6' W. Tropic bird "stowaway" released. Sea conditions poor, with breeze 12–14kts from ESE on swells to 8ft, from NNE. Tropical countercurrent flowing & colliding with wind-driven seas from ESE.

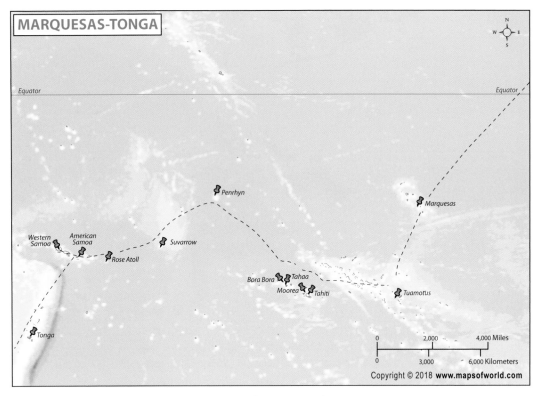

Islands of the South Pacific

We were underway on a non-stop voyage across the Pacific. Our destination was French Polynesia and the Marquesas Islands, 3,200 nautical miles away.

The first stop in the South Pacific dream.

But before we could get underway from San Diego, we had to get visas from the French Embassy in Los Angeles. This proved to be the worst embassy experience I would have in my entire life. Rude, arrogant, and blatantly disrespectful, the French Embassy staff were a disgrace to their country. Weeks of driving back and forth from San Diego to Los Angeles to satisfy their ever-changing demands for documentation made us late getting underway. In all the different embassies and consulates, in all the different countries we visited, none (not even Venezuela) compared to the way we were treated in Los Angeles.

To compound our late departure, in the "eleventh hour" we discovered a problem in our port main engine gearbox (marine transmission). Returning from the fuel dock, lube oil was found to be leaking from the air vent, at the top of the gearbox. Jay and Joubert immediately began the difficult and time-consuming repair, which involved lifting the main engine off its mounts and completely removing the gearbox. Once it was disassembled, they discovered

Taiohae Bay, Nuku Hiva

special vibration-absorbing parts inside had mysteriously hardened, cracked, and failed, prompting an oil seal to leak. The manufacturer provided different replacement parts they felt would be a long-term fix, everything was reassembled, the engine was realigned to the propeller shaft, and we were finally ready to go. But what about the starboard gearbox? With the same hours and wear and tear, we knew the same parts that failed on portside were most likely in bad shape on starboard. We were already late, and to make the same repairs on the other engine would ruin Michel's plans to meet us in the Marquesas.

To operate a boat in remote, primitive locales, far from support services, requires the will and confidence to make things happen. In this case, I elected to make a very long trip happen. We purchased the gearbox parts, a chain hoist, and a huge, wooden beam that we lashed to the portside deck stanchions. In the case of failure on starboard, Joubert and I would make the same repair as before. But where? Without shipyard assistance? How long would the worn parts last before the gearbox failed completely? It was a roll of the dice and not my usual conservative approach, but we got away in time to meet Michel's schedule.

Nuku Hiva fuel depot in strong surge

Captain's log, March 31

2035, anchor down in 35ft, sand, Taiohae Bay, Nuku Hiva

With the day's fading light, and Michel's excited voice coming from my satellite phone, we came up on the range, and idled into beautiful, calm Taiohae Bay, on the island of Nuku Hiva, in the remote Marquesas Islands.

It had been a long trip. Twelve days and twelve nights, to the steady drone of diesel engines and the unending motion of a boat in tough, open-ocean conditions, *Moana* proved to be the ocean-crossing vessel she was designed and built to be. Sometimes surfing down towering swells, sometimes punching through wild rain squalls, it was a bit of a marathon, and it required a strict mindset. The top of every hour, day and night, meant engine room checks of all the equipment, and a running log entry of position, speed, RPM, weather, and any maintenance issues. Given the seriousness of crossing the Pacific Ocean in whatever weather or equipment problems we encountered, boredom was ruled out and we were kept focused at all times. Indeed, the awareness of what we were doing provided an unspoken sense of excitement for us and, at trip's end, a wonderful feeling of accomplishment. It also cast in stone the strong bond of respect, confidence, and loyalty between Joubert, Pascale and me, which would last for years.

We had paced ourselves well and the boat ran perfectly, which was a good thing because Michel and guests had arrived in Nuku Hiva two days before, and after exploring the island on horseback, were ready to go. The very next morning, we cleared in with customs and refueled at a commercial and wild seawall.

Thanks to satellite communication and our exceptional ship's agents in Tahiti (I had yet to meet them), I made arrangements the week before to fly fresh food and supplies into Nuku Hiva. Most of it actually came from New Zealand, and the quality was amazing. Bruno, our agent's supplier, even knew to ship ripe, medium, and green produce, much to the approval of Pascale. On day two, we completed all maintenance items and stowed aboard all the supplies and fresh food, and at 0829 the following morning we were on our way.

The Marquesas are spectacular, towering young islands. Covered in lush rain forest, the cloud-covered mountains rise straight up from the sea, with no surrounding coral reefs. This is a bit of a dilemma for visiting boats because it often means anchoring in deep water, close to the shore, where strong winds fly down vertically from the high mountain peaks, making for spinning and exciting but uncomfortable anchorages.

Captain's log, April 5

1800 pos 11° 14.1' S, 140° 41.9' W. Green flash sunset, rolly, but good traveling weather.

We enjoyed the wildness of the Marquesas for two days before departing for what was termed the "Dangerous Isles" of the Tuamotu Archipelago. These low, coral rings, or atolls, only a few feet above sea level, were all that remained of the reefs that surrounded volcanoes that had sunk into the depths, eons ago.

Almost impossible to see at night, the atolls were given a wide berth by seafarers for centuries. In the middle of nowhere, with beautiful, calm lagoons inside the coral rings, we loved them.

We were surprised to find many of the lagoons in the Tuamotus filled with oyster farms. The clear, clean waters of the lagoons were perfect for raising the famous Black Pearls of the South Pacific. A lucrative business that depended on the pristine water, the farmers were very protective of their farms. When we asked to anchor inside, they escorted us to an anchorage but requested we not allow any wastewater to go overboard—not even dish or laundry soap!

We first visited Apataki, Rangiroa, and Fakarava. These huge atolls were visited by scuba divers from all over the world. The divers came mostly in big live-aboard dive boats from Tahiti to dive the passes, or openings, in the atolls. Every kind of sea life, from the smallest plankton to large sharks, dolphins, tuna, turtles, and all manner of reef fish, gathers outside the passes, waiting for the flood tide. Timing a dive to this flow of water into the lagoon, was flying underwater effortlessly in slow motion, completely surrounded by a breathtaking mass

Sunset, inside the lagoon, Tahanea

of beautiful marine creatures. Every dive was different, and every dive was a fantastic experience. It was on Rangiroa where we met the professional diver who told us about Tahanea.

Tahanea was paradise. The uninhabited coral ring of the atoll was made up of connected "motus," or small islands. They were a little higher than most of the other atolls and had enough decomposed coral, sand, and bird droppings to support small trees, bushes, and coconut palms that dotted the motus and encircled a stunning lagoon, fifteen miles across. Ages ago, natives lived there for many years, but life was simply too hard and they moved off. At the time of our visit, it was considered a sacred place to the Polynesians, as described on a very weatherworn wooden signpost on the largest motu. The pass and lagoon were uncharted, and we found current running down the atoll, so we had to wait until the sun was overhead to safely enter. Inside, we had no problems navigating the clear waters of the beautiful lagoon, passing several little islands that were densely forested and home to thousands of birds. We anchored in fifty feet, over a white coral sand bottom, behind a motu on the far end. With the low, coral barrier of the motu only yards off our bow, I marveled at the sight of powerful, dark blue, wind-driven seas slamming the windward side of the motu, while *Moana* floated on the calm, turquoise water inside the lagoon. For me, this was a unique experience, and I loved every minute of it.

Afternoon feeding time

We stayed at Tahanea for nine days, a long visit for us. It was a magical place and simply too fascinating to leave. Everything we loved was there. Diving the pass, snorkeling the reefs and coral heads inside the lagoon, playing in tide pools with marine creatures we had never seen before, kayaking from one perfect "Gilligan's Island" to another, beachcombing the motus where ancients last walked, feeding our little blacktip sharks, watching the bird show at sunset, barbecuing fresh fish, and sleeping in calm water—it was all there.

From the boat, I could see all the way across the lagoon and all the motus that made up the atoll. It was sobering to understand how difficult life must have been for the ancient Polynesian natives—no fresh water except for rain, very little "soil" that could support anything other than coconut trees, and no protection from the cyclones that visited these latitudes. There was plenty of seafood and an abundance of bird eggs, but life here had to be day-to-day survival. The fact that modern day Polynesians revere Tahanea as sacred and special suggests the ancients knew far more than we understood. All alone, *Moana* floated in what, for us, was a magical, pristine paradise. I pinched myself at every sunrise and felt privileged to experience such a wonderful place in my lifetime.

Captain's log, April 23

0703, A/C to 050° to exit pass. Port main fails!

Running the passes in atolls can be difficult, serious business. When a pass is narrow and the depth is shallow, with coral reefs close alongside, current sweeping across the reef, or with breaking waves, entering or leaving lagoon passes is reason for experienced judgment and intense concentration. On this day, our port main engine failed just as we were entering the pass to leave Tahanea.

Instantly, I considered and reasoned:

- Fuel? No, tank has plenty.

- Engine or gearbox? No RPMs, must be engine.

- Wrapped something in prop? No, no vibration.

- Starboard engine okay? Yes, RPMs constant, gauges look normal.

- Could common problem shut down starboard engine? If so, room to drop anchor without swinging into reef? No, pass too narrow.

- Will added power to starboard engine, to stay in center of pass, make it fail also?...

In the microsecond this flashed through my mind, I came on with more power to the starboard engine as I concentrated on the small waves and current running across the seaward side of the pass. This pass was a short one, but with the strong current capable of pushing us onto the reef, the moments needed to reach the safety of the deep, blue water outside the atoll were an eternity. It is remarkable to transit a pass in water only three to four feet under the boat, and in moments, see the bottom drop off to over a thousand feet. I probably held my breath.

It took two days of troubleshooting to find a very unusual problem. At the end of the build, the electricians discovered a requirement of the engine manufacturer they had not planned on. It was simply an extra cable running directly from the batteries to each Caterpillar control panel. Behind schedule and under pressure to finish their work, they elected to do the quick solution, instead of the right one. The added cables were undersized; and instead of the nice, commercial circuit breakers we normally used, they hastily installed small, in-line fuses. Over time, the undersized cables overheated, melting the plastic of the in-line fuse holder. The molten plastic flowed around the fuse, breaking the electrical connection, and the engine died. I was relieved to find and correct the problem but not very happy with our electrical contractor who had gone thousands of dollars over his estimate for the job.

Our first South Pacific adventure with the family aboard was over. We ran to Fakarava Atoll and anchored in the lagoon, less than 100 meters from the airport terminal. In the dinghy, I found a small hook in the volcanic rock seawall and ferried luggage, guests, and kids ashore.

Dinghy in hook on coral seawall; I never told Michel black bags were considered bad luck by mariners of old

Last to go ashore were Michel and Martine, and when I again maneuvered the small boat into the hook, Michel stood and faced me. Over the last month, we had successfully completed a first chapter in something he had dreamed of for years. He and his children and guests were going home with priceless memories, and I could see he was overcome with emotion and struggling to express his appreciation.

"On your bed… the Maori war club."

"Michel, I am your captain, and I can make a lot of things happen, but you are the man with the dream. You are our leader."

With tears in our eyes, we shook hands once again, and they departed for the airport. We raised our anchor and got underway at the same time their plane ran down the runway, 100 meters alongside. It was a beautiful day and a special way to end a trip.

While in the Marquesas, Michel had purchased an authentic, traditional Maori war club from a famous native carver. A beautiful work of art, it was made from a carved and polished marlin bill, attached to a long, wood handle, carved in the traditional Maori style. When I returned to the boat, it was resting on my bunk. It will forever remind me of a special time, place, and man.

Mola from San Blas (top), Penryhn fan (bottom), Maori war club from Marquesas (right)

Captain's log, April 26

0000 pos 16° 47.3' S, 147° 38.7' W. Underway on run from Tuamotu's to Tahiti in very good weather, clear, starry sky.

Just ahead of approaching bad weather, we took advantage of our speed capability and arrived in Tahiti in only nine hours. But during the run, lube oil began leaking out of the starboard gearbox vent. My roll of the dice in San Diego had worked out, but now we would have to make the same repairs that we made to the portside. I smiled to myself, remembering the exchange I had with Michel, somewhere in the Tuamotus. After weeks of seeing the big wooden beam lashed to the deck, Michel finally asked what it was for. When I told him about

Papeete gearbox repair

my decision, so we could get underway and make his schedule, he was stunned. He well knew how conservative and cautious I was.

"You… Lew?"

"Well, it was that, or ruin your trip."

The gearbox job proved to be the most difficult maintenance job Joubert and I performed alone. With no outside help, and the wakes from passing ferries dangerously rocking the boat, we somehow hoisted the gearbox out, replaced the worn parts, and put it all back together. Three hard days at Bounty Quay in Papeete, Tahiti, the difficulty was offset by the honor of working alongside Joubert, a fantastic engineer and dear friend.

I liked Papeete. The French capital of Tahiti, it was a harbor city, alive with activity, and an interesting blend of old and new, locals and tourists. Med-moored (stern-to a seawall, with anchor off bow, and stern lines to wall) to a seawall close to city center, *Moana* was the only power boat alongside many sailboats. It was here my opinion of sailboat people changed. Growing up on fishing boats, my captains and crewmates were constantly amused by the "Sunday sailors" who never really went anywhere, and were certainly not to be found offshore in the rough weather we worked in all year long. Sharing the same seawall with us were six to eight, thirty- to fifty-foot sailboats. Not a sailor myself, it was still easy to see most were very capable boats. As the days went by and I met several of the owners, I learned most of them had sailed from California, using our same route. But the thing that impressed me the most was the shared sense of purpose, the camaraderie, between the boats that traveled together, usually in twos or threes. At sea, they constantly stayed in radio contact with each other, sharing each boat's situation, and encouraging each other during hard stretches. Here, in Tahiti, they pooled their resources and expertise to help each other prepare for the next voyages. These were real sailors, and it was a pleasure to share our time in Tahiti with them.

They probably remember us as well. With the afternoon breeze coming up harder than usual and sweeping down the seawall, our sailboat neighbor alongside began to drag his anchor. Dragging an anchor while med-moored with other boats is like falling dominoes, on a terrible scale. As each boat drags into the next, the increased load overwhelms all the anchors, and they can all wind up slamming into each other and the seawall. We were laying on our big "Bruce" anchor, set far off our bow, so I had confidence we could hold another boat and threw him a line. An hour or so later, when the breeze was howling, I went forward to check everything and was astonished to see a line between the bows of the next five sailboats downwind. We were holding not only *Moana* in a hard beam wind, but five sailboats as well!

It was also in Papeete I learned the meaning of "moana." In walking distance from our seawall was the big wharf where visiting cruise ships tied up. Adjacent to the wharf was a huge, concrete landing where dozens of small kiosks sold typical tourist stuff to the cruise-ship passengers. At the end of the landing was a raised gazebo where musicians, in corny Tahitian garb, played equally silly music to inspire the tourists to stay and buy. When a cruise ship was in town, the small city was overwhelmed with tourists. The locals endured the invasion, knowing the city benefitted from the influx of money, but they clearly disliked the chaos, congestion, and frustration that went with the hordes of people. This all changed in a remarkable way when there was not a cruise ship at the wharf. The souvenir kiosks were replaced with small food trucks, and the gazebo was manned with local, amateur musicians, playing authentic Tahitian music. The food trucks and tables were set up on the other end of the landing, serving every kind of local, delicious food imaginable. The space between the trucks and the gazebo was a huge, circular area, resembling a dance floor, and ringed with benches. With no ship or hordes of tourists in town, the landing was transformed into an old-fashioned city square. As the sun went down, everyone from small children to grandparents arrived to sample the food, sit on the benches, listen to the music, and watch all the kids dance or act silly on the "dance floor." The food, the music, the friendly people, and warm, tropical breeze created a wonderful ambience that drew me to the landing night after night. And night after night, I heard the word "moana" in song after song. I did not understand the lyrics but loved the tempo and romantic feel of the music. Curious about this word that seemed to be included in every Tahitian song, I asked our favorite taxi driver the true meaning. She hesitated, giving me the look a mother might give a child who was asking something everyone understood, and said, "It is our world. It is everything. It is us."

Father's Day came while we were in Tahiti. Joubert and I rarely talked about the price we paid to be so far from our children on holidays or family events. It was too emotional, and it never got easier. When email came along, it was one of the best things that ever happened to me, and while aboard *Moana* my loneliness and guilt was often turned around by letters from my daughters. On this Father's Day, I received a letter that every father would cherish forever.

Subject: Happy Fathers Day!
Date: Sun 15 Jun 2003 0400
From: thecht@thetwoRascalsglobal.com
To: "Lew Maurer" moanacapt@gmail.com
It's Fathers Day!
Here's what you are according to Webster's:
Father: Male Parent
Dad: Father

Seems pretty limited when you consider what each of us thinks of when thinking of our fathers. We all envision our dads being in a familiar place and have an overall feeling about them when they are in our thoughts, conversation, and presence.

When I think of you, you are standing in front of large windows overlooking a blue-gray, vast, empty space. The light is bright but filtered. There is always a cup of coffee and paper or a journal before you.

When I talk about you, I refer to you as Dad. When I say "Dad" and I'm referring to you, the word sounds notably different than if I'm using the word in general terms. I always feel a sense of pride when I talk about you, introduce you, or show someone your picture.

While there has almost always been a great deal of distance between us, I found recently that you really aren't so far away. I went for a walk on the farm, and eventually sat down on the bench at the pond. After sitting for a few minutes, I realized I was sitting on a bench that you assembled, drinking tea from my "Lawaia" mug, while admiring how nicely the paint had held up on the bridges you painted two years earlier.

You're always in my thoughts, Dad, and I'm proud to be your daughter.

Hope you have a great day!

I love you,
Tiara

Unnamed, uninhabited island

Captain's log, July 27
Anchor aboard, 0857, dep Bora Bora, idling outbound on range, CC 280°

With family and guests aboard, we visited the principal islands of French Polynesia—Moorea, Huahine, Tahaa, and Bora Bora. All different, all beautiful.

We most enjoyed the anchorages where, at night, under a million stars and a nice offshore breeze, we could hear locals playing traditional music, smell dinners cooking, and hear roosters crowing in the distance. In some of the small, traditional villages, life was simple and slow.

With a little more rain than we wanted, we continued to work our way west and on July 29 idled through the shallow and very beautiful pass on Penrhyn Island, in the Northern Cook Islands. Typical of atolls, the coral heads inside the lagoon are uncharted and can be very dangerous, so we entered with the sun overhead, picked our way through, and anchored in front of the small village of Omoka. The motus and lagoon of Penrhyn were absolutely stunning, and everyone aboard was excited to explore this seldom-visited tropical paradise. We were the only visiting yacht, and after clearing in, we crossed the lagoon and anchored in front of the small village of Te Tautua.

Bora Bora, outside reef

The first thing we noticed was near the village, in the area where they disposed of garbage in the ocean. There, several large sharks were swimming with children, and it was easy to see by the children's relaxed nature, this was not an unusual event. Next, a small boat came alongside with a friendly young man who greeted us and was very informative. We had caught several reef fish already, and he was happy to let us know which ones were safe to eat, and which ones were likely to contain the ciguatera toxin. As we spoke, he asked for a beer, and after only a little while, I was amazed to see he was getting drunk. Before leaving, he asked for another beer and told us his father was the Iriki (village elder and religious leader). This was interesting because our research and the people in Omoka told us there was no Iriki in Te Tautua at that time, due to some undisclosed incident. Normally, we would go directly to a village chief or elder, and ask permission to visit the island, but in this case, we were assured it was unnecessary.

It was very quiet in the small village, and we soon learned almost everyone had traveled to Rarotonga, the largest of the Cook Islands and far to the south, for a traditional holiday. We had a lot of nicely wrapped gifts for children and were happy to find the school teacher and pass them on. It was then we met the most talented weavers in the South Pacific. The women at this village were famous for the beautiful hats, fans, and other items they made from specially treated young palm leaves. The smooth, fine, tight weave of their white fibers was so amazing, it was hard to believe they could be made by hand. But as we watched, four very talented women sat cross-legged and, while casually socializing, fabricated the island's most valuable export. Of course, we bought several.

We moved to the far end of the lagoon and anchored just off a beautiful, palm-tree-studded motu with a surrounding white-sand beach. Immediately, everyone was off snorkeling or exploring, while a small boat approached. It was an old man and his wife, in a very worn-out little boat, with an equally old, sputtering outboard engine. The man introduced himself as the village Iriki and went on to let me know we had not followed proper island protocol. First, we had passed by his house without visiting him, an act he assured me was very disrespectful. Second, we had got his son drunk, causing quite a stir in the village. And third, because we had come to the far end of the lagoon, we had caused him to use precious gasoline to visit and lecture us. I will always remember the most hilarious part of this episode, which was the man's wife. A very large woman, she sat completely motionless like a mannequin, staring down into the boat and, in a continuous monotone like an echo, repeated every word he spoke. I felt sorry for the deposed Iriki. It was the strangest non-conversation I ever had, and it was hard not to laugh as his wheezing little engine returned him and his wife back to the village.

For me, the most memorable event of our visit to Penrhyn came that night. While in Moorea, Michel had purchased a coconut crab, and we learned the giant, nocturnal land crabs were found on many of the remote islands of the South Pacific. After dinner, Thomas, Louis, Rachel, and Donald decided to go on the nearby motu for a coconut crab hunt. At that time, we did not know much about the incredibly powerful and delicious crabs, but we figured a densely forested island such as the one next to us, with lots of coconut palms, would be perfect habitat. Armed with several powerful flashlights, they motored over to the small island and began walking through the trees and bushes. From the boat, we could easily see exactly where they were by the bright beams of light. At first, the beams were aimed down at the ground, but after a few minutes the beams went up into the trees and were wildly flailing about. On the boat, it looked strangely comical, and I was laughing, trying to understand what was going on in the darkness.

A little while later, we could see our hunters stumbling out of the trees, onto the beach and towards the lights of *Moana*, the only thing they could see in the total darkness. Minutes later, they were back aboard, laughing, and in the bright deck lights we saw they were covered head to toe in spider webs! Hair, faces, arms, legs, it was a complete victory by the island spiders, but even more hilarious when the kids told us they saw rats everywhere! The hunt for coconut crabs quickly changed to avoiding spiders and rats, which explained the beams of light directed into the trees and bushes. A very funny night, and high marks for the kids and their adventurous spirit.

Our research told us Penrhyn was "a pearl in the Pacific," and we agreed. Everything about it—the motus, the reefs, the lagoon—was utterly gorgeous. The fantastic bird life even included nesting red-tailed tropic birds, my favorite. Strangely, the clear water of the lagoon did not support oyster farming. This was a disappointment for the locals but nice for us, as the lagoon was easy to navigate without all the lines and buoys.

Captain's log, August 9

Underway in South Pacific en route Suwarrow Atoll in poor traveling weather. 0000 pos 12° 01.7' S, 161° 43' W

From Tahiti, this was the first time the family traveled long range between destinations, and I was impressed at how they handled the open-ocean conditions. Stiff trade winds at twenty-plus knots, on big, multi-direction swells, were our day-to-day reality. *Moana*, ever the perfect ocean voyager, pushed on effortlessly, but the bodies inside were constantly reminded they were in a very different environment than "home, sweet home." The constant drone of the big diesel engines, noise of the seas impacting the hull sides, and never-ending boat motion made eating and sleeping a challenge. Occasional rain squalls, with their dark, intense frontal winds and lightning, provided reminders of where and just how small we were.

When it was just too rough, I would sometimes idle slowly down swell on one engine, to allow Pascale to prepare some food, and everyone to have a calm meal. With everything cleaned up and put away, I would again come up on our course and speed. This cost us a little time and distance, but was a nice break in our monotonous, tiring routine, and a reminder of how much we would enjoy the next calm lagoon.

Suwarrow was a large atoll, lying in the middle of the westward cruising routes for yachts. It had an easily navigated pass and good anchorage in the lagoon, so it was popular with sailboats. It also had an interesting history because of Tom Neale, a sailor who famously lived alone there for several years and wrote a book about it. The atoll was now uninhabited except for two park rangers who lived in a house built by Neale, many years before.

As we came through the pass and entered the anchorage in the lagoon, Joubert had already begun washing the boat, and after the anchor went down, he continued with his long, thorough routine. Soon after, a woman neighbor from Tahiti rowed over from "Abracadabra," to borrow some dish soap and make a little conversation.

Question #1: "Lew, please tell me that is not fresh water."

Question #2: "Is it true the owners already have their plane tickets to go home from one of your next destinations?"

We rarely shared anchorages with anyone, but when a sailboat would come into a lagoon or anchorage, these two questions sometimes came up. They had to ration every precious drop of fresh water in their small tanks, and watching Joubert washing the boat and the kids taking two or three showers on the aft deck every day, probably bordered on pain for them. They would have been even more amazed to know how much fresh water we used in the galley, clothes washer, etc., or that our watermakers produced more than 1,200 gallons of fresh water daily.

Never knowing exactly when they would arrive at their next destination, sailboat people were forever amazed at how *Moana* could use the ocean like a private highway, arriving in a port just in time for the family and guests to catch a taxi and make their prearranged flights on time. For us, this was our normal, and how we could maximize time aboard for the family and be sure they had seats on their plane for the trip home. We were definitely a different operation and were the subject of radio conversations we sometimes overheard between sailboats.

We had a good time at Suwarrow. The diving and fishing were excellent on the spectacular coral reefs inside the lagoon. Thomas caught his first coconut crab there, after a long, determined effort to drag it out from its home in the roots of a tree. Notable were the pretty motus of Seven Islands, home to thousands of sooty terns. When we were anchored nearby one night, they protested loudly until we turned off all our bright lights. We found this same behavior, particularly with large tern species, throughout the South Pacific. I loved and respected the beautiful sooty terns. Wonderfully streamlined and capable of the power required to fly directly into the strong trade winds, they mated for life and defended their nests against all predators, even the vicious frigate birds. So incredible was their flying ability and eyesight, they sometimes followed us at night, diving into the turbulence close astern, to catch small fish.

Captain's log, August 16

1111 pos at anchor in pass, 43ft, Rose Atoll. Current streaming out of pass, holding boat nicely.

From Suwarrow we ran 288 nautical miles west-southwest to Rose Atoll, the world's smallest atoll. It was alive with life! The narrow pass into the lagoon had a choke point in the fringing coral that prevented *Moana* or any other boat from entering the lagoon. With very deep water all around the atoll, the only place to anchor was in the pass entrance; and that was not a safe place to anchor overnight, so commercial fishing boats could not easily fish around the atoll or take refuge in the lagoon. This prevented exploitation of the marine life, allowing us to see an unbelievable variety of fish and mammals swimming in and out of the pass. Dolphins, turtles, sharks, and schools of huge dogtooth tuna passed so close alongside *Moana* we could clearly see their eyes (looking up at us?). Meanwhile, just 200 yards off our beam, a family of humpback whales was putting on a diving and splashing show, right next to the atoll! This breathtaking continuous sight was a normal day in the life of this tiny atoll in the middle of nowhere. As usual, we were all alone in this remote, untouched paradise.

Captain's log, August 17

Underway for Western Samoa in stiff trades, big wind-driven seas & long ocean swell from S. 0000 pos 14° 13.3' S, 169° 14.2' W

The summer trip was over, and we ran to Apia, the capital of Western Samoa. The family caught their flights home, and the crew and I caught our breath in a new and different country. We were in Western Samoa only a few days, but I was very impressed with the people, culture, and beauty of the faraway island country. Just the scenic drive along the seashore to the airport showed us we were in a very different country. The two-lane road skirted the sea to the west with one village after another on the lush hillsides to the east. There was little traffic on the well-maintained road, and the homes and villages were tidy and clean. Police patrol cars were not to be seen, apparently replaced by traditional meeting houses where people gathered peacefully to discuss everything from politics to social issues to personal problems. The meeting houses were easily seen in every village along the way, and their importance to the Samoan culture could even be seen on their money.

At the small customs office, the large and obviously Polynesian officer raised his brow and smiled at my papers.

"The name of your boat is *Moana*? We will need to get you on your way with no problems!"

Captain's log, August 23

0800 pos 14°10.8' S, 171° 05.1' W, in good traveling weather with 10–12kt breeze from ENE, on swells 3–4ft from SE, wind driven seas 3–4ft

From Western Samoa, we ran east to Pago Pago in American Samoa, where Pascale and I flew out for vacations in France and the US. We needed to keep the boat in a safe place while I was gone, and American Samoa was well known as one of the best "hurricane holes" in the South Pacific. For us, it was also the biggest disappointment of all the major ports in that part of the world. Most of the US tuna fleet of huge purse-seine vessels moved there in the '70s, when cheap labor, along with public outcry over killing dolphins, lured them away from San Diego. They delivered their catches to several US-owned canneries located on the waterfront. The canneries were a major player in the economy and operated with impunity regarding the environment, dumping untold tons of liquid and solid waste into the harbor. Combined with years and years of discarded trash of every description lying on the harbor seafloor, visiting boats had a very hard time penetrating the trash and holding the bottom with their anchors. On our first night there, a stiff breeze came up, and almost all of the twenty-plus sailboats dragged their anchors, some colliding in the darkness, and calling out in panic to each other on VHF radio.

A few days later, while Joubert was washing the boat, a harbor department patrol boat came alongside and warned him he would be fined if he continued to allow soap suds to run into the harbor waters! This hypocrisy was over the top, and I was in the harbormaster's office immediately. With headaches of his own, the harbormaster turned out to be a nice man, and he helped us immensely by assigning us the only small vessel berth in the harbor. It was a rough concrete seawall, with few cleats or bollards for securing the boat, and no electricity. A single freshwater faucet was over fifty yards away and trash was everywhere, but we were happy to have it. With Joubert aboard to watch over the systems, and the concrete wall to safely secure the boat in strong winds, Pascale and I went home for our vacations.

Returning to the boat after a vacation was always interesting because of Joubert. He was easily the best engineer I ever had, and he took his job very seriously. I never had to worry about anything in my absence. But the interesting thing was how popular he always became with everyone in a marina or anchorage. He was observant and sociable, ready to help anyone, and always with his famous smile. In this case, I returned to find he had made himself quite the hero with all our sailboat neighbors. He allowed them to raft up (tie side to side) to *Moana*, so they could get fresh water and be able to walk to nearby stores and markets. I later found out he had two or three boats at a time, rafted to our outboard side. On my first day back, the rafted boats had returned to the anchorage and a couple of them passed by, outbound on their next trip. Each time, a chorus of "Hello Joubert," came from the smiling, waving sailors. Wherever we went, everyone loved Joubert.

Fortunately for the Indonesian crew on a local commercial fishing boat, Joubert was also from Indonesia and could speak their language. He met them one evening when the boat crew were unloading their catch, and they were happy to find someone they could talk with, to reveal the conditions aboard. I was unsurprised to hear the owner treated them badly, but I was shocked to hear they were leaving on their next trip with a problem that would leave them drifting at sea and unable to return if the main engine was turned off or failed. The engine would have to run day and night, and judging by the smoke coming from the exhaust, the entire crew was in serious danger. Before we could do anything, the boat departed, and Joubert and I hoped his friends would be okay.

Blacked out, the boat returned at night, a few days later. Joubert went to check on his friends and immediately came back with an incredible story. The owner had plane tickets for the Indonesian crew and was taking them to the airport that very night. He refused to give them any money for the three months they had worked on the boat, and he was sending them home! To silence them, the owner threatened to turn them over to Immigration, telling them they would go to jail and never see their families again. Scared, unable to speak English, and not knowing how to get help, they were going to go home, unpaid for months of terrible treatment.

Growing up on commercial fishing boats, I needed no one to tell me how hard life was for crew in that business. This could not stand. I hit the button on my VHF radio and asked the sailboats if there was a lawyer in the anchorage. Indeed there was, and after hearing my story, he volunteered to intervene. I had no way to know someone else heard our conversation, and that person came on the radio to let us know the police would be coming very soon. It turned out the owner was well known on the waterfront for bringing in and abusing undocumented workers. It was his turn to be intimidated, and with the police and Joubert there he made no effort to defend himself and paid the crew with cash. I was very proud of Joubert as he shook hands with his countrymen and wished them well. They were momentarily scared when the police asked them to get into the patrol car, but broke into wide smiles when Joubert explained they were getting an unofficial ride to the airport.

Captain's log, October 7

Underway in South Pacific, en route Kingdom of Tonga in good traveling weather. Low swell 4–5ft from SE, light trades and seas from E. 0000 pos 16° 37.5' S, 172° 29' W.

We needed to work our way south, to get below the latitudes infamous for the terrifying cyclones in the South Pacific. Tonga was Michel's choice for one more trip before we would run for New Zealand. Tonga, never a colony of a European country, was a modern-day kingdom that seemed to me to be caught in a time warp between a very old culture and modern times. A taxi ride to the airport, for example, would almost always include dodging pigs in the road—the same road that had the largest satellite dish I had ever seen. The 169 islands in the archipelago run in a 500-mile-long, north-south arrangement, with the largest and most frequently visited islands of Vava'u and Tongatapu the farthest north and south, respectively. Scattered between are many small and uninhabited islands and coral reefs. Due to the difficulty of navigating and anchoring safely, few boats attempt to explore there, opting to visit the two main islands only.

After leaving Vava'u, we saw no other boats as we explored our way south, enjoying spectacular little islands and extensive coral reefs. With only Michel and Martine aboard, the atmosphere on the boat was very relaxed and slow. Unfortunately, the trip was plagued with a little more rain and wind than we expected, but it did not seem to bother Michel and Martine, who enjoyed the serenity of a kids-free trip.

With three days left on the trip, we approached the picturesque island of Kelefesia, slowly passing between wild surf on two large coral reefs. Boom! Serious impact noise and vibration! Instantly, I looked at the fathometer and took the engines out of gear. We were in 108 feet of blue water and I had not felt hull impact, so I knew we had not hit anything. With a stiff breeze on our beam and the close reefs, we did not have room to drop the anchor, so I put the engines back in gear, one at a time. The starboard engine was fine, and we idled forward. But there was definitely something wrong with the port engine, and at the same time, I realized we had no steering! After a hasty trip to the port engine room, Joubert reported the engine was running fine and the propeller shaft was turning, but there was a strange noise coming from the propeller shaft tube. We knew the port engine was not driving the boat, so we

David and "boys," preparing new propeller shaft

quickly realized the shaft had broken. This meant the broken shaft slid back and the propeller slammed into the rudder, jamming the rudder and producing the loud impact noise. Visualizing the propeller against the rudder, I turned the helm back and forth in small degrees and was able to work the rudder free just enough to steer the boat. We idled into the anchorage, dropped the anchor, took a deep breath, and assessed the situation.

With the twin hydraulic cylinder system aboard *Moana*, Joubert was able to lock and isolate the port rudder, allowing full travel on the starboard, and we finished the trip on one engine

Propeller installation, "Tonga method"

and one rudder. The last two islands we visited were absolutely stunning, the weather fantastic, and Michel and Martine enjoyed a great finish to the trip. But now we were in Nuku'alofa, the capital, and not exactly a boat repair center.

With the same hours and wear on both propeller shafts, I did not want to risk running to New Zealand on one engine. There would be no backup system if we broke the starboard shaft on the 1,500-nautical-mile run. We would be completely disabled at sea, not a situation I was willing to risk. I decided to replace the broken shaft, but after seeing the small boat yard could not haul us out of the water, I knew it was going to be a real challenge. But being a waterfront guy, it did not take long to find David and his "boys."

David was a part time salvage diver, part time aquarium-fish supplier, and full-time opportunist. If it was in the water, physical, and difficult, David was the man. And if you needed some serious muscle, he had his "boys." Young Tongan men, they said very little, but I remember thinking they would probably follow David into anything he asked. The very next day, we were double anchored in shallow water, over a soft-sand reef.

At low tide, we almost rested on the bottom, perfect for the job at hand. We dropped the rudder and pulled out the broken shaft and propeller on the first day, taking care to plug the holes and not sink the boat.

Having built the boat, we had aboard the exact specifications of the propeller shafts so, with care, it was not too difficult to have a new shaft fabricated in New Zealand and shipped to Tonga. With David's help, airline workers, customs agents, and transport people were properly "taken care of," and we soon received the new shaft. But installing the new shaft, fitting the propeller, and reinstalling the rudder, all underwater, was a never-ending movie going around and around in my head. Joubert and I went over every detail and finally came up with a procedure to deal with a situation made more difficult by the fact we would be inside the boat and unable to communicate with David and his boys, underwater.

David and his boys arrived in his small boat at breakfast time. Relaxed and nonchalant, the boys proceeded to have breakfast, which consisted of a quart of orange soda poured over a big hunk of unsliced white bread. Joubert, Pascale, and I were amused at what seemed to be their standard operating procedure. Next, I went over in detail how we would complete the jobs at hand. I was a bit wordy, but I wanted to make sure David understood how I envisioned it all coming together. After listening carefully, he nodded in apparent agreement. Then, he turned and, in Tongan, told his boys what we were going to do. Except his version was quite different than mine, and definitely shorter. The boys stood up and threw the shaft into the water and sat down again. Before I could say a word, David jumped into the water, picked up the shaft, walked across the bottom, and pushed it all the way into the tube. Next came the propeller.

Bang! Onto the shaft, and nut tightened in place. When David came up for the rudder, which was on a long, heavy shaft, I cautioned him about how it would be very difficult, even with help from the boys, and he again nodded. The boys stood up, threw the rudder into the water, and David jumped in again. I was absolutely astonished to watch David pick up the heavy rudder, walk across the bottom, and slam it all the way up into place, alone, and on one breath of air! An amazing show of strength and confidence!

Joubert completed all the engine room and lazarette work the following day, and we celebrated a seemingly impossible repair with a small party for David and his wife that evening. He seemed amused that we were so impressed by a job that was, for him, quite ordinary. We assured him we would not forget him and his boys any time soon.

We were ready to roll, but our favorite taxi driver insisted we take a tour of his island. So early the next day, we were off on a fun adventure. It was a great one-day trip around the island that included everything from pigs in the road to the Royal Palace. On our way to a spectacular blowhole on the coast, we passed by a very large cemetery. Far from the city, in a beautiful, grassy, but uneven plot of land, it ran alongside the dirt road we were bouncing along in our taxi. The social standing and wealth of the deceased were quickly made obvious by the shrines built directly above the graves. Some were really elaborate, with frames covered with colorful tapestries, cloths, or rugs, and with painted statues inside; others were more modest, depending, I assumed, on the wealth of the relatives. Near the end of the cemetery, Joubert, Pascale, and I could hardly contain ourselves with the sight of a newly interred Tongan. The gravesite was a fresh mound of red dirt; and instead of a shrine built over, the mound was decorated with no less than fifty empty beer bottles! Neck-down, into the dirt, the bottles seemed to say, "Here lies good old Joe. He really knew how to party." Out of respect for our driver, I resisted the strong urge to take a photo, but the one in my head will live forever!

Captain's log, November 22

Underway in South Pacific between Minerva Reef and New Zealand. Bumpy, uncomfortable seas slowly improving. Black, cloudy night sky. 0100 pos 26° 02.8' S, 179° 39.6' E.

We had stopped at North Minerva Reef, a large, spectacular coral reef located 270 miles southwest of Tonga. It was well known to the sailboat people as a good place to take shelter on the open-ocean run from Tonga to New Zealand. Swarming with fish, sharks, and lobsters, the lagoon inside the circular reef was very calm in spite of the rough sea conditions outside. We were the only power boat in the huge anchorage we shared with nineteen sailboats, all of us driven there by lousy weather. From Minerva Reef to New Zealand, 1,230 miles distant, sea conditions were a serious issue, so the constant topic of radio conversation was weather forecasts. Six days later, our weather forecasting experts gave us the green light, and we were on our way. We had good traveling weather most of the way but got roughed up the last day. With our speed, we were the last to leave Minerva Reef, and the first to arrive in the Bay of Islands, New Zealand. We were very glad to get out of the miserable weather and felt sorry for our friends, who we knew would take a beating from full gale-force winds for the last 200 miles.

Captain's log, December 2

0300 pos 40° 08' S, 173° 29' E, in wild beam seas, screaming breeze from SW. Dangerous snap rolling, spray everywhere.

We were in the notorious "Roaring Forties" latitudes, and they lived up to their reputation as we fought our way down the west coast of North Island, New Zealand. The trip had started from Opua, and we had great weather around the north end of the island; but we really paid our dues on the last miles into Nelson, on the north end of South Island, New Zealand.

Nelson was quickly our favorite place in all the thousands of miles and many ports in our journey to date. We came to Nelson to avoid cyclones and complete never-ending maintenance, not dreaming we would fall in love with the rugged, unspoiled beauty of the area and its friendly people. One of the original designers of *Moana* was part owner of a boat yard there, so it was an easy decision to bring her to Nelson.

In New Zealand, the native people are Polynesian but more commonly known as Maori. When we saw the ferocious weather common to those islands, I had tremendous respect for their forefathers who completed epic voyages of thousands of miles all over the South Pacific. Without any of our modern instruments, much less electronics, they were the undisputed finest sailors and navigators the world has ever known. Beyond the physical difficulties, their relationship with the ocean was spiritual, an integral part of their being, so it was no surprise to me to find the locals loved the beautiful lines of our boat. Like their ancestors' double-hulled sailing canoes, *Moana* was a catamaran. We were often the subject of photos by the locals, but the absolute approval came when one of their religious leaders offered to conduct an authentic Maori blessing of the boat. I will always remember his question.

"Do you know what 'moana' means?"

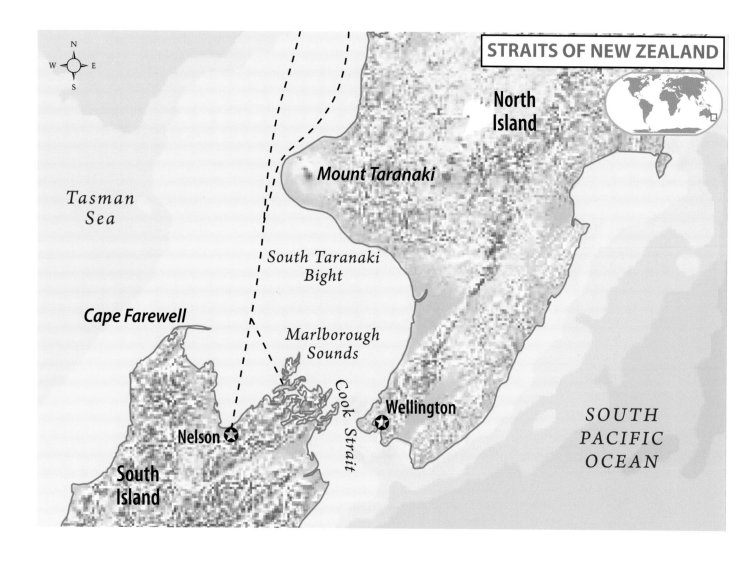

STRAITS OF NEW ZEALAND

North
Island

Tasman
Sea

Mount Taranaki

South Taranaki
Bight

Cape Farewell

Marlborough
Sounds

Cook Strait

Wellington

SOUTH
PACIFIC
OCEAN

Nelson

**South
Island**

N
W E
S

2004

AUSTRALASIA, OCEANIA

Captain's log: March 24, 2004

1200 pos 40° 05.1' S, 173° 49.3' E in miserable weather. A/C to 296° to get better angle. Breeze W @ 20kts, seas beginning to "stack." Drop RPM to 1200.

With a nice current astern, it looked like we would finally make it across the South Teranaki Bight, separating North and South New Zealand. After taking a terrible beating and turning back on two prior tries, conditions looked better. With a stiff breeze and mixed seas that were uncomfortable, we anticipated better weather once we had crossed the Bight. Suddenly the low, wind-driven seas on our bows changed to waves unlike any I had ever seen in my life: Twelve to fifteen feet high, extremely vertical and close together, with hissing crests about to collapse. Impenetrable, overwhelming walls of water, it was a death zone.

I pulled the engines out of gear and kept the bows straight into the first wave, trying to coast over as slowly as possible. But with the current astern, the sharp bows of *Moana* drove mid-wave into the wall of water. Four feet of solid blue water instantly covered the entire forward deck, all the way aft to the main cabin. The tonnage of water overwhelmed the boat, and she went into a sickening roll to port. I got the helm hard over immediately, keeping the angle, letting the water run off and at the same time getting the stern around to the next wave. As the boat stabilized, the current sucked us backwards into the face of the next wave, and I came on hard with the throttles. Time stood still. And then *Moana* surged forward, overcoming the current and accelerating out from under the next monster that would have buried the entire stern of the boat, swamping us and laying us broadside to the onslaught of waves that stretched as far as I could see.

These were the "standing waves" I had once read about but never before witnessed. Nor did I know any boat captain who claimed to have seen the phenomenon either. All I knew for sure was that I would not make the mistake of running through the South Teranaki Bight on an ebb tide again. As an ex-commercial fisherman who experienced terrifying waves at the entrance to the Columbia River on the Oregon-Washington border, I well knew the danger of running the bar, known as "the graveyard of the Pacific," on a strong ebb tide. But the South

Teranaki Bight was not a bar, where a big ocean swell can create huge waves when opposed by the ebb tide current. No, our death zone was in deep water, which in theory would not allow the waves we witnessed.

And for the third time, we retreated to safe anchorage in Marlboro Sounds, a popular cruising area east of Nelson, on South Island, New Zealand. It was in Nelson, while clearing out with customs, we were told quite sternly, "You must depart the country directly and not re-enter. I don't want to hear about you cruising around Marlboro Sounds." I had heard this speech in other countries, from different customs officers, but resisted arguing that the safety of my crew and boat were more important than immigration law, which ironically, was exactly why we were anchored in Marlboro Sounds.

To the east of Nelson is the notorious Cook Strait, where the north and south islands of New Zealand are relatively close. In the strait, giant power catamaran ferries run back and forth daily—except for the many times ferocious seas force them to stay in harbor. To the west of Cook Strait is the South Teranaki Bight, a large, bay-like body of deep water adjacent the southwest end of the north island, and a stretch of water I will never forget.

In my commercial fishing career, I had never once turned back at the beginning of a trip due to bad weather. But here I had been beaten into submission not once, but three times. Each time, I learned my mistake, and each following time I was sure we would be okay. At this point I wanted no part of what the South Teranaki Bight could dish out if I made another mistake, but there was another problem. It was now March 24, 2004, and our next trip was to visit the French island of New Caledonia, 1,260 miles distant. Martine was to arrive a week early and stay aboard the boat, waiting for the family who would arrive on the 5th of April, a week later.

All over New Zealand, the locals listened to Bob McDavitt, the undisputed guru of weather forecasting. I had purchased his book and listened carefully to his forecasts before departing, but they were not really specific to the South Teranaki Bight, so we were surprised. This time, I called Bob direct and was again surprised. "Lew, you will not get the weather you need until mid-April, or possibly even May." Not what I wanted to hear.

Aboard *Moana*, Pascale and Joubert, our French cook and Indonesian engineer, had traveled thousands of miles and crossed oceans together in every kind of weather imaginable. We were a team that truly trusted and relied on each other. Not once did they question my judgment or navigational skills, but after our last, fearful experience I could taste silent anxiety. I promised myself to get it right, to not make my faithful crew fearful again.

Anchored in Marlboro Sounds, we were safe, surrounded all around by the raw beauty of the tall, sparsely wooded, rugged islands that blocked the open ocean seas to the west. Bright sunshine and clear, cobalt-blue skies belied our reality. We were at 41° 15' south latitude, in the infamous "Roaring Forties." Screaming winds, aptly called "bullets," blasted straight down on us from the island ridges in gusts reaching sixty knots. On the other side of the islands, that same wind was flying through the South Teranaki Bight.

"Bullets," straight down, gusting 60kts

Six windy, restless nights later, Bob forecast a small easing of the winds, and we got underway again. My plan was simple: I would forget deep water theory and treat the death zone the same as a breaking river bar. I would time our arrival for high slack; the moment when the tide is neither rising or falling, and current is near zero. And I would stay to the south, increasing the distance around but hopefully skirting the dangerous area I had accurately charted.

The day dawned bright but cold, and as we cleared the islands of Marlboro Sounds, we were encouraged to see a definite drop in the winds, with low, wind-driven seas. Three hours later, and pushing against the last of a flood tide, we approached the southern edge of "the zone." The pilothouse was silent as our eyes strained to see the slightest change in the sea surface, but we saw nothing. Nothing. The South Teranaki Bight had gone eerily calm. Not a single ripple could be seen on a calm sea that stretched across the Bight, all the way to snow covered Mount Teranaki, towering in the clouds over New Plymouth on the southwest corner of North Island.

Our good weather window lasted twenty-four hours, enough to allow us to escape the worst of the Roaring Forties. As we passed Three Kings Islands, off the north end of North Island, I chose a course to take us off to the east, in anticipation of the strong trades. One day later the

Cyclone victim: Capsized fishing boat, no survivors

strong east-southeast trades caught us, and a course change put the big seas on our starboard stern for a wild but good run to New Caledonia.

Our good fortune to "escape" was tempered the next day when we came upon a capsized fishing boat. It was a very capable, sixty- to seventy-foot steel boat and appeared to be in good condition. Lying on her side and occasionally rolling almost upside down, the big seas were slamming into the superstructure and living spaces with incredible force. It was easy to imagine the terrified crew trying to hide inside, and being driven out by the fury of the elements. The unknown crew were my fellow seamen, and I felt a deep sadness for them. There was no debris around, nor any oil slick, and there were no survivors. We stared at the scene for long moments as I called in the location of the hazard to navigation to French authorities. (We learned the boat had been caught in a cyclone, two weeks before.)

We arrived in Noumea, the capital of New Caledonia, on April 5, the same day Michel and the family arrived. I could not put into words how fortunate they were that we had arrived in time for their next trip, or what the crew and I experienced to make it possible.

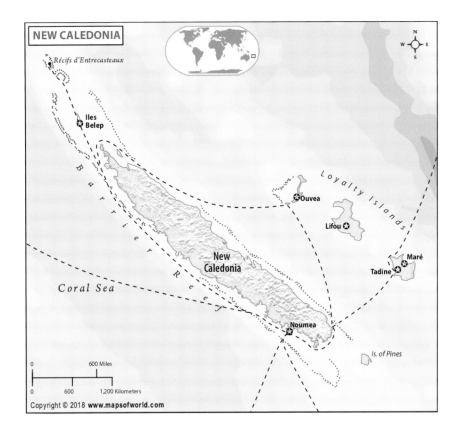

Captain's log, April 8

Underway in South Pacific on run from Noumea to Ouvea in tough weather. Surfing down big, wind-driven seas from stbd quarter. Gusty, SE breeze, 25–30kts.

After only one day to clear customs and provision and fuel the boat, we were underway once again. Pascale, our wonderful French cook, performed a minor miracle to somehow purchase and stow aboard, all in one day, all the food we would need for another two weeks. It helped that New Caledonia was a French island, but it was truly remarkable.

Our next trip took us to Ouvea, an island in the Loyalty Group, east of New Caledonia. It was also a French island, with an interesting history of unrest, and even a rebellion by a tribe of natives, some years before. We quickly discovered that not all of the island's chiefs were welcoming to anyone speaking French, the family's first language. This could have been a big problem for us if not for our US flag, flapping in the breeze. During WWII, New Caledonia became a strategic staging island, where the US brought in all the war materials and troops they would need for the coming battle with the Japanese in the Solomon Islands. It was the

Melanesian natives' first experience with Americans, and the result is well known to this day. For the first time in their lives, they saw black American officers commanding white soldiers, and being saluted and respected. The black skinned natives were shocked to see something they never thought possible. Our American boat, with traditional custom gifts for the chiefs, was very welcome!

Ouvea and its smaller surrounding islands were pristine jewels in the South Pacific. It was difficult to visit and largely unknown to the travel industry, and we loved the unspoiled beauty and fabulous dive sites shown us by our native guides. In our travels, we often walked on the most beautiful sand beaches imaginable, but Ouvea had the most spectacular beach I had ever seen. And in the middle of the long, laser-white beach was a small inlet, leading into a lagoon. From a low bridge over the inlet, in the crystal clear water, an amazing variety of fish, turtles, and other marine creatures could be seen flowing in and out of the lagoon. While the family was out diving, Pascale and I peered down from the bridge, certain the wonderful show of nature below our feet was unchanged since the beginning of time.

On our first day, with *Moana* anchored just offshore the beach, the boys and their guest built a huge sand castle while waiting for Michel to pick them up in the dinghy. From the pilothouse, I could see in my binoculars how much fun they were having, even decorating the corners of the giant castle with dead palm fronds they found laying on the beach. By the time Michel arrived, the castle was quite impressive, with high walls and palm tree "flags" flying. And as soon as Michel arrived and the boys waded out to the dinghy, a group of teenage native boys, who had been sitting nearby, immediately went to the castle and carried away the palm fronds. They did not destroy the castle, but simply took the fronds a short distance down the beach and dropped them on the sand. Had the boys shown disrespect? Was there something sacred about the palm fronds? We were always careful to respect the many customs of natives in our travels, but unfortunately I was never to learn the significance of the young men's actions.

Captain's log, June 28
Alongside wharf, Tadine

Running for cover. Passing Mare Island in the Loyalty Islands, our weather boys in New York called to say an unusually strong weather front was going to sweep through our area. Mare was not a high island and did not offer a good lee, so I opted to run for the small RoRo harbor of Tadine. On my chart, it was obviously a man-made harbor, but it jutted out from the island in a "C" shape that looked to provide a safe haven. As we lined up to run the channel, I could see wind-driven seas and swells beginning to wrap around a far point on the island, and I could feel the breeze picking up fast. By the time we came alongside the long, concrete inner wall, the swirling winds were ominous. This was no typical rain squall. In fact, there were clouds flying over the top of the island, but they were not black, and there was no rain at all.

Giant waves crashed over the seawall, including the concrete shelter

Within an hour of securing the boat to the big bollards on the rough concrete wall, the channel was impassable. Huge breaking swells were sweeping through the channel and raging into the small harbor. Coming into the harbor, I did not notice there was not a single anchored boat, or docks for fishing boats, typical of every harbor in the world. And as the swells impacted the harbor sides, the deflected energy produced a surge that explained why we were all alone. Even with the boat secured with our heavy lines and all our very capable fenders between us and the wall, the surge began throwing the boat into the wall with frightening force. Huge waves began crashing completely over the seawall, and churning white water two feet thick was rushing across the adjacent apron, smashing broadside into *Moana* and compounding the violent motion that was now throwing us off our feet. It was difficult to watch, to be a part of a situation that was going to destroy our boat.

Farther down the wall, perhaps 200 feet, was the ramp for the roll-on, roll-off cargo ship. It faced us, with its outer concrete corner some sixty feet off the main wall. On the corner, I could see some kind of rusty steel structure that looked strong enough to hold a line. Between sets of wild white water, I jumped onto the wall top and fought my way down the apron while

Joubert fed me our longest line. The rusty steel turned out to be an old ladder going down into the water, but it was heavily made and the angle from there was just enough. Joubert winched the long line tight, and our home surged forward and off the wall. White water continued to explode all around the wildly snapping, bouncing boat, but she no longer impacted the wall. Soaking wet and shaken to my core, I stood there, frozen by a scene that would have made the cover of every boating magazine in the world.

The storm was powerful, but it was moving fast. Soon it moved off far enough that the angle of the generated swells changed. It was as if someone threw a switch, and everything changed. The sun came out, and before everything that was part of the flying salt water could dry, the harbor went calm. The only lasting testament to the fury of the storm was two huge steel plates, moved down and almost off the ramp.

Captain's log, June 30
Anchor dn in 72ft, off Quarantine buoy, Port Vila

The family met us in Port Vila, the capital of Vanuatu, the starting point for our summer trip that would take us to the Solomon Islands. Port Vila was an interesting little city, bustling with activity and friendly locals. We found good local markets for provisioning, much to the relief of Pascale. We also met expats from many different countries who were allowed to bring their money of questionable origin, as long as they kept a low profile with the government.

My lasting memory of Port Vila was with Michel, when we were approached by a street vendor who was selling ivory bracelets made from pig tusks. The vendor explained they were made by removing the two chewing teeth opposing the tusks of the pig, which allowed the tusks to grow long and circular. He also claimed a bracelet gave a male wearer fantastic sexual power, which of course, justified the considerable price he was asking. We began to laugh when the vendor unabashedly showed us he was wearing a bracelet on both arms! They were quite beautiful, however, and Michel closed a deal. I never asked how it worked!

And knocking out teeth was not just for pigs in Vanuatu. After seeing several women there, with one of their front teeth missing, we learned of a custom I don't think will ever be popular in most countries: If a woman pleased her husband in every way, she was allowed to ask her husband to knock out one of her front teeth, as proof to the community of her feminine qualities!

We had poor luck with weather and passed though the islands of Vanuatu quickly, arriving in Honiara, the capital of the Solomon Islands, on July 31. This was a different country for us in many ways, and it would prove to be one of my favorites. We arrived at the very time an inter-island war was winding down, thanks to RAMSI, a police force made up of agents from other island countries, mostly Australia and New Zealand. The police force had an interesting tactic to stop the killing: they traded food for all the guns. It seemed to work well, but there

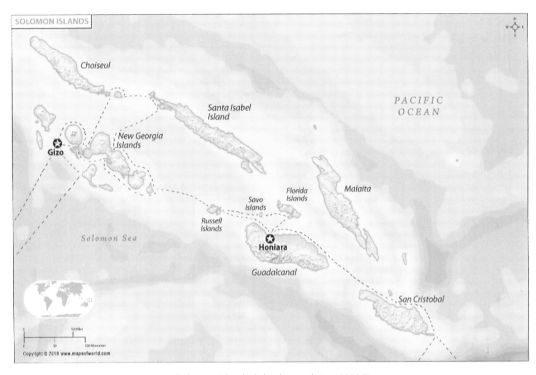

Solomon Islands, little changed since WWII

was still a lot of animosity between the tribes of Guadalcanal and Malaita. Nevertheless, the fighting ended while we were there.

The main island of Guadalcanal, the scene of heavy fighting during WWII, seemed little changed from those long-ago battles. The original capital, on another island, was destroyed by bombing, so Honiara became the new capital. Like most island cities, it straddled the main road that ran alongside the waterfront, but since it grew from necessity rather than planning, it was a curious mixture of commercial, government, residential, and small-town shops, all crammed together in no apparent order. Between the occasional rain showers, the road was dry and dusty; and with the black, smoke-belching trucks and taxis, no traffic lights, and people milling about everywhere, downtown Honiara was quite a scene for any newcomer. But probably the biggest adventure for anyone on foot was to avoid the flying betel-nut spit of anyone walking nearby.

Betel-nut chewing is very popular throughout Melanesia, and it was one of the most disgusting habits we witnessed in our travels. Almost every man in Honiara had a small bag, much like a woman's purse, slung over his shoulder. Inside were Areca nuts, betel leaves, slaked lime, and sometimes other ingredients that made up his daily supply of betel nut. The nut was usually wrapped in betel leaves and lime and, when chewed, instantly produced *buai pekpek*, a bright red mucous that the locals spat out continuously and everywhere.

The devastating result of long-term chewing is black, eroding teeth, oral cancer, and other terrible side effects. Like tobacco in other cultures, the locals know about the impending downsides, but the custom is so popular, they continue to ignore the danger. Of course, the kids and I had to try it once, just for fun. Never before had my glands produced mouthfuls of crimson red slime, or the need to get rid of it immediately!

Honiara was without a doubt the most primitive city we had yet visited. Every day was a new experience, beginning with our first day, clearing in with Customs and Immigration. Our yellow quarantine flag drew no response, so I walked to their nearby offices in some old, rundown buildings. Like most of the Melanesian officials we came in contact with, they were very friendly and polite, and the formalities would not have been remembered except for large posters on the office wall. End-stage results of horrible diseases were depicted in vivid color, to warn visitors the Solomon Islands were not without serious dangers. Our research had told us the same, but I will never forget those posters.

Pascale was to discover the next adventure in Honiara. For her, finding the best markets for provisioning was a personal challenge she loved, but in this case it was more exciting than she imagined. She soon learned of a huge farmers market near our downtown anchorage and was off to see what she could purchase for our next trip. A beautiful but independent and hard-headed French woman, she had no idea the attention a blonde, young, white woman would get while surrounded by over a hundred Melanesians of varying degrees of civilized behavior. Pascale was not naïve, but the aggressive tactics of the locals to steal her money surprised even her. She soon returned to the boat with hard-to-believe stories, the wildest being an old lady who slit her backpack open with a razor blade. A day or two later, I accompanied Pascale and was shocked at the size and primitive nature of the open-air market. Under a giant tin roof, the sights and smells of all the things for sale, ranging from animals to fish, fruits, vegetables, cooking supplies, native spices, firewood, etc., combined with the stifling heat and humidity and distinct body odor of the natives, overwhelmed my senses. And in the midst of this, a man held up a baby for sale! Even by local standards, this was too much, and the man was arrested. On the evening news, we learned his wife gave birth to a baby by another man.

Typical of island countries, the outer islands away from the cities are the most unspoiled and pristine. This was certainly the case in the Solomons, where there were only two real cities on two different islands. The rest of the chain was cruising into a time machine that seemed to take us back to a primitive time and place. Many of the places we visited were uninhabited, but where there was a nearby village, the shy and friendly natives never failed to paddle out and greet us in their canoes. Almost always, our greeter would have a few vegetables in the bow of the canoe, to offer in trade for our store-bought items that were so precious in the remote places. I loved these opportunities to meet the local people and learn all I could. First, I made sure to ask permission to anchor near their village, which always drew a smile of respect. Next, we were always very generous with the trading goods we carried aboard. Clothes, fishing gear, school supplies, food (tinned beef, rice, flour, and sugar), flashlight batteries, aspirin, and even fingernail polish for the chief's wife were our standard trading items.

All of the natives spoke *pisin*, a kind of pidgin English, but because missionaries had passed through the islands years before, many of the natives spoke good English. This really enhanced our experiences and the many things we learned from them. And on our first stop after leaving the capital, the natives' good nature and sense of humor were clear to see.

Thomas and his buddies bought a pig when we were in Vanuatu. It was completely pre-pared for cooking, and their idea was to roast it on a beach somewhere. "Somewhere" turned out to be a beautiful sand beach on one of the Nggela Islands, also known as the Florida islands. It was a hilarious adventure from start to finish. Instead of a small pig, Thomas purchased a pig large enough to feed a small army. We had to offload it with our dinghy davit and struggled to get it to the beach. Fortunately, we had Joubert organize a plan, and after setting up a bed of coals and fabricating a spit, the pig was slowly roasting. But it was too large to roast easily and required more and more firewood and attention to turning, to prevent burning.

While this was going on, a canoe arrived on the beach nearby, and a nice family appeared to be getting ready to have a picnic. But no, our native friends came to see the crazy white people trying to cook a pig, and from time to time walked over to give us some advice. More coals, turn more often, etc. It really was hilarious to be coached by natives who probably could not read or write but who certainly knew how to cook a pig and were willing to help. At the end of a very long day, the roasted pig did indeed taste delicious!

Our next stop was Savo Island, an extinct volcano. Eons before, the volcano sank down and part of the cone fell away, allowing the ocean to enter and create a small, beautiful lagoon inside. We double anchored, with a stern line to a huge tree, and enjoyed the mirror smooth water and densely forested walls of the volcano that rose high in the sky, all around us. We were in a spectacular, ancient amphitheater that included schools of tropical fish below, and beautiful, yellow monitor lizards in the rain forest. (I later learned Savo was a favorite refuge for fishermen, who also told me the big lizards were well known for coming aboard their boats and stealing food.)

With so many wild and beautiful places to fish, dive, and explore, it was difficult to choose one island over another, but my favorite was the small village of Peava, on the island of Ngga-tokae. Directly in front of the village was a small, beautiful lagoon created by a natural, cir-cular coral reef. Some years before, the locals dynamited a small opening in the reef to create a pass into the lagoon, and it was one of the most picturesque anchorages in the Solomons. The natives there were exceedingly friendly and made us feel welcome. We stayed at Peava for several days, enjoying the hospitality of everyone in the village. This included a small group

Joubert, master engineer and pig roaster

of young boys who visited *Moana* daily and entertained me with their never ending laughter and enthusiasm. It also included Tokapae Moses, the village fisherman, who quickly became a hero in the eyes of Louis.

Tokapae was not only a very good fisherman, but a quality man we came to know and appreciate. A slightly built and dark Melanesian, his quiet manner and sincere smile made him our favorite. When the boys could not find any lobsters on the reef, he took them out one night and taught them the local techniques, and they came back with over a dozen. On another occasion, he took Michel and the boys to a nearby island, and they returned with several large coconut crabs, nocturnal creatures well known for how difficult they are to catch. When he learned I was an ex-commercial fisherman, he was very interested to share our knowledge of the fish species he typically caught for the village. I gave him some fishing lures I suspected would work well, and indeed they did. Before we left, I promised to send him more, but he surprised me with a look that suggested he doubted it would happen.

We soon discovered the Solomon Islanders were world-class woodcarvers. Everywhere we went, a canoe would appear very soon after the anchor went down, and inside would be some

Beautiful, typical wood carving

of the finest wood carvings imaginable. The woods used were often rare tropical hardwoods, and inlays of other woods or exotic shells such as nautilus were used with beautiful effect. The detail and highly polished finish of these creative carvings spoke of countless hours of talent and labor. We also learned the tools used were hand-made, often fashioned from pieces of WWII tanks and steel relics the locals found in the jungles. We could not resist such unique treasures and purchased many bowls, utensils, masks, and fish and animal carvings. They made wonderful gifts, and over the years the ones that remained aboard became integral, a part of *Moana* and the inseparable memories of people and places.

Closing the deal: Clean bottom for food

We had a great summer trip in the Solomons. The fishing was fantastic, as almost everyplace was teeming with untouched schools of all the fish we loved to catch and eat. As was sometimes the case in our faraway places, we had difficulty finding the very best dive sites, but we still found some great ones. Still, the exploring and the friendly natives were the best. Day after day of one wonderful memory after another.

Captain's log, August 30

1410 anchor dn in 72ft, Port Mary. Nice anchorage after very tough day.

We were underway for Australia, after seeing the family off in Honiara, but the weather blew up on us before we could transit the Coral Sea, forcing us to wait it out in a nice anchorage at Santa Ana Island. It was a small, remote island and the scene of unforgettable memories for me.

On our first day there, a local man came out in his canoe to welcome us. He could speak English because he had visited Honiara many times and had learned how to make a little extra

Pascale and shampoo hysteria

money from visitors and tourists. We were rare visitors to his island, so he did not want to miss an opportunity. It was fun to negotiate a deal with him, and soon we agreed to pay some of his men to clean the bottom of the boat. This was always important for us because the increased efficiency of a clean bottom meant fuel savings on long transits. The "pay" was actually to be food, as money in such a remote village had little immediate value.

The following morning, several canoes came out with very enthusiastic native men. I handed out masks, fins, snorkel tubes, and cleaning pads, while describing how I wanted the cleaning to be done. The boss relayed this to his men and they jumped into the water. Almost immediately, they popped up, gagging for breath, their masks full of water! They had never used snorkels before and assumed they were some kind of magical tool that would let them breathe underwater! I could not contain myself and laughed at the good-natured natives who laughed back. Undaunted, and with big smiles, they tossed the snorkel tubes back on the boat and got on with the cleaning. When they finished, I told them to send back their wives for the food payment, and they returned to the village.

Next to arrive were three little girls. In remote villages, there is always the fear children will take a canoe and paddle off exploring, just as children might do in the city on their little scooters. But in their world, the danger of being swept out to sea and lost in winds and current they could not paddle against was very real, so the fathers hide the paddles where the children cannot get them. Our cute little visitors were as clever and mischievous as little girls could be—they simply went into the jungle and cut some crude paddles of their own.

Laughing all the way, it was plain to see they were quite proud of themselves when they arrived. Quite impressed and laughing along with the girls, Pascale rewarded them with their first ever ice cream!

Soon a dozen canoes with the village women and young boys arrived, and we handed out a real bonanza of food. It was our last visit in the Solomons before going to Australia, so we cleared out our trading stock and took care of the entire village.

As the women paddled off, I decided to go under the boat and see if the men had done a good job, and Pascale joined me. As always, when coming out of the water, I rinsed off with the shower unit adjacent the aft boarding area and walked forward to dry myself. Suddenly, laughter broke out on the stern. The laughter turned to screaming hysteria as I witnessed children laughing like I had never seen before. Pascale had washed her hair with shampoo and noticed the young boys staring at her, mouths open in wonder, so she proceeded to lather up their heads. They went absolutely wild! Soon, they had the bottle of shampoo and were lathering up their entire bodies, all the while laughing hysterically. It was a scene impossible to really capture, but I grabbed my camera and got off a couple of shots I will treasure forever. Pascale and I recounted this scene many times, trying to understand what it was exactly that sent the boys into such hysterical behavior, but we never figured it out.

The wind refused to let up, so we just worked on small projects, enjoyed the friendly kids who visited daily, and waited it out. The strong breeze made me wonder if any village fishermen had ever been lost at sea. With only paddles for power, it was easy to imagine how they could be caught offshore and overwhelmed by a sudden storm. Our village spokesman told me it had happened a few times, but very rarely because they always knew about coming bad weather. He explained further that the village elders could very accurately predict the weather, and the fishermen depended on them. Via satellite email, my weather routing experts in New York had already told me we would not get a decent weather window for at least four days, so I was curious to know what the elders thought. "You could try to leave in three days, but it would be safer to wait for four," was their advice. In a remote village with no modern communication with the outside world, I was impressed. We left in four days and had good weather across the Coral Sea.

Captain's log, September 7

Underway in Coral Sea on last leg to Cairns, Australia. Fair to good traveling weather in strong, variable currents through offshore reefs. 0100 pos 16° 17.2' S, 147° 25' E.

We arrived in Cairns, Australia, in the late afternoon and anchored out, as requested by customs. As darkness fell, we were stunned at the lights of the city. Cairns is not a huge city, but we had been in wild places for so long, where the normal light at night was only a fire in the village, we had forgotten how the lights of a real city could light up the sky.

Donald, teasing potato cod

Cairns quickly became my favorite city. Located on the spectacular Trinity Inlet, it is the gateway to the famous Great Barrier Reef, just offshore. It was home to a fleet of fast, luxurious power catamaran tour boats that visit the reef daily, and we fit right in with the friendly locals. The marina and management were first class, and most of what we needed for our operation was close at hand. It became our home away from home, and we loved it.

Captains log, September 10
   Dep Marlin Marina, 0659, idling into ship channel in light rain, cloudy sky, NE breeze.

We were underway for the Great Barrier Reef, armed with a nice list of the best spots to visit, courtesy of the very friendly Aussies, who freely shared local knowledge that guaranteed a great trip.

First stop was Cod Hole, a unique area in the coral reef, and home to a resident school of huge potato cod. Like many areas of the Great Barrier Reef, the Australian government understood the true value of its resources, and Cod Hole was totally protected from any kind of fishing or commercial exploitation, which explained the very tame behavior of the big groupers. It was really fun to swim and play with such large fish that were completely unafraid of us.

Next was a stop at Lizard Island. The island had an interesting history, including a visit by the famous Captain Cook, who climbed to the top of its highest peak to survey his difficult situation sailing through the reefs. It was also one of the best anchorages for miles around, an important issue for anyone cruising in the stiff breezes and big seas lashed by the powerful trade winds. Like Cod Hole, the waters around Lizard Island were totally protected, which made the diving and snorkeling fantastic. Here, we swam with some of the largest fish in all of Australia, including a grouper large enough to swallow a small child, and, on two nights, a visit by a very large tiger shark.

Two of the big dive boats operating out of Cairns specialized in trips to Osprey Reef, our next destination. Offshore the protection of the Great Barrier Reef, we never saw another pleasure boat at Osprey. There was a lagoon inside the reef, but anchoring was difficult and it did not offer protection from the big swells that passed over the reef at high tide. It was a rolly, wild place to visit, but the big dive boats came almost daily with their hard-core divers for one reason only: At the North Horn, Osprey Reef, you are guaranteed to swim with big sharks! I learned this in a very exciting way, on our first visit.

Arriving alone at the reef, I looked over the lee side for a good anchorage, and finding a heavy duty mooring at the North Horn, we tied off. It was obviously a mooring put in place by the big dive boats from Cairns, but, ever cautious, I snorkeled over to inspect the attachment of the heavy line to the reef. As I slowly swam over, enjoying the fantastic visibility of the blue-purple water, I saw a large school of small sharks in the deep water, directly below me. In moments, the small sharks became very big sharks, as they rose from the depths and circled close around me. There is something very cold and totally impassive about the eyes of sharks, and when seen very close, you understand you are not looking into the eyes of the family dog. These were the big boys, and their unusual behavior was unnerving. Normally, big sharks are actually shy and slow to come near humans. (We learned the dive boats trained them over time by feeding them.) This was great for their divers who paid a lot of money to see big sharks up close and right away, but quite the breathtaking surprise for me! Silky sharks, silvertips, and other species were all so aggressive they were biting our marlin lures, an unusual behavior. We moved down the reef and, despite the rough, rolly conditions, had a fantastic trip fishing, diving, and snorkeling in the pristine waters of Osprey Reef.

2005

ACROSS THE CORAL SEA

Captain's log, March 20

1000 pos 17° 11.6' S, 154° 13.5' E. Sky clouding over, slight dip in barometer. Grinding it out, hand steering.

"Of course" it was at night, in heavy weather, and in the middle of the Coral Sea.

It was a real slog, but we were grinding it out when, inexplicably, the port rudder jammed hard over and then snapped in half from the intense pressure of being dragged sideways. Joubert centered it up and locked it off hydraulically, and we continued on. But losing a rudder is never a good thing. In our case, the boat steered so well on one rudder, we could not feel a difference, which was a good thing because it would be almost a year before we could make the necessary repairs.

After hauling out and taking care of yearly boat yard maintenance on the Gold Coast, near Brisbane, we were underway for Papua New Guinea and offshore, remote islands. It was a tough course, the length of the Coral Sea, and I was happy to see the weather lay down as we approached Jomard Entrance, a pass through the reefs separating the Coral and Solomon Seas. I will forever remember this pass for the terrifying, coal-black clouds that descended low, blotting out the entire night sky. They were so low, it seemed I could reach up and touch the massive, black monsters that experience told me were about to unleash their deadly energy. Not a breath of wind stirred over the suddenly glassy calm sea, and in the eerie, electric silence, I was aware the hair on the back of my neck was standing up. A few hours seemed like eternity, but dawn broke, the sun came out, and the monsters of the night disappeared like something out of a scary Hollywood movie.

Unforgettable.

The Easter trip took us to Milne Bay, a wild area off eastern Papua New Guinea that was well known for spectacular diving. Several live-aboard dive boats frequented the area, and their friendly captains freely shared the locations of the dive sites with us. The sites were home to endless varieties of small but beautiful fish and other life we had yet to see in our

Milne Bay, Papua New Guinea

travels. It was here we also experienced "muck diving," a name given to sifting through loose coral rubble in the shallows, to see an amazing variety of tiny and exquisite sea creatures. For days on end, it was world class diving in perfect conditions, and the entire family had a great time.

To the northwest, the rarely visited islands of Normanby and Egum Atoll were irresistible. Normanby was difficult to approach and anchor, so we pushed on to Egum Atoll. This lonely atoll, with its one small village, was a member of the Kula Ring, a group of far-flung islands in the Solomon Sea that practiced a well-documented and fascinating tradition of gift giving among the many tribes. The traditional, large sailing canoe used on these voyages was on the beach, and I could not resist seeing it up close. The villagers were very friendly and happy to show the big canoe to Pascale and me, but my fascination with the construction of the canoe, which had not a single metal part, was overshadowed by the happy children who quickly surrounded us.

Pascale with children, seeing themselves for the first time on video

Captain's log, April 13

1800 pos 9° 50.2' S, 152° 11.7' E. Boat motion increasing as SE swell picking up. Steady rain.

After our previous trip to the Solomons we could not resist another, so on April 20 we dropped anchor in the small anchorage behind the yacht club, in downtown Honiara. The yacht club could not be much smaller, consisting of a traditional, palm-covered meeting room with picnic benches outside. There was a small pier, but visiting dinghies just hauled up on the sand beach. The club officers were really friendly and welcoming, however.

Visiting yachts were rare in the Solomons, so when Pascale and I noticed a nice sailboat sizing up the anchorage, we immediately went over in the dinghy to help our new neighbors find a good spot. And this is how lifelong friendships with real boat people begin. Otto Lehrack, a retired US Marine and famous author of several books on the Vietnam War, and his Canadian wife, Pierrette, were on a circumnavigation in their sailboat, the *Hana Hou*. Alongside, after helping them get secured to a strong mooring, we were about to return to

Moana when Pascale detected Pierette's French accent. Never in my life had I witnessed two women become inseparable friends in a matter of moments. Pascale refused to drop the line between the boats, and while Otto and I just smiled at each other, the two of them enjoyed their native French like a couple of teenage school girls for what seemed like a very long time. And at the end of every day, their hilarious laughter could be heard coming from the picnic benches behind the club. At the same time, Otto and I became good friends too, and he inspired me to write this book.

Our second time in Honiara, we knew our way around. We understood the basics of provisioning, and importing parts and supplies, two of the most important issues for trip preparation and maintenance. But in a wild place like Honiara, there seemed to always be a surprise like the one I received from our young taxi driver. Bleary eyed one morning, he explained that he did not get much sleep the night before, because of the arrival of one of his "*wantoks*," a *tok pisin* word meaning literally, "one-talk." Wantoks are a group of people who are bound together by an agreement to help each other at all times. The group includes families, but it can also include outsiders. Generations ago, it was a beneficial mechanism that ensured survival of the wantok by members' unconditionally helping each other, but modern times made the system work against itself. My tired taxi driver explained a wantok family had arrived at his home in the middle of the night, and he and his family had to take them into his small home.

"How long will they stay?" I asked.

"As long as they want," was his answer.

This explained why many of the small shopkeepers in Honiara were Chinese. If a shopkeeper was a local man, any member of his wantok could come into the store and take whatever he wanted, without payment of any kind. The wantok could not be refused. It also explained corruption at the highest levels of government, as the largest wantoks controlled the votes and appointed their wantoks to all the political positions. Months later, my poor taxi driver was still housing and feeding his wantoks.

"Whiskey, whiskey!"

Drunken men in a small boat were alongside a nearby neighbor, banging on their boat and demanding alcohol. In the darkness, I could see the terrified occupants pass something down to the loud, aggressive, Melanesian men. And in moments, they were on their way to *Moana*. These were not the shy and friendly natives we normally met on the outer islands. These were unpredictable local thugs who could create a nasty situation. I decided to simply lock the cabin door, but before I could, they were alongside. To my horror, Joubert walked across the deck to confront them.

Joubert reached the side of the boat at the same time the four large men began to scream again. Their boat was close to our cockpit, making it very easy for them to board, and as I looked down from the upper deck, I considered bringing out the gun. A double-barreled 12-gauge shotgun loaded with lead slugs is a devastating weapon at close range, but Joubert proved to be even more effective. Leaning over the bulwark, he pressed an index finger to his lips, and with a loud "shhhhhhhh," like a mother scolding misbehaving children, quietly told the men, "We are Seventh Day Adventists here. We have no alcohol." The effect on the men was absolutely stunning!

"Oh, oh," they muttered, and with their open palms raised in a gesture of complete submission, sat down in silence. Utterly shamed, they motored off into the darkness as Joubert looked up at me with his famous smile. "So, Joubert," I teased, "we are now Seventh Day Adventists?" Hilarious beyond words!

Our second trip in the Solomons was really memorable. We returned to our favorite islands and villages and enjoyed the warm welcome of natives who were like long lost friends. At Peava Village, four children who had been my favorites called out, "Captain Lew, Captain Lew!" as they paddled out to greet us. They were later followed by the village elders, who apologized for not coming sooner, due to that day's being their Sabbath and they were all in church. They were still dressed in their best clothes, wanting to greet us as soon as possible. It was this kind of honest friendship with the natives that was special to the family and me. Again, we traded beautiful woodcarvings for the trading goods they valued so highly, but for me, I could hardly wait for the arrival of Tokapae Moses, my fisherman friend who had been so nice to the family, especially Louis.

While in Australia, I had ordered a complete, professional woodcarving tool set. It really was an impressive assortment of almost every tool needed for high-quality woodworking. On our previous visit, Tokapae shared with me that although he was a skilled and respected fisherman; he really wanted to be a carver. He worked hard to provide the village with fish, so had little time to pursue woodcarving, and had to borrow tools from friends when he had the chance. He showed me a spectacular "turtle bowl" he made from a very large tree, so his considerable talent was obvious.

When he finally came alongside in his boat, I said nothing as I handed over the tool set, encased in its nice wood box. Staring at the razor sharp, beautiful tools, he gave me an interesting look and began to explain he was unable to pay me anything. It took a few moments for him to understand, followed by an incredible smile, when I told him it was a gift. The village went crazy, with everyone he knew borrowing tools. And a beautiful turtle bowl resides in my house to this day, reminding me of a very special man.

We worked our way northwest, visiting some new islands and finding great fishing, diving, and exploring. The natives know where all the WWII battles were fought and where all the relics from crashed airplanes to gun emplacements lay in the jungles, and were happy to share some with us. This included a small shrine the natives put together on an island near where John F. Kennedy and the rest of the crew washed up after PT 109 was run down by the Japanese. The display of memorabilia was not much, but the natives were hoping tourists would one day pay money to see what they had salvaged from the historical battle that night long ago.

While anchored there, I realized the "bug bite" I received on my leg a few days before was developing into something serious, as the small red spot had grown into a golf-ball-sized lump, oozing a strange fluid. My leg from the knee down was swelling, and when I noticed red lines appearing under my skin, I remembered the horrible posters in the customs office.

"It's too late for the twig," a passing fisherman declared. He knew immediately about the fly that laid its egg under my skin, and the local treatment, which used a tiny, harpoon-like twig to spear the egg and pull it out before infection took over. "Now, you will live or die depending if you can get antibiotics."

The nearest real city was Gizo, and we got underway immediately. On board were two very complete first-aid kits that included every kind of medicine and bandages imaginable, including antibiotics. We had done our homework and were ready for just about any medical emergency, but we made one mistake: The antibiotics were penicillin base, and I was allergic to penicillin. A few hours later, we arrived off Gizo and launched the small boat, and Joubert took me to the beach. Limping on my swollen leg, I hired the first local I found to take me to the hospital. It was almost funny when he drove all of fifty yards and stopped in front of an old wood building. Hollywood could not duplicate the condition of the aged, windowless building, and I was so surprised I blurted out, "This is the hospital? Are you sure?"

At the top of the stairs, several mothers with crying babies were rocking back and forth, obviously distraught. The only door into the hospital was locked from the inside, and a hand-written note attached declared:

No plasters

Only deep cuts and infectious today

The door finally opened and a doctor looked me up and down and then ushered me inside. The building was built on pilings over a tidal mud flat, and as I followed the doctor I had to watch my step to avoid the holes in the floor, where I could clearly see decaying trash in the black mud below. A nurse provided an old wooden crate, and I sat in front of her desk, which was piled high with stacks of old forms and papers. While answering her basic questions, I looked around in disbelief at the conditions of the "office." Everything was very old, bare wood and, most disturbing, dirty. Behind me, yellow-orange fluid oozed from a pile of used bandages, heaped high in a big sink. A distinct odor filled the air. This was definitely Third World.

"Do you have a history of diabetes in your family?"

"No, doctor."

"I am going to test you for diabetes."

"Doctor, I have a very bad infection."

Big fish, serious knife; Joubert feeding the village

As the nurse approached with her blood sampling tools, I could not help but wonder if I was about to receive an infection that would be terminal, but she sterilized her needle in front of me, and took the sample to another room. The doctor returned, and stared at my swollen, bandaged leg, not sharing his thoughts. And at that moment, I remembered that in many countries, "plasters" is another word for bandages. The hospital had no clean bandages! They would not be able to give me a fresh bandage, which was why the doctor was too embarrassed to remove mine. I pointed out the window to *Moana*, lying at anchor nearby, and said, "Doctor, that is my boat. We have lots of bandages aboard, so you don't have to put a new bandage on my leg." And without another word, he ripped my bandage off, took one look, and declared, "Wow! You have a very bad infection!"

The hospital did have non-penicillin–based antibiotics, and I was soon on my way. But not before I had to pass the many open rooms where people lay on old war-surplus bunkbeds surrounded by anxious family and friends. A steady breeze blew past the sunbleached curtains, passing through the windowless building, and helped carry off the strong odor of bodies,

Turtle tied to a stake

medicine, cleaning agents, and the black mud flat. Even the flies, swarming over the stagnant mud, seemed deterred by the smell and seldom entered. As Joubert picked me up in the small boat, I cast a long look at the hospital. It took two months and two regimens of antibiotics to kill the infection. Plenty of time to wonder about natives in remote areas, unable to obtain antibiotics and "too late for the twig."

Two days later, we were returning to an anchorage, with a huge blue marlin aboard. Normally we released marlin, but on this day I was very happy to bring it on the boat. The big fish would feed an entire village, and I was looking forward to making good on my promise of the day before, when we anchored near a small island. The privately owned, unnamed island was home to a group of people who worked raising and harvesting coconuts, and the village chief and his son paddled out as soon as our anchor had hit the water. Visitors were very rare to this particular island because the chart offered no suitable anchorages, so the natives were surprised by our arrival. I had found an interesting shelf with clear sand bottom that would provide a decent overnight anchorage and, most likely, excellent snorkeling. But the chief's son, who could speak English, gave us reason for some serious fishing.

The island natives were asking the owners for more money (food, actually) for their labor, and the owners were refusing. The owners stopped the supply boat from visiting, to force the natives back to work, and the natives, who were not fishermen and had no other source of food, were in desperate shape. We were near the end of our trip in the Solomons and did not have a lot of spare food aboard, so I promised the chief we would go out the following day and catch some fish for his village. And as we approached the island the next afternoon, Joubert was busy cutting the giant fish into huge, cross-section "wheels," as all the village canoes were already paddling our way. I will forever remember placing a big piece of the fish into a young girl's canoe and watching her paddle off with a huge grin and tears in her eyes.

We finished our second trip in the Solomons in the Manning Strait area. We were alone in a pristine, beautiful paradise most of that time, but we also had some memorable experiences with the natives when near villages. For me, it was heartwarming to see children from such different cultures and circumstances playing together. With his big smile and never ending enthusiasm, Louis was a favorite with the young native boys, and it was not unusual to see him paddling off in a canoe with his new friends.

On one such occasion, while paddling to a nearby village, Louis pointed out a turtle to his companions, who immediately changed course and caught the turtle. At the village, the boys tied the turtle to a stake at the waters edge, where it would remain alive until later cooked and eaten.

Poor Louis felt guilty, knowing the beautiful, helpless animal would be killed and eaten because of him, and he found a clever way to untie the line while the natives seemed distracted. But natives see everything in the village, including the funny white boy who was relieved to find the natives actually laughed as the turtle swam off. They fully understood why Louis released the turtle, and they saw the humor in his ignorance of their culture. His friendship was more valuable to them than a turtle. This was not lost on Louis, a very sensitive and thoughtful young man.

Captain's log, September 10

Underway for Port Moresby, capital of Papua New Guinea. 1414 pos abeam Duchateau Reefs. Spectacular 60ft sailboat wreck, broken in two, high on beach.

Rated "the most dangerous city in the world to visit" by various international travel agencies, Port Moresby deserved its reputation. Fortunately for us, the yacht club was the safest place in the city, due to a high fence topped with razor wire and patrolled day and night by armed guards and dogs. During the day, there was one taxi driver we found to be safe, but we went nowhere at night. Two supermarkets were safe to visit, but only because armed guards patrolled not only the parking lots but the aisles of the markets as well! To walk past

Headlights on

Shrimp on anemone

Hiding in the coral

Leaf fish

black-clad, deadly serious security guards who toted pump shotguns inside a supermarket was a reminder we were not in Kansas anymore, Dorothy! A trip to the bank was equally memorable, with electronically controlled access/isolation doors and chambers, bulletproof glass everywhere, and workers impossible to approach closely.

It did not take long to understand most of the problems. The divide between the rich and poor was beyond anything we had ever seen before. The government provided no education or medical help to the local people. All the decent paying jobs were held by foreign workers, brought in and housed in a walled, guarded compound. They, like the politicians and officials, came to work in bulletproof cars, driven by professionals. Local people, many of them illiterate natives from the highlands, were lured to the city by rumors of jobs and money, only to find no opportunity whatsoever. In not so many years past, highland tribes were well known for their brutal warfare, where any gain justified killing or maiming. Now, their descendants were ill prepared for life in the city. Broke and hungry, they roamed the streets in desperate gangs, ironically called "Rascals."

Michel knew of a dive boat named *Golden Dawn* that specialized in trips to Eastern Fields, a reef system offshore Papua New Guinea, in the Coral Sea. It was a wild place that prompted Craig Dewitt, the owner/captain, to warn would-be customers not to come if they were prone to motion sickness. Just our kind of place! Michel and the family flew into Port Moresby and we were on our way.

Extremely fortunate for me, I was able to meet with Craig before our trip. A great guy and unselfish captain, he passed on crucial information learned from years of visiting the reef. And it was all about the dangerous current that swept across the reef with incredible power. Combined with the seas driven by the strong trade winds, knowing where and how to anchor inside the reef was essential—not for enjoyment, but for survival. Inside Eastern Fields, dragging anchor at night was certain disaster.

With Craig's GPS numbers, we visited great dive sites and had a sensational trip. The reef was incredibly pristine because, except for *Golden Dawn*, no other boats from Port Moresby dared to venture inside or were willing to deal with the rough weather. Huge schools of every tropical fish imaginable swam in crystal clear water over jaw-dropping beautiful forests of hard and soft corals. Day after day, we enjoyed a wild and wonderful diver's paradise. And it was here I noticed the qualities of Louis's underwater photos take on the look of a professional. Free diving to twenty meters and spearing large fish had become routine for him and he enjoyed the attention he received from his siblings, so it was interesting to see him use those considerable underwater skills with a camera. Many times, I saw him lying on the bottom, absolutely motionless, waiting patiently to get a shot of a fish or tiny creature so perfectly camouflaged no one else would have noticed.

But of course, the wild places can come with a price, and on one of our last days inside the reef, Joubert woke me up early to say the dinghy was gone. Our small boat was more than just a dinghy. It was our shore boat, dive boat, fishing boat, even sometimes a tugboat. Highly customized, our little "sea truck" was vital to everything we did, and as I looked around, my heart sank to see it was gone.

How could this happen? I wondered. I dreaded facing Michel with such terrible news, as I tried to re-create the circumstances in my mind. Slowly, a time-lapse picture emerged. Because of the strong current that swept through the reef, reversing itself at every tide change, it was necessary to double anchor *Moana*, aligned bow and stern into to the current, so the current could not drag the boat broadside and overpower the anchors. This meant that, tied mid-ship on a single line, our small boat streamed off the stern when the current came from the bow and then streamed off the bow when the current changed and came from the stern. This would not normally be a problem on most boats, but *Moana* was a bulbous bow catamaran, with razor sharp "cutters" on each bow, to prevent commercial fishing long lines from being snagged on the bows, and winding up wrapped up in the propellers. The piece of our small boat's bow line, still attached to our port side, and just long enough to reach the cutter, completed the picture in my mind: When the small boat was streaming off the bow, the current changed, and instead of passing aft, down the side of *Moana*, the line was long enough to allow it to go around the bow and into the cutter. We had cut off our little boat!

But I knew at what time the current changed in the night, so it was easy to calculate the time the line of the small boat would have gone into the cutter. "It just happened, Joubert!" I almost yelled. It had to happen just before daylight, less than two hours before. And as soon as I looked down current in my binoculars, I saw her. Drifting fast, and outside the reef, she was a speck on the horizon.

"It's a very narrow pass, and on a dog-leg, so you will need to be careful," Craig explained, giving me the GPS numbers on a pass through the reef I needed to use. Two hours later, we had her in tow, and Craig was the hero of the day.

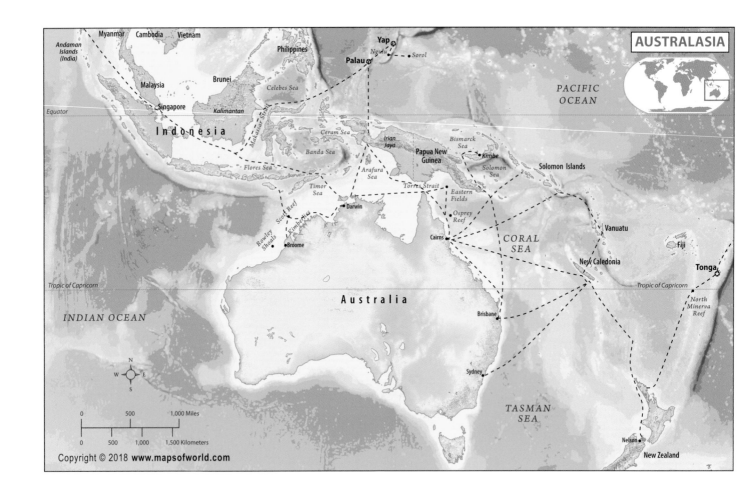

AUSTRALASIA

Andaman
Islands
(India)

Myanmar   Cambodia   Vietnam

Philippines

Yap
Ngulu   Sorol
Palau

PACIFIC
OCEAN

Malaysia   Brunei
Singapore   Kalimantan
Celebes Sea

Equator

I n d o n e s i a

Ceram Sea
Banda Sea
Irian
Jaya
Papua New
Guinea

Bismarck
Sea
Kimbe
Solomon
Sea

Solomon Islands

Flores Sea

Arafura
Sea

Timor
Sea

Torres Strait

Eastern
Fields

Scott Reef
Kimberleys

Osprey
Reef

Vanuatu

Rowley
Shoals
Broome

Darwin

Cairns

CORAL
SEA

Fiji

New Caledonia

Tonga

Tropic of Capricorn

Tropic of Capricorn

INDIAN OCEAN

A u s t r a l i a

North
Minerva
Reef

Brisbane

N
W   E
S

Sydney

TASMAN
SEA

0   500   1,000 Miles

0   500   1,000   1,500 Kilometers

Nelson

New Zealand

Copyright © 2018 www.mapsofworld.com

2006

ACROSS THE CORAL AND ARAFURA SEAS, INTO THE INDIAN OCEAN

Captain's log, March 31, 2006

0300 pos 20° 46.1' S, 155° 02.8' E. Rough seas, heavy rain.

In Pascale's doghouse again, we were grinding out another tough slog up the middle of the Coral Sea. Swells generated by a passing cyclone created massive waves that closed out the Seaway Tower channel, south of Brisbane, delaying our departure from Australia. Pascale was a wonderful chef and real team player, and I always tried to arrive at least a week before the family, to allow her to find markets and provision with all the fresh food we would need. Now, she would have to perform a minor miracle in one day, in a wild place we had never been before.

Pushing hard in the lousy weather, we still arrived two days late in Kimbe, a bay on one of the New Britain islands of Papua New Guinea. Ringed by densely forested islands and smoking volcanos, it was an exotic and wild place. Fortunately, Michel and the family were able to stay at a nice lodge while waiting for our arrival. Due to the spectacular diving on unique underwater reefs, canyons, and sunken volcanos offshore, Walindi Resort attracted professional underwater photographers from all over the scuba diving world.

Max Benjamin was one of those very interesting men we sometimes met in our travels. Undeterred by difficulties that would discourage most, he developed a first-class lodge in a wild place. And one of the difficulties he dealt with was finding a way to operate peacefully with the numerous native tribes in the area. Working with the chief of all the chiefs on the Willaumez Peninsula, he paid the chief fees for all the dive boats that operated out of his lodge. Upon return to the lodge, the boats would reveal all the places they anchored, and fees would be determined to pay each village chief for the boat to be in their waters. This, Max explained to me, discouraged young natives from demanding visitor fees over and over, at every dive site or overnight anchorage. And to make sure we had no problems, he gave me a letter in tok pisin to remind natives of the agreement he had with the head chief.

He also gave me a map of the entire area, detailing the name and precise GPS location of all the dive sites. It was really well done and took us directly to fabulous places we never could

Ben, "owner of the sea"

have found in the limited time we would be there. At each site, we dove down with a long mooring line and attached it to a big steel ring embedded in the bottom. This eliminated the damage that would otherwise be caused by anchors and chain, protecting the fragile corals for years to come.

All of the dive sites were fantastic. Two were inside the sunken cones of ancient volcanoes, where curious manta rays entertained us at close range. The water was absolutely clear, there was seldom current, and the sites teemed with life, including sharks and whales. We enjoyed day after day of superb diving until poor weather blew up and drove us close to the coast to find a calm anchorage.

I did not notice the three canoes arrive, but I certainly noticed the five or six natives who swarmed into the cockpit. We had never seen this kind of behavior with natives in all of our travels. The leader of the pack was immediately in my face, with obvious hostility.

"My name is Ben. I am the chief," and with arms outstretched for effect, declared, "I am the owner of the sea, and you will give us many things. Bring me a newspaper!"

I was shocked at his hostile, aggressive behavior, but handed him an old newspaper we surprisingly had aboard. He pretended to read the paper, to impress his fellows, while they looked about for something to steal. I presented him with the letter from Max, which made him furious. As he began to walk forward, as if to enter the cabin, I stepped in front of him and said, "This is our home. You cannot enter!"

"Out, out, out! You all out!" he yelled. And with that, we hauled our anchor and got underway as the natives paddled back to their village. Fortunately, this happened when the family was all forward, lounging on the big hatch cushion, so they did not experience the threatening attitude of the natives. Unfortunately, it also meant no one saw a native steal Michel's small camera.

Immediately after discovering the missing camera, I sent an email to Max, detailing the event and our location. Within an hour, I was astonished to receive an email apology from the head chief, and his promise to find the camera. Reading his email, I almost laughed out loud because we were off a very wild area on the Willaumez Peninsula, far from any kind of civilization.

The last days of the trip included diving on more of the unique sites off Kimbe, in beautiful, calm weather. While trolling back to Walindi Resort, Pierre, a best friend of Thomas, caught a large blue marlin that unfortunately died on the line. Of all the various marlin species, they are the best eating, so we elected to bring it in and give it to the cook at the lodge. As we came alongside the lodge pier, a crowd began to appear as the lodge manager approached the boat and told me the camera had been found. Further, she explained, the authorities were bringing the thieves to face me for punishment! This was their custom, and I was told that whatever I decided would be carried out.

An old WWII Jeep bounced out of the jungle, complete with a small "jail" on the back, and inside were two of the thieves who were on the boat. A big, shirtless native with a shotgun, and his driver boss wearing an old surplus army shirt, brought the trembling natives to face me, and the crowd went silent. With our US flag flapping in the breeze, I wondered how many Hollywood movies the natives had seen, and no doubt were sure an American would demand blood at the very least. I was disappointed that Ben was not one they caught, as he was clearly the instigator of the incident, and I felt sorry for the poor men before me, who were shaking so badly they could hardly stand. I could not tok pisin, so asked the officer to translate my sentence, which was: "Look me in the eyes, and shake my hand." A collective sigh of relief, followed by excited chatter came from the natives who were obviously pleased no one had to be killed or maimed. I later learned the men's real punishment would be rejection and humiliation by the entire village for weeks.

The following morning, the family and guests flew out in a small plane, and we got underway for Darwin, Australia. This required a fuel and provision stop in Port Moresby, and a big surprise for me.

As before, we were the only visiting yacht in Port Moresby, and after two days preparing the boat for the run to Australia, authorities informed me that I had broken a customs law and had to appear in court. The customs officer in Kimbe felt we had disrespected him by not telling him of our departure, and wanted us to be prosecuted under a law related to smuggling on commercial ships. If found guilty, the fine was to be around $5,000 kina, about US $450. We were tourists, aboard a private yacht, so the charges were ridiculous, but I had to appear.

I was surprised when my taxi drove out of the city, into a clearing in the jungle, where small pre-fab office buildings were lined up in a long row, comprising courthouses. At least fifty wild looking natives milled about, looking at the only white person in their midst. I had no idea where to go, and finally found a large information board that described the day's events, and charges against my fellow accused. Murder, armed robbery, kidnapping, and rape! I was in the jungle of Papua New Guinea, surrounded by primitive, desperate natives who knew only the rule of brute force, and not a single policeman was in sight!

At the end of the first building, a man behind a barred window directed me to my courtroom where, soon after, the door was opened by a young Melanesian woman, and I entered the smallest courtroom on the planet. A raised, classic judge's bench and four wooden chairs filled the small room. The young woman pulled on a robe and casually informed me the fine was now $50,000 Kina. I was surprised such a young woman could be the prosecutor, and asked how the fine could now be raised. "You are in Papua New Guinea," was her answer.

Moments later, a door opened from the side, and the Melanesian judge, wearing a classic white English wig and heavy, burgundy robe, went to his bench. "All rise," commanded the prosecutor, and the two of us stood in the tiny courtroom. It was an amazing trial. The prosecutor made her case, and the judge surprised me by asking her how a private yacht could be considered a commercial ship. She quickly held up a paper and declared, "Under Papua New Guinea law, any vessel propelled by anything more powerful than paddles is considered a commercial vessel." I was sure a "kangaroo court" was in order.

"This sounds so Draconian," the judge replied. "And how much is the fine?"

"Fifty thousand kina, your honor."

"And the minimum?"

To my astonishment, the judge was on my side, and even encouraged me to plead innocent! I really liked this man, but I explained we were already late getting underway for Australia and just preferred to pay a fine and be on our way. And with that, the gavel came down, we paid the minimum, and I became a convicted criminal in Papua New Guinea!

The real cause of this entire episode, my failure to clear out with the customs officer in Kimbe, was not because I did not know about the regulation. It was simply because I did not want the giant, overweight, stinky Melanesian on my boat again. In our travels to remote island countries, we learned that some of the authorities that came to the boat for customs and Immigration procedures did not practice modern hygiene, to say the least. Almost always courteous and very sociable, they often had a body odor, especially in the heat and humidity of the tropics, that made it difficult to be near them for more than a few minutes. When one of these pungent officials came aboard, I would take them to the pilothouse and seat them next to the large window at the portside dinette table. Even with our air conditioning system running, the intense sunlight coming through the window would cause our poor guest to sweat profusely and prompt him to conclude business right away. So, to avoid a situation bordering on comedy, I wound up an authentic desperado!

Captain's log, May 5

Underway in Gulf of Papua in beautiful traveling weather, mostly clear, starry sky. 0100 pos 9° 13.4' S, 144° 10.5' E

Running across the Coral Sea and then westward through Torres Strait put the strong trade winds and big seas astern, so we had a good passage all the way across the top of Australia, to Darwin. I dreaded the day, however, when we would have to run back, into the teeth of those notorious seas of the Arafura Sea and Torres Strait.

We loved the city of Darwin and its people. I was fascinated to learn of its WWII history, the Boxing Day cyclone that destroyed much of the city, and the "run up to the wet," a period of weather just before the onset of the rainy season so terrible many people leave the city until it is over. It was a real Wild West town, with a lot of very rugged souls! Also, there was an excellent shipyard and many support services, so it was a great stop for repairs and provisioning before pushing on to the west coast of Australia.

Captain's log, July 17

Underway for Scott Reef in very poor traveling weather with stiff ESE breeze 20–25kts on beam, wind driven seas to 6ft

140 nautical miles offshore in the Indian Ocean, Scott Reef was just the kind of wild reef system we loved. It was actually three reefs, swept by strong winds and seas that passed over the coral reefs, and there was not a single calm anchorage. It was not for the average boat with visitors expecting a good night's sleep and meals eaten without drama. But it was home to yellowfin and dogtooth tuna, snapper, grouper, and many other species of fish we loved to catch and eat.

Inside the lagoons of the offshore reefs we visited, there were sometimes beautiful small sand islands. Due to the remote location, these little islands were often home to many seabird species and were nesting sites for turtles. One such island was near our anchorage and, despite a fringing coral reef that made it almost impossible to visit, was irresistible for our adventurous family. Wanting to see turtles laying their eggs, Michel and the family found their way ashore

Donald to the rescue

in the dark, no small feat. They were rewarded, not by a nesting turtle but by hatchling turtles emerging from the sand and making their desperate run to the sea. Fortunately for the baby turtles that became lost in a large tide pool, they were rescued by the kids and released into the sea before the sun came up and the birds could eat all of them. We understood it is natural for the baby turtles to be eaten by the birds that needed to survive as well, but in all of nature, there are few animals as precious and vulnerable as baby sea turtles, so we always chose to help them.

This was the summer trip for the kids. It was winter in the southern hemisphere but summer in Europe, so the kids were out of school and enjoying a spectacular vacation on the west coast of Australia. Seven years had passed since we began our adventures aboard *Moana*. The kids were older, and I often wondered what they told their schoolmates about their summer vacation. How did they describe their adventures in our travels to the incredible places we

Shovelnose sharks, spawning in inches of water

visited? Did they even try? They came to the boat on every school vacation, so maybe it was so normal to them they did not think it to be special. We never talked about this, but I had no doubt that one day they would realize our adventures aboard *Moana* and the remote, wild places we traveled were indeed special. I also had no doubt the unsaid lessons they experienced would shape them in many ways.

The west coast of Australia and its offshore islands were wild and unspoiled. Operating out of the small city of Broome, we enjoyed multiple trips offshore as well as on the coast.

North of Broome and not far offshore the mainland, the low island of Lacepede looked uninteresting from a distance, but it proved to be one of our favorite stops. A nesting island for thousands of seabirds, it was also a major nesting island for green turtles, with a spawning lagoon full of shovelnose sharks and many species of fish we had never seen before. Ruggedly beautiful, it was a photographer's dream.

Turtle tracks and nests were everywhere on the long sand beach, so the boys, always ready for adventure, decided to spend a night on the island and see the female turtles come ashore to lay their eggs. The boys, older now, had a basic plan, but they understood we could not rescue them in the dark due to the rocks and surf on the beach. After all, what bad things could possibly happen on such a serene, peaceful beach?

Returning to sea

Home of the boobies, nesting area for turtles

What? Dive-bombing boobies? Crashing into kids wandering around in the dark? Boobies, like most birds, do not normally fly around in the dark, but they are not normally scared into flight by kids wandering around their sleeping spots on the beach, either. Large birds, with armored heads and sharp beaks and built for speed, boobies are also well known for crazy airborne antics when confused or surprised. In this case, the birds took flight when the boys frightened them, flew around in the dark and tried to return to the beach, only to become disoriented by the flashlight beams the boys used to try to defend themselves. After a few direct hits by the boobies, the boys shut off their flashlights, hunkered down on the sand, and the first International Boys/Boobies Peace Pact was successfully concluded. It was all worth it, however, when a few hours later, at high tide, turtles emerged from the surf and began crawling up the slope of the beach. Over and over, they saw the big females dig their nesting holes in the sand, lay their eggs, cover the nest, and struggle back to the sea; the boys had front-row seats to a true wonder of nature. As the sun began to rise, the boys called us excitedly on their radio to say a late arriving turtle had just begun to dig her nesting hole. Pascale and I immediately jumped into the dinghy and beached the small boat in time to see the amazing event. It is truly fascinating to watch an animal, guided only by instinct, perform things that border on the impossible. Using her rear flippers, and unable to see anything, the turtle digs the egg hole with incredible dexterity. Not one grain of sand falls back into the hole! It is a slow process, but the egg-laying is not. She lays 60 to 100 eggs in mere minutes, covers the nest with a clever, rotating maneuver, and, exhausted, struggles down the beach to the water. It is easy to understand why turtles prefer sand beaches that have a definite slope. Both the exhausted female and the hatchlings can reach the water quickly and with as little effort as possible.

Back on the coast, we anchored all alone in the hook of stunning Cape Leveque and enjoyed a beautiful panoramic view of long sand beaches, backed with a rugged landscape of orange and red cliffs and rocks.

The bay was so serene and relaxing, we stayed for two days without any diving or fishing, very unusual for us. It was all aboriginal land and known as Kooljaman in their language. Developed by the locals as a tourist destination, it featured clever, almost invisible cabins on poles, set back from the beach, in the trees. This was remarkable because it took three difficult hours in a four-wheel-drive vehicle to get there from Broome, and even more remarkable because European tourists made reservations a year in advance to visit the remote, unspoiled area. The aborigines offered several nature excursions that were the real thing, and Michel decided on a mud crab hunt in the mangroves. It duplicated how the aborigines of years past survived in the wilds, and by the time our hunt was over, we had tremendous respect for them.

"Our" mangrove swamp was a real-life nightmare of twisted tree roots, spikes, and rotting flora over soft mud.

Shaded by the dense trees, visibility was poor and every step uncertain. Slogging through the mud, trying not to lose our boots or fall down, with rivers of sweat running down our

Miles and miles of pristine beaches at Cape Leveque

Louis, Thomas, Rachel, and Donald. Young adventurers, six years on

Aborigine guide and Lew posing with one of Donald's crabs

faces and clouds of hungry mosquitoes surrounding us, we did manage to catch a few mud crabs before our guide called it a day. I noticed he was amazed at the determination and quick learning skills of Michel, Louis, and Donald (I did not find a single crab) and found it hilarious that he was the one to say "enough."

Captain's log, August 7

0834 pos off pass, Clerke Reef. A/C to various, to run down reef, watch whales, wait for better sun angle.

170 miles offshore Cape Leveque is the three atolls of Rowley Shoals. These circular coral reefs, two of them with passes into lagoons, are all that remain of volcanos that sank into the depths, millions of years ago. In the deep water and bathed in the offshore current of the Indian Ocean, they are unique and home to countless forms of marine life. Permits must be obtained from the Australian government before visiting these priceless but vulnerable gems, and strict regulations must be observed. The government rightly understands the value of Rowley Shoals and protects the reefs with daily flights of "Coastwatch" planes that record and photograph all boats in the area. When foreign fishing boats are caught illegally fishing in Australian waters, the crew goes to jail and the boats are burned on the beach.

With Joubert and Michel perched on the bows, watching for coral heads, we entered the narrow, dangerous pass of Clerke Reef. Charts help, but in the passes of coral reefs, it comes down to eyeball navigation, the correct sun angle, and experience. With the big beam of *Moana*, there was no margin for error, and I was very relieved to slide past the most dangerous area.

We stayed at Clerke for a week, spending two days exploring a low, windswept coral sand island inside the lagoon that at first glance appeared to be completely barren but was home to several bird species that nested on the open sand. This included two of my favorite sea birds, the sooty tern and the red-tailed tropic bird. I loved and admired these birds, especially the reclusive red-tailed tropic bird that lives in the vast desert of the middle ocean, where no other birds can survive. Wonderfully evolved, the streamlined and beautiful birds are normally difficult to see close, so to find these birds nesting at Clerke was a wonderful experience for all of us. With so few human visitors, they were unafraid when approached slowly, and they allowed us to take some excellent photos.

The water of the lagoon was a little green and cool, so we re-anchored outside, close to the coral reef. Due to the steep drop-off of the bottom, it was necessary to drop the anchor very close to the reef, where huge swells passed under us and thundering surf exploded less than a hundred yards off our stern. The family enjoyed great diving and fishing, but I was nervous around the clock. Here, we saw dogtooth tuna swimming with sharks, and we were amazed to find a small shark in the stomach of one of the tunas. Apparently, the dogtooth tuna were the real landlords of the reef!

Next, we visited Mermaid Reef, which had a much easier pass to enter. The regulations, however, were different at Mermaid than at the other two atolls of Rowley Shoals. Mermaid was a National Nature Reserve, and the reef, lagoon, and sea offshore to four miles were totally protected. We were not allowed to catch or touch anything and were allowed to anchor only in a small, designated zone inside the lagoon. Coastwatch flew over us every day, sometimes twice, but we all agreed the strict regulations had made Mermaid a paradise of sea life. Without any exploitation by commercial or sport fishing for years, the quantity and quality of marine life was really unbelievable. And nowhere was this more apparent than in the pass. At the turn of the tide, when fish of all size and description gather just outside the pass, we would join them and "fly" in on the flood. It is really the closest thing to flying, barely kicking with a fin, to stay horizontal, pushed along in the current while surrounded closely by everything from clouds of every kind of fish imaginable, to big sharks and even turtles and dolphins! Every day, it was the main event, and we never missed it. The only boat there, we were all alone in paradise once again.

Dangerous pass at Clerke Reef

Two feet of water over coral, five feet off hull sides; no margin for error

Potato cod begging Michel for food; we never fed them

Flood tide in the pass

Red-tailed tropic bird with chick at her breast

Captain's log, September 6

0200 pos 10° 57.6' S, 136° 36.9' E, abeam Wessel Island, 2.3 mi. Entering Gulf of Carpentaria.

Getting "home" in Cairns required sixteen total days, including ten brutal days of rough head seas in the Bonaparte Gulf, Arafura Sea, and Torres Strait, going east across the top of Australia. While *Moana* was a great sea boat, the bodies inside sometimes took a beating, and this was one of those times.

We finished 2006 with one more visit to Cod Hole, Lizard Island, and Osprey Reef. It seemed the big potato cod, schools of huge jacks, and sharks were waiting to greet us once again. Personally, I have always been fascinated with sharks.

I love the beautiful, efficient shape of their bodies and, except for a few unusual situations, love to swim with them. The entire family was comfortable swimming with sharks as well, but sometimes we had guests who were a bit overwhelmed by the curious predators that like to appear from nowhere and follow you around.

At Osprey Reef, we had the only shark attack suffered in all of our travels. I witnessed the attack from the pilothouse through my binoculars, and it was a wild event! Michel's sister, Collette, and her husband, Jean-Marie, were snorkeling along the edge of the reef, above the

Gray reef shark going home

drop off and deep water of the open ocean. Suddenly, the attack began, and they were driven back into a small cave of the reef. The relentless predator would not give up and pressed the attack, forcing its terrified prey to climb up onto the reef! Fortunately, Michel was nearby in the small boat, saw the white water flying, and came to the rescue. And at close range, Michel saw exactly which type of "shark" it was: a very large remora!

Remoras are not sharks at all, but very interesting fish. They have a large, flat-shaped sucking disc on the top of their head that they use to attach themselves to large fish such as sharks, manta rays, marlin, etc., where they get a free ride with a large predator and eat scraps of food at their host's mealtime. When a remora tries to attach onto a swimmer, which is not unusual, they come from behind. The sudden sensation of the rough sucker disc on bare skin is a shock, especially when there are already real sharks around! To make it worse, they release and re-attach as the swimmer rolls around in an attempt to discourage the "attack." Poor Collette and Jean-Marie had to suffer not only the surprise and unnerving habit of the three-foot-long fish but the endless teasing of everyone aboard *Moana*.

2007

MICRONESIA, INDONESIA, MALAYSIA

Cairns became our home base, and we loved the beautiful city on the banks of the Trinity Inlet. It had the feel of a real Wild West town because it really was in a wild area of Queensland, Australia. In any direction, in thirty minutes you could be in rain forest, white-sand beaches, mountains, or the deserts of the notorious Outback. Unfortunately, another wild aspect of Cairns was cyclones. The powerful and dangerous storms wreaked havoc on the Queensland coast almost every year. By January, all the large yachts in the Marlin Marina cleared out and ran to ports to the south. This usually included *Moana*, when we ran to the Gold Coast area near Brisbane to take care of our yearly boatyard maintenance. But this year, we elected to stay in Cairns and go to a boatyard later in the year. This meant we had to have a cyclone strategy, and for all the boats that stayed in Cairns, it was a crazy solution.

When the approach of a cyclone was imminent, all boats in the marina and those anchored outside would run further up Trinity Inlet and enter deep creeks in the mangrove forests of the hills surrounding Cairns. Some of the creeks ran far up into the tall, dense mangroves, providing enough space to hold many boats, but it was a very "iffy" strategy, relying on boat crews to understand how to anchor in a mangrove creek. The locals told stories over and over of how it once worked in a port north of Cairns, and the stories were quite colorful. Many boats were thrown into each other, and some were thrown so far into the mangroves it was difficult to get them back into the water. To make it even more exciting, all the wild creatures of the mangroves, including crocodiles, snakes, rats, and bats, took refuge on the boats.

I spent two days in the dinghy, finding a mangrove creek far away from the ones close to the marina, and filled my GPS with all the numbers I would use to get the boat to a safe spot, day or night. We were the only large yacht in the marina celebrating the January–March 2007 new year, and with no close cyclones, we were very glad we did not add the mangrove creek escape plan to our adventures!

Shipwreck on Helen Reef, Micronesia

Captain's log, April 21

Underway for Palau. 0200 pos 2° 43.9' S, 131° 33.9' E in Ceram Sea, off coast of Irian Jaya in absolutely beautiful conditions, flat calm sea.

It is a 2,000-nautical-mile run from Cairns, Australia, to the Republic of Palau in Micronesia. From Cairns to the top of Australia, through the notorious Torres Strait, across the Arafura Sea, around the west end of Irian Jaya, and finishing with a brutal 600-mile run into the far western reaches of the North Pacific, it was exactly what *Moana* was built to do. Rough weather, unlit fishing boats, logs and debris, dangerous reefs, and crew fatigue combined to make the run a real test of boat and crew, and passing the rotting corpses of ships aground on the many coral reefs was a reminder of mistakes made in years past.

Palau was a good destination for us. We came, of course, for the diving on its world-class reefs, but we made good friends there as well, something I loved about traveling to new lands and cultures. One of our first friends was Tina, who proudly let us know she was the only woman taxi driver in Palau. A wealth of information, she introduced me to the memories of the local people during and after WWII. One of the bloodiest battles between Japanese and American forces took place on Peleliu, one of Palau's islands, and is still talked about to this day. The people have been displaced so many times by the Spanish, Germans, Japanese, and the war itself that disputes over land ownership will never end; but due to the Americans' having driven out the Japanese during the war, our US flag was very welcome.

However, Ada, the head government ranger, was not impressed with us and initially denied our request for a permit to cruise within the reefs. It made no difference to him that we had cruised in remote, wild island nations before. So many visiting boats had piled up on the very dangerous and extensive reefs of Palau, I had to demonstrate the accuracy of our electronic charts and navigation system and personally promise we would have no accidents before he finally relented. In the end, he proved to be a good friend and a man who really cared about his country. But after a few trips inside and outside the coral reefs of Palau, I understood Ada's concern. Daily, we saw local dive and tour boats zooming around at high speed, operated by locals who grew up on the reefs, but we never saw another yacht, even at the famous dive sites of German Channel, Blue Corner, or Ulong Channel.

After several great days of diving inside the reefs of Palau, we ran north to Kyangel Atoll, on the far north end of Palau's many islands. Squeezing through a very narrow pass and dodging many coral heads, we entered a beautiful lagoon and approached the lone village on the main island. It was a picture-postcard lagoon, and we were excited to begin exploring, but it seemed the locals were not excited to meet us. The reason: A huge Chinese aquarium boat was anchored nearby, and the chief was selling the atoll's exotic and valuable reef fish. Our knowledge of the situation shamed the chief and embarrassed the locals. We left the very next morning without another word between us.

The island of Yap and its offshore islands and reefs were to be our next destination, and I could not understand why the government office that would issue our permit to visit was not responding to my calls or faxes. Michel suggested I fly over from Palau and meet the authorities in person, and it turned out to be a great idea. Not just because we needed a permit, but because I needed to resolve some interesting logistical challenges we had heard about, such as a place to anchor or a source of fresh food. We knew there was no marina, no electricity, and no water; but no anchorage? No fresh food?

I was told Bill Acker would be the man I needed to see on Yap, so he was first on my list when I arrived. Bill owned Manta Ray Bay Hotel, and also Manta Ray Bay Divers, a world-renowned dive operation that specialized in diving with the big manta rays that called Yap home. His dive masters were amazing and knew the location of every cleaning station where the mantas went to be cleaned by various cleaner fish. Over the years, they photographed each and every manta and, based on their individual body markings, even gave them names. It was a great operation, where even novice scuba divers could be almost guaranteed to see the big manta rays at close range in crystal-clear, shallow water, surrounded by beautiful coral reefs. I will always remember meeting Bill and our conversation when discussing Ulithi Atoll, a huge atoll we planned to visit. It was east of Yap, and made famous during WWII.

Stone money at the "Bai" (meeting house)

"Lew, if you have the boat you say you do, you don't want to go to Ulithi. You want to go to Sorol."

I had never heard of Sorol. The locals and fishermen in Palau told me about an atoll named Ngulu, but no one ever mentioned Sorol, which was quite far to the east. As luck would have it, Bill introduced me to a diver at his hotel who had been there on a research vessel several years before. The diver was on his way to the airport, with limited time to speak with me, but on a hotel dinner napkin he drew a chart of Sorol from his memory. Weeks later, after taking delivery of an old Admiralty chart, I was surprised to see how close to scale his napkin sketch proved to be. But most importantly, he located the small pass into the lagoon.

Next on my list was the government office where cruising permits were issued, and I almost laughed out loud to see the disabled fax machine. It certainly explained why my faxes from

Moored to typhoon wreck, Yap Island

Palau had gone unanswered. And judging by the old papers and electrical cords piled on top, repair was obviously not a priority. The very friendly official was curious about our coming visit but granted our permit on the spot. My first day on Yap was going well, and I was soon in the island's lone taxi, rolling down a scenic country road, on my way to see the chief.

Ignathio Hapthey was the "Chairman, Council of Tamol," chief of all the chiefs of the outer islands. A quiet, humble, and intelligent man, one look in his eyes told me all I needed to know. In long-ago times, I was certain this was the man who would have been King. There was surprise in his piercing eyes, and a gentle smile as I presented my customary gift (fresh betel nuts, wrapped in banana leaf) and explained why I had come. I knew tribal permission to visit offshore islands was not a legal requirement, but I also knew it was important far beyond government regulations. It conveyed respect for the local people and their traditions; and in a small community, I knew word of my visit would make a tremendous difference in my relationship with the native people. To this day, I treasure the personal letter he gave me, inviting me back to his home to receive our permit (we had to clear customs in Yap before the permit could be given) when *Moana* arrived.

If an American knew of Yap, the "Paradise Island of Stone Money," it would probably be because of an old Hollywood movie starring Burt Lancaster, who played the part of David O'Keefe, a legendary character who washed ashore in a storm and went on to become a famous sailor, trading goods and stone money in the islands now known as the Carolines. The huge stone discs are to be found all over Yap to this day, and much has been written about how money could be in such a unique form.

Captain's log, July 25
0654 pos entering Yap ship channel (Tamil), various NW courses

We solved the anchorage problem by dropping anchor just inside a coral reef and running a stern line to a wreck on the island. The wreck was a big steel barge that had been thrown up on the beach by a typhoon a few years before, and it was a grim reminder of the power of the monster storms that passed through the Carolines every year. Surrounded by reefs just below the surface, it was a tight anchorage, but with our dependable generators, watermakers, and small boat for going ashore, we were right at home. And Bill solved our fresh-food issues by letting us know we could give our shopping list to his daughter, who was in charge of flying in the hotel's needs from Guam.

We were almost ready to go, but I needed to visit Chief Hapthey and get our permit. After my previous visit, I looked forward to seeing the chief again, and this time for my customary gift I took a small cooler with a nice coral trout inside, and a loaf of homemade bread. I had no idea my visit would be the most memorable of all my visits with native chiefs. The chairman was happy to see me, and the smile from his wife let me know they loved my gift. We sat opposite each other at the long table where, I was sure, many chiefs sat during their meetings. The permit was already waiting for me, so business was finished quickly, and the talk became friendly and informal. In the midst of our conversation, one of the most beautiful native girls I have ever seen, naked above the waist, slowly walked behind the chief, and past my line of sight. It took every bit of my self-control to maintain eye contact with the chief as we continued to talk. Then she took a seat across the room, directly behind the chief. I could plainly see her mischievous smile and understood her fun with an American boat captain! The chief and I finished business with a warm handshake and he presented me with a beautiful, handmade sarong, but my everlasting memory will always be of the game played on me by the beautiful young girl who turned out to be the chief's teenage granddaughter.

The big manta rays were indeed the stars of the show on Yap. The family spent several days swimming with them in various beautiful locations, all recorded by Louis with his ever-improving skills with a camera. But after hearing about Ngulu and Sorol, we were soon on our way. We had the boat, we had the crew, and we had Michel, the man with the dream.

Beautiful, graceful manta ray: Yap Island

Coral reef close astern, impossible to see in the dark

Green turtle hatchling, one day old; survival in doubt

Captain's log, July 28

Drop engines to idle, entering pass on various courses, Ngulu

Sixty-five miles south-southwest of Yap, the atoll of Ngulu looks like a big pork chop on a nautical chart. Over twenty miles long and about fourteen miles across at the widest point, it was a different and challenging atoll for me. The eastern flank of the reef was totally submerged and offered no shelter from swells. On the northwest part of the reef, we found deep, wide passes into the deep central lagoon, but good anchorages were not to be found in the north end of the lagoon. We worked our way south and found spectacular dive sites, but every night was a nightmare for me. The best anchorages I could find were closely encircled by nasty reefs, just below the surface. With very little room to swing on the anchor, there could be no mistakes. As soon as the anchor went down every afternoon, I dove down to make sure it could not drag in the intense rain squalls that sometimes swept atolls such as Ngulu. And at every sunset, I dreaded the coming darkness. Night after night, my sleep was interrupted by wind or current changes, forcing me to stare endlessly at my electronics, revisiting childhood nightmares, alone in the dark and unable to escape.

Chief Mike, kids, and Alison

Of course, those same wild reefs and the unbelievable water visibility provided incredible diving and fishing for Michel and the boys. We could sometimes see the bottom in 100+ feet of water, and as we worked our way south in the atoll, the deck freezer filled with all our favorite fish.

On the south end of the atoll, we visited Chief Mike at his lone village on one of the nine tiny islands that dotted the atoll ring. All of the islands together made up less than one-half square mile of land, but the best two islands were here. Mike was a nice man whom I had met at Chief Hapthey's on Yap. He had invited us to visit, and we were quite impressed with his little settlement. The traditional palm-thatched homes were set back from a pretty sand beach, in the shade of many coconut palms, and the grounds all around were immaculate. His family and the other people only numbered about a dozen, including children, and they all seemed to be happy and healthy. So far from Yap, it was amazing to see how resourceful they were to thrive in such a remote place. They caught rainwater, grew food, and collected abundant seafood. A supply boat visited every month or so, bringing items from the outside world.

Mike directed us to a nearby island, and it became our favorite base on Ngulu. He knew we would like it because it had, by far, the best anchorage on the entire atoll and the fringing reef was alive with fish and lobsters. But, he warned, a saltwater crocodile had been seen on the beach there a few months before, so we had to make a very thorough inspection of the entire island. We found no trace of the croc on the small, beautiful little island, and instead found our first mascot to live aboard *Moana*.

Returning to the small boat, Thomas and Pierre came upon hatchling turtles emerging from their egg nest in the sand and making their desperate run for the sea, only yards away. As was usually the case, they had to somehow get past waiting predators. And among the predators were crabs. In the moment's long frenzy of a hatchling's struggle to reach the water, birds, lizards, and occasionally a land animal catch a single turtle. Not so the cruel crabs, who run from turtle to turtle, and by crushing a flipper in their strong claws leave them paralyzed on the beach. One by one, they are then eaten alive. This drama is usually played out at night, when the turtles have the best chance to make it to the sea. But on this sunny day, strictly by chance, humans came upon this scene and the course of history was changed in a small way. Of about fifteen baby turtles, birds caught a few, and at that very moment, a large crab broke the flipper of his tiny prey. Thomas and Pierre returned to *Moana* with both the crab and the turtle. We ate the crab and placed the poor turtle in a bucket of seawater.

Crippled and in shock, she almost died before we learned how to feed her. She lived in our bait tank for forty-eight days, during which time she grew markedly, her flipper healed completely, and we released her back into the wild.

When Mike got word of our return to Yap, he asked if he could catch a ride back with us. Of course, we were happy to help him out. We laughed the next morning when he approached with a boatload of "cargo," and several members of his family.

Captain's log, August 6

Underway Sorol Atoll in terrible traveling weather. S breeze steady @ 25–30kts, gusting 40kts on steep, close seas and backing into W. Multiple swells and confused, wind driven seas making for miserable night @ 5–6kts over bottom.

If there is a place on our planet that defines paradise, it is the uninhabited atoll of Sorol. Only about eight miles long, all of the small islands together occupy less than one square mile. But the beautiful lagoon is three square miles of calm, blue water, with only one dangerous coral head. And right where our diver friend drew it on the restaurant napkin, we found the small, shallow pass into the lagoon. Double anchored off the bird island, on our very first day we knew Sorol was indeed a paradise on earth.

With a shape resembling a seahorse on a nautical chart, with the belly being the lagoon inside the coral reef, the atoll lies 160 miles southeast of Yap. Several small islets dot the reef perimeter, but only the four largest are vegetated, and each of the four is home to life not found on the others. Apparently, there is just enough water separating the islands to prevent

Coconut crabs

animal migration. The principal and largest island, to the south, was home to monitor lizards. The next island, to the northwest, was home to various sea birds; the next was home to turtles, and the northwesternmost island on the head of the seahorse was home to a huge population of coconut crabs and frigate birds. We found this unique diversity fascinating, and it made for endless exploring and photo opportunities.

As with the other wild places we visited, we spent a lot of time exploring. We knew the very first day that we would return, so we spent many days looking for the best anchorages, dive sites, fishing grounds, and islands for exploring. It was an exciting time for the entire family, as there was something wonderful to see and experience for everyone. We caught tuna and marlin outside the reef, and grouper and snapper in the many caves and canyons on the reef. We barbecued monitor lizards and ate the unbelievably delicious coconut crabs that were in numbers we had never seen before. Beachcombing was fantastic because a current passed through the lagoon and deposited a time capsule of lost fishing gear and hundreds of pieces of flotsam on a sand bar between the south and bird islands. Turtles could be seen every day, mating in the shallows next to their favorite island. We were blessed with safe anchorages, gentle trade winds, and crystal clear waters. Time passed quickly, and we were soon on our way back to Yap for new guests and supplies.

Sorol lizard, 5 feet long

We made another trip to both Ngulu and Sorol that summer. Because of our previous trips, we went directly to our favorite spots and had one wonderful day after another. *Moana* performed perfectly, thanks to the loving attention of Joubert, and the weather was almost perfect. It was typhoon season, however, and the Caroline Islands, including Yap, Ngulu, Sorol, and Palua, were in the crosshairs of the monstrous storms. This was the reason a capable Japanese fishing boat sat wrecked on the reef, and a big steel buoy could be seen high in the trees at Sorol. We never saw another boat at Ngulu or Sorol. We used a reliable weather forecasting service that sent us daily email forecasts and could call us directly via satellite if a typhoon was bearing down on us. Still, it required us to have the range and speed to run south, into the latitudes where the storms known as typhoons, cyclones, or hurricanes cannot

August 3, Rachel's birthday, with very close siblings

live, before they reached us. Few boats in the world, and especially in the size range of *Moana*, could dare to use this strategy.

Captain's log, August 27

Underway for Bitung, Indonesia. 1149 pos abeam Morotai Island light, 6 mi. A/C to 247° into Molucca Sea in very good traveling weather, clear sky and hot sun.

Indonesia had been on our radar for some time. We were excited to visit the legendary Spice Islands, home to active volcanos, Komodo dragons, and some of the most unusual marine life in the world, on over 17,000 islands. Professional underwater photographers from all over the world made the long flights to reach the well-known dive sites via hotel dive boats, but we had the ultimate dive boat, and we had Joubert. A native Indonesian from Manado, on the northeast tip of Sulawesi Island, he knew where, all alone, we would find the most spectacular diving and exploring on the most remote islands. But, sadly, it was not to be.

According to the Indonesian website, Bitung was listed as a "visa on arrival" port, meaning we did not have to apply for our visas weeks in advance. This was good news for me, but I should have known Joubert was skeptical for a reason. Within moments of coming alongside at the port, a large crowd gathered and we heard several of the men chanting, "Big fine, big fine!" This was our welcome to one of the most disappointing and corrupt ports we had yet to visit. I was not new to developing-world locals trying to take advantage of an opportunity to intimidate by threats of fines or big problems to make some money. I quickly chose Danny, a street-smart kid, to be our agent. He knew the game every one of the hustlers was trying to play, and I almost laughed out loud to see them walk off, disgusted that Danny had ruined their day.

Danny arranged for all the real government officials to visit and clear us in, letting me know exactly how much the bribe would be in each case. It was an interesting procession of blatantly corrupt officials, but after more than four hours, it was finally over—or so we thought. A day later, we were escorted to the chief customs officer, who asked quite directly, "Did you have any problems with my men?"

"No sir. Your men were professional in every way," I lied.

I was not at all surprised by this exchange but had no idea just how badly it could have gone if I had elected to provoke him by complaining. A few days later, an unbelievable rumor went out on the radio, and we were immediately underway for Singapore. The rumor, which proved to be true, involved a previously undisclosed customs duty. This duty gave a customs officer the power to assess the value of any foreign vessel in Indonesian waters and demand up to 50 percent of that value, in cash! The penalty for refusal to pay the duty was seizure of the vessel. The money was to be returned to the owners on their departure from Indonesia, but no one entertained the thought of robbery on such a scale. A mass exodus of yachts, mostly sailboats, fled Indonesia.

We were one of the first yachts to reach Singapore. The very next day found me at the Indonesian Embassy, across the desk from the very man who wrote the law. To my astonishment, he admitted he was the law's author, but he refused to discuss the intent, enforcement, or any details of the most egregious customs duty ever enacted in any country. We never visited Indonesia again.

Captain's log, September 17

Underway in South China Sea in good, downhill traveling conditions, with mixed seas & breeze square on stern. 0300 pos 1° 52.3' S, 107° 30.3' E.

With Indonesia off the table, we tried to take advantage of our location in Singapore and haul out the boat for our annual underwater maintenance, but a boom in everything related to oil drilling and exploration had all the shipyards committed to huge steel projects. We were small potatoes and soon on our way, all the way back to Australia.

2008

MALAYSIA, MICRONESIA, AUSTRALIA

Captain's log, January 27

Underway in Timor Sea in beautiful, calm seas, starry sky, 0000 pos 10° 39.3' S, 124° 21.1' E

We did find a boatyard in Singapore that was willing to haul us out, but after seeing clouds of tiny steel particles flying toward us, downwind from the nearby yards, we had to decline. Landing on *Moana*, especially on the non-skid decks, the overnight dew would transform the tiny specks of steel into embedded rust, destroying our high-tech polyurethane paint. Now, after traveling over 1,850 miles, back to Australia, we were to experience yet another boatyard problem, and a serious one at that.

Australia is a wonderful country. Wild and beautiful, it is vulnerable to all kinds of invasive creatures that could seriously damage the fragile marine ecosystem. For this reason, Australian Customs is very strict and enforces standards that are far higher than those of most countries. This includes the use of sniffer dogs and highly trained personnel on boat interiors, and even divers, for underwater inspections. Clearing into Australia from a foreign port was often a long, boring process due to their thorough inspections, but I appreciated the intent of their people and, after our many visits, came to know many of them on a first-name basis. One of their most dedicated customs inspectors was Sue, the underwater dive inspector. And on this inspection, she had some very bad news.

"Lew, I have found some small mussels inside the sea chests. If they are the species I believe them to be, we have a serious situation here."

Marine biologist experts were brought in, and they confirmed we had black-striped mussels, one of the most dreaded of all invasive species, living in our sea chests (sea water inlets, providing cooling water to engines and machinery). I had paid a good diver in Singapore to clean the bottom and running gear "antiseptic clean," but he did not inspect the sea chests, and Sue had found four to six of the mussels that were smaller than a fingernail. This set off an amazing series of events, as we attracted the full attention of the Australian government, and especially the multimillion-dollar pearl farming industry, south of Darwin. The tiny mussels had no natural predators in Australia, and they could reproduce rapidly, attaching themselves to the pearl oysters in such numbers that they would destroy entire farms by consuming their food supply.

The top-heavy bureaucracy of the Australian government swung into action, and we immediately had biologists and experts swarming the boat. Special chemicals were flushed through every salt water pipe in the boat, to kill any mussels that might be alive inside. But that was not enough. We then had to anchor offshore, in a quarantine area, before hauling out at a shipyard, where the bottom of the boat and all thru-hull piping was pressure washed with a special chemical. Nine years before, a cruising yacht brought the same mussels into Cullen Bay Marina, in Darwin, and it required killing every living organism in the marina, and millions of dollars to eradicate them. The government was rightly concerned.

Our boatyard headache seemed endless. Overwhelmed with multiple vessels and priority work, the yard initially refused to haul us out of the water, but with our mussel problem, and after we agreed to do all the work on the boat ourselves, they relented. With *Moana* hauled out, and pressure washed, they set us off to the side of the yard. We then experienced what the "run-up to the wet" really meant. The oppressive heat and humidity was so severe, and with no air conditioning inside the hauled-out boat, I checked us into a hotel.

Entering the boat the following morning was unbelievable. At eight o'clock in the morning, the temperature gauge in my pilothouse read 120° Fahrenheit! The inside of the boat was an oven! The heat was so intense I could not think clearly, and I retreated to the shade underneath the boat. Needless to say, work went slowly, and there was no problem with the paint drying.

Captain's log, March 7
Underway in Seram Sea, 0900 pos 3° 50.6' S, 131° 46.8' E

Another 1,800-nautical-mile slog into the strong trade winds on another journey to Palau gave me plenty of time to reflect on my job description as captain on *Moana*. Our operation was certainly unusual, as were many of our destinations, and required solutions to problems not to be found in any cruising publications; that was for sure. I grew up on fishing boats, where my captains only worried about catching fish. Here, I needed to be not only a captain but a Customs and Immigration regulations expert, banker, purchasing agent, maintenance expert, marine biologist, lawyer, meteorologist, and USA ambassador. Add to that, the happy barbecue chef when the family was aboard. A full plate, as they say. Even so, there seemed to be no end to the surprises, such as the next one waiting for us in Palau.

We arrived and cleared in with the usual officials we knew from before, with no drama, and med-moored the boat to the seawall at Neco Marine. Friends from our previous visit welcomed us back, and we were happy to hit the sack early, to rest from the long trip back to the North Pacific.

"Everyone out, now," the chief customs agent screamed over and over, interrupting our quiet breakfast. "Now, now, everyone out now!" We looked at each other as if to ask, "Us?" We shuffled out on deck and were shocked to see six to eight men in military fatigues, rifles at the ready, accompanied by two sniffer dogs and their handlers, a couple of agents that I recognized from before, and some guy who looked like ex-CIA from a Hollywood movie. The agent running the show continued barking commands, making sure everyone knew who was in charge. This was a deadly serious customs inspection. I was instantly furious.

It was not the first time in my career that I was boarded by armed men, but unlike how I was probably afraid that first time, this time was different. I knew my crew, and I was 99 percent sure there could be nothing aboard to justify such a military type operation. It became very heated between the chief and me, as I made it very clear he was acting like an idiot. Of course, in the company of his men, he did not take lightly his being disrespected, so the atmosphere spiraled downhill fast. As the other agents took my crew inside, one at a time, the "movie guy" told me to shut up, whereupon I told him the only reason he was there was because he could no longer sell his worn out "expertise" in the States. It was ugly.

A large crowd gathered at the seawall, only a few yards away, when a loud voice called out, "You guys are messing with the Billy Graham of boat captains," followed by, "The newspapers are on their way." This increased the anxiety of the chief, who I could sense, was worried that my behavior signaled we had nothing to hide. The searches inside were not going well, and as Alison, our new cook, and the agent who had accompanied her came out, a big and jovial (from a previous clearance) agent went inside. As he passed next to me, I noticed he had his betel nut bag slung over his shoulder. I waited a minute until he passed below into a cabin.

"Your inspection is over now, chief," I calmly stated. "You allowed a man to enter my boat unaccompanied by me or a member of my crew, with a bag over his shoulder. Now, drugs or contraband can be mysteriously "found" inside the boat. Get off my boat. Your credibility is gone. It is over for you."

As the chief's expression showed his shock at this turn of events, the agent who had been with Alison took me aside. "Lew, there has been a big mistake, and we will be off your boat in a few minutes."

Our previous cook's name was Allison, spelled with two l's. Prior to our arrival on this trip (we were later told), the authorities in Palau received a report from Australia naming her as being involved in some kind of illegal activity. Judging by the inspection team that boarded our boat, it must have been something very serious. When we cleared into Palau, and customs saw "Alison" on our crew list, they assumed it was our previous cook, and the bust was on. The local newspaper was not kind to the chief who refused my handshake two weeks later.

Michel and big grouper

Captain's log, March 18
1417 pos abeam S end of fringing reef on Yap, slight lee, A/C to 057°

2008 was a great adventure in Micronesia. We made multiple trips to Yap, Ngulu, Sorol, and Palau, revisiting favorite places we had found on previous trips, and rekindling friendships. For me, return visits were much easier. All the research and endless challenges required to explore remote places for the first time were known, allowing me to really enjoy how truly extraordinary our trips were. Sure, the weather was always a variable, but we had the perfect boat, a great crew, a family that thirsted for adventure, and, most of all, we had Michel: the man with the dream, courage, and determination to make it happen. Year after year, these elements were the driving force that made our operation successful, and the reason we never saw other boats in the really remote, wild places.

Paradise

We did see another boat at Sorol one morning. It was the one and only government patrol boat, and the captain called me on the radio to let me know we were going to be boarded. Their boat was a typical patrol boat design, about the same size as *Moana*, and they were idling just outside the reef. When I saw they were getting a small boat ready for launching, I told the captain he could come inside the reef, through the pass that we had marked with a buoy, and anchor in the calm waters of the lagoon. A cautious, experienced captain, he was unwilling to trust a stranger with the shallow, dangerous reef pass. His boarding officer was soon in my pilothouse, and his stern attitude told me he expected problems. In less than five minutes, he asked to use my radio and called his captain.

"Captain, they have a permit from the chairman! From Chief Hapthey!"

"Very well. Tell the captain thank you, and we wish him a good day."

The native Micronesian boarding officer also saw my official government permit but did not mention it to his captain, who did not ask about it. The bright yellow permit from the "Chairman, Council of Tamol," and his personal letter of friendship were all they needed to see.

We had many good days at Sorol, the atoll that probably describes paradise better than any other. In every direction, it was visually everything people might imagine in their dreams of

Joubert and Michel, unloading baby giant clams

a place so perfect and remote as to be lost to the outside world. The prolific animals and birds that had never seen humans and were unafraid of us made it easy to imagine we were the first to ever set foot on the small islands. Of course, we were not, but the prolific life also included the waters surrounding the atoll, where the boys once hooked three marlins at one time in the small boat, and Michel speared a giant grouper that fed us for many days.

At Ngulu, we had some new, memorable experiences. On one visit, Chief Mike told us how illegal foreign fishing vessels had wiped out the giant clams on his reefs. The clams were a valuable food source for his little settlement, and he wanted to reintroduce them to his atoll, but he had no way to purchase them from an aquaculture facility on Palau and bring them to Ngulu. This was the very thing we loved to do, and on our next trip to Palau, we purchased 1,500 baby giant clams, kept them alive in special plastic trays in our bait tank, and brought them to Mike. We became good friends with Mike and his people, and like to think they will be eating our clams for years to come.

As the years pass, I mark up my charts, indicating important things I don't want to forget on future voyages. Usually, the notes or marks are navigation or safety related, but sometimes they locate good fishing/diving spots, and so a very special place I named "Leopard Shark Pass" was noted on my chart of Ngulu Atoll. This pass through the reef was one of the most

Sleeping leopard shark

spectacular of all the reef passes we found in our travels. On one particular dive through the pass, the family came back aboard in silence, each waiting for one of the others to be the first to try to describe what they had witnessed. Finally, Louis looked at me and simply said, "Lew, it was probably the finest dive of my life."

But another dive they will remember forever happened on our last trip inside the reef, on Palau. We had returned to dive Ulong Channel and were anchored off a small island of the same name. Fishermen had told us of an underwater cave at the island that could be found by swimming through a narrow tunnel under the island. We were told it was difficult to find the tunnel, but the cave, lit by sunlight coming from a hole in the ground above, was spectacular. Thomas, Louis, and Pierre swam off, determined to find such an exciting place.

As I came up the pilothouse stairs, I heard Joubert burst into laughter. His voice then became serious as he pointed out the boys returning to the boat. White water trailed the boys as they half-swam, half-ran across the water in a frenzy to reach the boat. They had found the cave and come face to face with a saltwater crocodile! We routinely swam with sharks, even very big ones, but saltwater crocodiles are a completely different animal. Creatures unchanged from the time of the dinosaurs, the silent, powerful predators attacked and ate people every year we were in Australia. Word of our discovery reached Bert, the dive master at Neco Marine. A crocodile attack on a tourist in Palau could be devastating to their business, so he asked us to show him the cave. I was not surprised to see Michel take him in. Photos were taken at close range(!); and it was determined the croc was not quite fully grown but still a serious threat to any human. We never knew the final outcome, but I am very sure the government sent a hunter in to eliminate any possible problem for the lucrative dive industry in Palau.

Captain's log, September 2

Anchor dn in 19ft, mud, lee of Kolepan Island

We were homeward bound for Cairns but had to anchor offshore Kolepan Island, Irian Jaya, waiting for the wind in the Arafura Sea to calm down. It was one of the ugliest anchorages we had ever used while waiting on weather. It was a low, swampy, mosquito-infested coast, and home to some of the most primitive people on the planet. Missionaries passed through almost all the islands of Australasia, but this particular area of Irian was so inhospitable they did not make contact with the native tribes. I remember wondering how long a shipwrecked sailor might last, trying to survive in such a place.

After waiting a week, our weather gurus at WRI finally told us we could make our run across the Arafura Sea. "Lew, it will be tough, but based on the weather you have been able to endure in the past, you will be able to make it. If you do not go now, it may take a month to get a better window."

As always, our weather experts gave it to me straight. This was the reality of operating in areas notorious for terrible weather. We got underway at first light and hoped for the best. And feeling the boat bouncing off the bottom, two miles offshore Ug Salah, in water charted to be forty to fifty feet deep, made me wonder if this would prove to be a really bad trip. It was.

We slowly pushed through the uncharted shallow mud bank and rounded the point, and before we could increase speed to more than six knots over the bottom, we took on the powerful head seas of the Arafura Sea. It was one of the worst beatings we would take in years, and we rolled into Thursday Island, Australia, fifty-two hours later. The boat was fine, but we were trashed and spent two days resting up in the lee of the island.

There is nothing romantic about running long range in heavy weather. How many times have you needed to crawl across the floor at home? Ever had forty things in your face when you opened your fridge? What's that? You don't like to sleep on the floor, for only two hours at a time? Yes, taking a leak is a sit-down deal, men. And you had better be hanging on. The reality is, sooner or later, you will have to deal with it, and every experience will be shaped by how well you are prepared, the condition of the boat, and the experience and seamanship of the crew. For us, we had a time-tested battle plan that prepared the boat and every system for however long the fight would be. We had well-defined rules to minimize the risk of injury, or of exhaustion due to lack of sleep. No one was allowed outside on deck. Hourly engine room checks (going down ladders) were out. Cooking and galley work was done only when idling down swell.

For me, there was always a lot to consider. I had the option to change course and speed, two elements that could dramatically lessen severe boat motion. But I sometimes had to consider maintaining a lousy course and speed because I expected the weather to worsen and needed to get the boat to calmer water as soon as possible. Sometimes I veered off and ran a hundred miles or more, to position the boat for expected heavy weather coming from a different direction. But in the end, it always came down to doing the right thing for as long as it took.

And I can tell you, there is no finer sleep than that of a captain who is finally in a safe, calm harbor. Hour after hour of wonderful, silent stillness….

Captain's log, December 17

Anchor dn in 22ft, sand, Lizard Island

Our last trip of the year was a return to Cod Hole, Lizard Island, and Osprey Reef, all in the area of the famous Great Barrier Reef of Australia. After the last, rough trip to Osprey, this was a "boys' trip only," with Michel, Thomas, Louis, Donald, and Michel's nephews, Charles and David.

Cod Hole and Lizard Island were as fun as before. The huge potato cod gathered to greet us as soon as we picked up the mooring, and at Lizard Island the huge jacks again went into a feeding frenzy under our underwater lights. It was always an amazing show when a hapless bait fish would appear in the bright glow of the lights, and be attacked by the fast, aggressive jacks. Rarely, the bait fish would manage to escape, putting on a show of desperate maneuverability as one fast predator after another snapped, lunged, and boiled on the small fish.

A million bright stars lit up the warm night sky over a rare glassy, calm sea on our way out to Osprey Reef. Making unusually good time in the calm weather, we arrived off the reef in the middle of the night. I shut down the engines, let the boat drift, and stretched out on the big cushion on the forward hatch. There was not a breath of wind, not a hint of swell. Floating so completely motionless, it was easy to imagine we were not a boat at all, but another star in the night sky. In the open ocean, this was extremely rare, and a marvelous feeling to fall asleep in such serenity.

Two days later, I stared stupidly at the large, treble hook buried deep into my wrist. This can't be happening to me, I thought. Me! The captain! The man who has handled more hooks than all the people on the boat will ever see in their lifetimes! And to make it worse, the jack on the other hook of the big, popper lure was shaking and thrashing, driving the hook into the bone. As adrenalin began to flood my system, I sat down on the deck.

Until that moment, we were having a great trip at Osprey Reef. Calm seas, blue-purple water, and wonderful fishing and diving. And now, ruin the trip by running all the way back to Cairns for medical help? Or... deal with it? My second, and equally stupid thought was, I wish this was happening to someone else. Fortunately, Charles wasted no time getting the fish off the other hook on the lure, and then cut the hook from the lure. Now, there was no longer any pressure on the one hook, but with the barb buried deep below my skin and the sharp tip of the hook into the bone of my wrist, it was "deal with it" time. First, I pulled back on the curve of the hook until I could feel the point come out of the bone, and Charles cut the other two hooks of the treble hook off. The big barb of the hook, designed to prevent it from backing out of a fish, now prevented me from backing it out of the flesh of my arm. With a pair of pliers, I got a good grip on the shank of the hook and began twisting the point upward. I was astonished at the force needed, but the tip and barb slowly emerged through my skin, and I pulled the rest of the hook through. Strangely, I was so focused, I felt little pain. The new hook, having never caught a fish, was clean, so my arm healed quickly.

Of all the kids, including nephews, Charles was borderline "maniac" when it came to fishing. Energetic, excited, and tireless, he was hilarious to be around when the action was hot. At Osprey Reef, though, I was very happy to experience his clear thinking in this situation.

2009

AUSTRALASIA, MALAYSIA, BAY OF BENGAL

Year 2009 would prove to be one of the most difficult, adventurous, exciting, and rewarding years. *Moana* traveled thousands of miles to reach places with names like Recifes d'Entrecasteaux, Kimberlies, Broome, Rowley Shoals, and Andaman Islands. Few people know of these places, and fewer still of the wild islands and reefs within.

But our perfect boat was now nine years old. Even with the extraordinary skills of Joubert, and our professional maintenance program, *Moana* was showing her age. Thousands of miles of open ocean weather and the hot sun of the tropics had taken the shine off our home. Joubert, Pascale, and I ran south, to the Gold Coast of Australia, for some serious shipyard maintenance. Every system and all components were evaluated, serviced, and/or upgraded as necessary, and the entire exterior of the boat was repainted. It was a huge undertaking, and by the time *Moana* was back in the water, we were totally, utterly exhausted.

Captain's log, April 25
1300 pos 27° 32.7' S, 154° 13.2' E, A/C to 055°. Slow, miserable slog @ 8kts.

Having a schedule sometimes meant we had to run in terrible weather, and this was one of those times. Customs are always strict about clearing in and out of countries and in this case forced me to depart Australia just as a nasty storm arrived. The crew and I were already exhausted from the shipyard experience, and by the time we crossed the Coral Sea and entered the Noumea ship channel of New Caledonia, we were physically running on empty. But Noumea was only a pit stop, and after a hurried reprovisioning we were underway again.

Captain's log, May 3
Anchor down in 36ft, sand, off Art Island, Belep

An interesting tree, symbolizing a giant penis, and taller than all the others in the village, marked the location of the chief's home. This made finding the chief's house easy, as we motored in with the dinghy to present the Kastom gift. This was the main village in the

Like brand new

islands of Belep, offshore the far northwest tip of New Caledonia, and home to a very nice tribe of Melanesian natives. Along with the customary tobacco and colorful cloth, I presented the young chief with a framed photo of *Moana*, signed by the crew. He seemed to really like the gifts, which was good because he owned a diesel pickup truck, one of the only cars on the island, and promised to be our "taxi" when Michel and guests arrived at the landing strip the next morning. But when a chief is speaking French, and I am speaking English, a lot can be lost in translation, and when I arrived at the chief's house the next morning, the chief and his truck were already gone.

Knowing about where the dirt-strip airport was, at the top of a nearby hill, I set off walking and soon saw the small plane fly overhead. But after walking in the general direction for a while, I came to a fork in the seldom used, dirt road. Not knowing which led to the airport, I sat down in the shade of some bushes. Moments later, along came the chief, with Michel, guests and luggage, bouncing along in the back of the pickup. The chief stopped when he saw me at the side of the road, and I stood up. For Michel and guests, this must have been hilarious because they did not see me at first, and then when they suddenly saw their captain at the side of the road, in the middle of an island wilderness, they burst into laughter. I hopped into the truck and joined in with the laughter as our smiling chief

Michel in pickup-truck taxi

delivered us to a tiny, man-made harbor. This was typical of our operation in the remote places, and we loved it.

A long day's run north took us to one of the wildest reef systems on our planet. It consisted of five or six major sunken reefs, spread out over more than sixty miles, with only one known anchorage, and it was raked by strong trade winds and dangerous currents. No one came here. Once again, we were all alone in a wild, exciting place.

The area was discovered in 1792 by Bruni d'Entrecasteaux, commander of the French vessel *Recherche*. He and the crew were surprised to find the unknown reefs and small islands and thus named the first one they saw "Surprise." They did not stay long but named the other tiny islands of Fabre, Leleizour, and Huon, after crewmen on the ship.

Some of the atoll-like reefs had no islands or passes into lagoons and were so difficult to visit, we passed them by. Pelotas, the first one we reached, had no pass on my nautical chart; but after a cautious approach, we found a serpentine route into a beautiful lagoon. We were probably the first vessel ever to anchor inside this reef. Schools of bait fish and diving birds all around signaled fantastic diving and fishing, but a big swell swept over the reef and rolled the boat heavily. We left after only a few hours, to look for a calm overnight anchorage, not knowing this was to be the normal situation at the "Récifs d'Entrecasteaux."

Collette, Michel, Joubert, Jean-Marie, and tuna for the barbie!

The fishing all around the reefs and the exploring on the islands were extraordinary, but the current was so strong, diving was out of the question. A big swell rocked us without mercy every night, so we spent a lot of time anchoring and re-anchoring as we passed through the reefs. It was a tough trip, but the wildness of the reefs and the incredible fishing were irresistible to us. On one occasion, off Huon atoll, we came upon an area of feeding yellowfin tuna that made me wish *Moana* was my old commercial tuna boat. We could have easily caught many tons of tuna that day!

Huon atoll had a small island and the only calm anchorage. It was a nesting island for hundreds, if not thousands, of green turtles. We spent several days there, exploring the island, watching the big turtles coming and going, and enjoying our first nights of good sleep. We even did a little diving in the calm, perfectly clear water. I could find very little information in my pre-trip research to the reefs, but one interesting passage regarding Huon talked about the time of year when the turtle nesting was at its peak, and the water in our anchorage was red with the blood of turtles being eaten by packs of Tiger Sharks.

Fabre and Leleizour had extensive fringing coral reefs that made it almost impossible to reach their small islands, but Michel always seemed to find a way. The strong, ever-present current was dangerous, a fact made clear by the skeleton of a sailboat deep inside the reef near

Juvenile shearwater stowaway

Leleizour. It was sitting perfectly upright, with no mast and no planking on the frames, and only visible at low tide. Nothing in my research or on my charts noted the existence of the old wreck, and knowing it would have been out of radio range of possible help, I had to wonder the circumstances and outcome of the disaster. Did the people survive? Or, in such a remote place, did they simply vanish unknown to the outside world?

At Fabre, we discovered a stowaway. A very young shearwater flew downwind, off the island during the night and landed on the boat. He huddled in a corner in the stern, where Joubert found him. Over the years I have seen this happen many times, and it was almost always a death sentence for the young bird whose only fault was to be a little more daring than he should have been. He was too young and not strong enough to fly back to the island, against the strong wind. At his age, he did not have enough oil in his feathers to keep him dry and warm, so if he landed on the sea, he would soak up water and drown, or be killed by a passing frigate. By instinct, he knew this and took refuge on the boat. If only he stayed in his burrow until his parents finished caring for him, only another three to four weeks, it would have made all the difference.

I threw a towel over him, wrapped him up gently and took him in the dinghy to the island. Just off the beach, I pitched him into the air, so he could fly to the island and hopefully, be seen by his parents. Just as I feared, he could not make it that far and fell into the water. He was actually paddling around looking quite at home in the water, but I could see he was soaking it up quickly and would soon drift downwind, away from the island. I maneuvered the dinghy behind him and herded him onto the sand, where he hopped up on the island and disappeared into the dense foliage just beyond the sand. I was happy to have done all I could, and I wandered around taking photos of all the different bird species swarming just overhead and resting in low nests in the foliage.

Walking back to the dinghy a while later, I discovered my little shearwater on the beach, sitting very still and looking very alone. I walked up close and took a photo, and as I stepped back, he put his little head down and walked toward me, having a little difficulty padding along with his webbed feet. When he reached my feet, he sat down in the sand and looked up at me. My heart sank. The implied message was heart rending. I had done all I could. I had brought him home, but unless his parents found him, he would surely die. I turned and walked away, unable to look back. On the sand, he had the best chance of being spotted by his parents, but with his black feathers, he would eventually overheat and die. I had no way to know anything more, only to hope for the best.

For me, the memory of the reefs that will be with me forever was the evening bird show at Surprise. Unfortunately for sea-bird lovers like me, no one will be able to capture the epic event with any kind of camera. It was similar to what we saw at Isla Coco, off Costa Rica. But here, the nightly drama of life, death, and piracy was played out on a scale of unbelievable magnitude. Night after night, I watched one of the most fascinating shows on earth.

In the late afternoon, flocks of noddy terns would begin to gather just offshore, above the island. As it grew later, the flocks became clouds of the brown, robin-sized birds, numbering in the hundreds of thousands. The clouds slowly circled, rose, fell, and flowed in a constantly moving black mass, around the island. This beautiful, flowing spectacle was a defensive strategy to avoid the frigate birds hovering in the trade winds, above the shoreline. If a single noddy ventured too close, a frigate would immediately attack and break off a wing, and I would see the poor bird spiral down, into the ocean. This cruel behavior is not solely because the frigates want to kill noddy terns. It is because the survival of the frigate depends on his flying skills, and the act of killing a noddy is another of the many exercises a frigate employs daily to hone those skills. (I have seen frigates kill other birds, usually juveniles, many times. They are indeed one of the cruelest animals in nature, and they use this behavior to reinforce fear in their prey.)

The frigates were awaiting the return of the brown boobies who were coming home from a day of fishing far offshore. One after another, perhaps forty or fifty boobies would pass by the frigates unmolested, when suddenly the frigates would attack a lone booby. Watching this carefully in my binoculars, I could not see any difference between the birds the frigates allowed to pass and the ones they would attack, but the attack was immediate and effective. Frigate is another word for pirate, and indeed, the birds were pirates. Without any oil in their

The falls at the head of Mitchell River

feathers, hollow, lightweight bones, a long, razor sharp beak, and huge wing span, frigate birds have evolved to be the masters of aerial acrobatics and warfare. They cannot land on water but can catch their food by stealing from birds, and their favorite victims are the boobies. Boobies are large, fast, powerful, diving birds who put up a strong resistance, but their fear of being injured by the sharp beaks of the frigates eventually prompts them to throw up the fish in their belly. Sometimes this happens high in the air, and it is impressive to see the huge frigate catch the fish before it hits the water. After watching the behavior of the frigates closely after many years, I am still not sure if they see a slight bulge in the belly, or if they can tell by the way a fish-laden booby flies, but they know. And in that moment they know, in a fleeting, split-second moment few people ever see, they project a predatory posture and a truly sinister look flashes in the frigates' eyes. The attack is on.

While all of this is going on, many other bird species, by the hundreds, return to the island, unmolested. This includes the white, blue-footed boobies, who approach the island from very high in the air, and when over the island, drop almost vertically to their nests, without interest by the frigates. The poor brown boobies fly straight in from the sea, running the gauntlet, every evening. Perhaps they are the youngest (dumbest?). Then, in that moment when the sky turns from dark to black, all of the frigates, all of the noddy terns, and the rest of the returning

My big dogtooth tuna

brown boobies, swarm onto the island and land on their favorite trees, bushes, or beaches. Thousands upon thousands, possibly a million birds, all landing in mere seconds. It was a breathtaking spectacle I waited for night after night.

Captain's log, June 25
0848 pos abeam Cape York, "top of Australia," 2 miles, A/C to 247° en route Darwin

Darwin, like Cairns, was becoming another home to the crew and me. We were meeting new friends, learning where everything was, and generally enjoying the Aussie spirit. Historically, the wildness of Australia demanded strong people, and their "can do anything" attitude was alive and well in Darwin. Our operation seemed to fit that spirit, as the locals loved *Moana* and were sincerely happy to help us with anything. This included advice on the very best places to visit on the west coast of Australia.

Tiny uncharted pass at Scott Reef

Martine at Cunningham Island

Rugged climb for clifftop view

Joubert vs. shark

Crocodile patrol

Michel and Martine

The Kimberlies were at the top of most lists. A rugged, red rock labyrinth of narrow channels, filled with calm water, snaked for miles and miles into the wild, uninhabited outback. The area was so vast, charter boat captains claimed they had been visiting for over thirty years and still had not yet seen it all. We spent a week there, and it was everything they said. Carefully navigating the Mitchell River all the way to the falls, we were rewarded with a spectacular anchorage. With both saltwater crocodiles and sharks continuously swimming around the boat, no one dared the water; but the hiking and exploring were so wild, it was easy to imagine coming face to face with a dinosaur.

Captain's log, July 16

Underway in Indian Ocean for Scott Reef. 0600 pos 14° 02.7' S, 122° 30.9' E, in low seas, no wind, very nice ride.

This, our second trip to Scott Reef, was as spectacular and exciting as before. In postcard-beautiful weather, it included my dinghy catch of the boat record dogtooth tuna, and the discovery of a tiny pass and access to Cunningham Island. Michel and Martine are two of very few people ever to walk on the snow-white sand of the spectacular, reef-locked island.

Running this extremely narrow pass, and crossing the lagoon to visit a place where few humans have ever walked, was a good example of not only the adventurous spirit of Michel and Martine, but also Michel's navigation skill and incredible sense of direction. At the time, our little sea truck did not have the sophisticated electronics we installed later, so Michel had to understand two very important things: How to run back across the lagoon and find the tiny pass again, and do it before the sun angle changed too much. If they stayed too long at the island, the sun would no longer be on an angle allowing them to see the edges of the reef, and they would be unable to find their way out. Over the years, Michel drove me crazy by fishing out of sight, outside reef passes, and like a frigate bird returning to its tree in the last moments of light, blasting through the pass and coming alongside with laughing kids and a boat full of fish. Never did he hit a reef or ding a propeller.

July 29, 2009

Hi Rascals:

For the first time in this trip, I have the time to tap out a letter. I have a little time for writing because we are stuck inside the lagoon of Mermaid Reef, some 160 miles offshore Western Australia. The weather has really blown up on us, making it risky to run the pass out of the lagoon. It would not be such a bad place to be stuck, except it is a marine park and fishing or spearfishing is forbidden. It is such a sensitive area, we can't touch anything on the reef and we can't throw food scraps in the water, much less pump out our black tanks. Even underwater photos can only be amateur. The Australian gov't has put down moorings so that visiting yachts are now prohibited from anchoring, and "Coastwatch," a gov't plane, flies over us every day to make sure we are following the rules.

The upside is a fish population that has exploded in recent years. We were here three years ago, and Michel was here in '92 with the old Moana, *and from what he has seen, the fish and marine life have increased markedly. One of the biggest thrills here is to snorkel through the pass into the lagoon on an incoming tide. It is truly unbelievable how many fish gather just before the flood, and accompany you as you seemingly "fly" through the pass, with just the effort to keep your body pointed forward. When the current and visibility is just right, it is a world class experience. Unfortunately for us, with this poor weather, the huge surf pounding just outside the pass has made for poor visibility, not to mention the wind driven seas that make for tough snorkeling. With no way to leave and run to a different atoll, we are stuck until we get a break in the weather. Michel and family are playing board games and making the best of it, and we have a world class cook aboard, so no one is suffering.*

The moorings, put in right after our last visit in 2006, are of questionable engineering. We were given permission to use the largest one, rated for vessels up to 50 meters and winds to 40 knots.

The mooring buoy is attached to a 3in. hawser with big eye splice, which indeed looks very strong. It probably is very strong but seems to be rigged without any chain near the bottom, or at least with very little chain. A nice length of chain would provide the natural shock absorbing feature needed in times of big swells when the vertical motion and pitch is dampened by the scope and weight of the chain rising and falling. We discovered this oversight in a way I will never forget.

We arrived at the mooring buoy at low tide, and secured Moana by passing two one-inch lines through the big eye splice and securing them port and starboard. This places the pull of the mooring line on a bridle on the centerline of the boat, and displaces the load and chafing area on four lines. We have used this method of tying to moorings for some time, with never a problem.

At high tide, just after 0200, the portside lines broke. The stbd lines held for some time before chafing on the stem and parting. Broadside to the wind, Moana took off in 30 knots of wind for the huge reef .5 mi astern. Everyone was asleep, including me. It was one of the highest tides of the year, still rising and about to rip the bottom out of Moana and place her hopelessly lost on top of the reef.

Luck can be an amazing thing. When anchorages are rolly, I can't sleep in my pilothouse berth because the motion is simply too much. Over the years, I have come to enjoy sleeping on the deck when we are underway in rough weather or rolly anchorages. The fresh air, stars overhead, and nice motion are great for sleeping. And this is where I was when the boat broke free. When the boat went broadside to the wind, I was awakened by the sudden breeze coming over the side and trying to blow off my sheet. At first, I thought it was a change of current (tide) and the boat simply swinging around, and almost rolled over to go back to sleep. But before nodding off again, I waited just a moment to feel the bow come around. The bow did not come around and instead, I felt the sideways rolling of a boat adrift.

Knowing several smaller reefs were close by and the main barrier reef was right behind us, my only hope was to get the anchor down as quick as possible. The mooring lines that parted were still wrapped around the capstan and, as luck would have it, were jammed in the chain wheel. It was probably only seconds but seemed like eternity before Joubert and I got the line off the windlass and the anchor down. It was pitch black and we had no way to know if a reef was nearby, waiting to rip into us when the anchor dug in. We swung several times with good water under the boat and increased the scope, little by little, until we were pretty comfortable with the situation. Then, I had time to look at my electronic chart plotter and see where we had gone, and how far. It turned out to be truly amazing how fast I woke up, realized the situation, and anchored the boat. We had drifted just past a very nasty reef and stopped only about a football field away from the mooring buoy. In the dark, at the time it was happening, I had no idea how long the boat had been drifting and was terrified we would feel the grinding impact of the reef at any moment.

My heart is apparently in good shape because it was severely tested that night. Had I been sleeping in my pilothouse berth, I doubt I would have been awakened by the drifting motion of the boat, which is very gentle compared to the rolling and pitching when moored or anchored. I shudder to think of what could have been.

We now have the same setup as before, but with our big storm lines. The more I thought about what happened, the more I suspected there was something strange going on. We had tied to mooring buoys many times in the past in the same way, without any problems. When the tide came high again, I looked closely at the mooring line and saw that there was no stretch or gentle rising and falling of the line. Instead, as a swell passed under the buoy, the line went instantly vertical and yanked down on our bridle lines with a tremendous shock load. We did not see this when we tied to the mooring because it was low tide at the time. At low tide, there is more line from the bottom to the surface, but more importantly, the reef blocks the swells from rolling through the lagoon. We went to sleep that night before high tide and had no way to know what was in store for us. I learned an incredible lesson at 0214 the following morning.

I plan to tell the Australian gov't about this, for the simple reason that it will happen again with catastrophic consequences for some poor, unsuspecting people. Even now, with our huge storm lines in place, the shock load and chafe are amazing at high tide. With gallows humor, we agreed at dinner last night that my sleeping on deck should be standard practice from now on. Needless to say, I got up and checked the lines several times.

Aside from the above, we have had a great summer trip. Before coming out here, the weather was perfect, day after day, and we enjoyed fantastic fishing, spearfishing, snorkeling, and exploring, everywhere we went. I guess the law of averages caught up with us.

It is amazing how fast the days go by on these trips. It is a 24/7 blur, with no personal time outside of a shower in the afternoons. I really do love what we do, but it's a real effort to make every trip as special as possible. In the meantime, I hope your days are not quite as dramatic as mine, and you are having a great summer.

I hope to get around to sending some digital photos when we get back to Darwin. We got some great ones!

All my love,

Dad

The wonders of high technology, including satellite communication and email, helped lessen the guilt I felt, being so far from my "Rascals." If my now-grown daughters resented my faraway life, they never mentioned it, and I tried hard to stay as close as possible with my letters and emails.

The run from Scott Reef to Rowley Shoals was in a very different ocean, and terrible weather cursed us. At Mermaid Reef, we thought it would be just a matter of days and the weather would improve, but it never did. The mooring nightmare was followed only two days later by one of the most frightening episodes in all of our travels.

Michel and Donald had found a small pass through the reef and, despite the terrible weather, had decided to go fishing just outside the reef. I was astonished to see them trying to troll in the nasty wind chop. Being a lifelong surfer, I knew returning would be very risky. After my call on the radio, Michel immediately tried to return, but it was already too late. Big surf shut off their return route in the small pass; and when they arrived at the main pass, giant storm surf crashed across the entrance. It was a real dilemma. The pass would not be safe until the tide came to high slack, but that would not happen until after dark, and in the total darkness Michel would almost certainly crash on the reef. On *Moana*, the late afternoon sun made seeing the reef edges and coral heads impossible, so I could not navigate the pass and come to their rescue. In the binoculars, I could see Michel idling around in a calm spot, beyond the breakers, just outside the reef. He and Donald would have to stay outside the reef until dawn, but how? The drop off was so severe, their anchor would not reach the bottom, and their fuel supply would run out during the night.

The huge waves in the pass were wild, stormy, and unpredictable. They were not the clean, cyclical waves with nice lulls between sets that surfers love. I could not offer any advice to Michel. He was in a terrible situation. And he was with his son.

Our radios went silent and, as I continued to try to think of a solution, Michel took off. Using speed and maneuvering in a manner to make a professional surfer envious, he drove across the face of a towering wave, all the way to the other side of the pass, cut back at the bottom, outran the breaking white water, and rode the back of the next swell into the calm water of the channel! It was an exhibition of skill and courage I will never forget. Alongside, Donald hopped on the boat without the slightest expression of anything out of the ordinary, but Michel knew just how lucky he was, and (comically, to me) blurted out, "Thank God Martine was not with us!"

Captain's log, July 31

Underway in miserable, grinding weather to fight our way back to mainland. 0800 pos 18° 20.8' S, 121° 17.09' E, SOG 4–5kts.

The bad weather finally drove us out of Rowley Shoals, and we ran back to the coast. The locals told us of some nice anchorages and beautiful beaches to the south of Broome, and they were right as usual. Eco Beach proved to be the warm, calm, and absolutely gorgeous stretch of coastline we

Eco Beach landscape

needed after the tough weather offshore. Turquoise water in the anchorage, and stunning red rock landscapes made Eco Beach a fantastic place to finish our second trip to Western Australia.

Captain's log, October 31

Underway for Singapore, in Java Sea. 1200 pos 4° 18.6' S, 108° 38.3' E.

The acid rain of Singapore was worse than Panama. It had an orange-brown tint when it first hit the boat, but if allowed to dry it turned into a black haze that was almost impossible to remove. Poor Joubert washed the boat almost every day, and sometimes twice in a day, all by himself. But the acid rain was not the only problem when staying at Raffles Marina. Over the years, many boats were struck by lightning there, including Michel's previous *Moana*, when Joubert was almost killed.

Singapore was a vibrant, exciting place to visit, especially for tourists who fueled things like Orchard Road, the unbelievable shopping district where huge malls flanked both sides of the street for miles. The malls were fronted by outrageous, high tech displays of the world-famous brands within. Dior, Chanel, Versace, Tiffany, Gucci—they were all there. A shopper's paradise, it was absolutely overwhelming for me. The sensory overload of noise, colors, shapes, lights, food, and thousands of people drove me out in less than an hour.

But it was a good place for provisioning, bringing in parts and supplies, and catching up on the endless maintenance. Our next trip was to be the Andaman Islands, an archipelago in the Bay of Bengal, far offshore Burma, but owned by India. This meant a trip to the Indian Embassy to obtain visas for the crew, and it was a preview of Indian officialdom. I will never know how I talked the only sympathetic and very pregnant official into granting us our visas, when all the others we pleaded with insisted each crew member would have to return to their home countries; but after almost a full day in a giant madhouse of confusion, we had our precious visas.

Captain's log, December 10

2000 pos 2° 30.7' N, 101° 38.3' E. Underway in heavy ship traffic, Malacca Strait.

Everything from rowboats to supertankers plies the Malacca Strait, the narrow, 550-mile stretch between the Malay Peninsula and the Indonesian Island of Sumatra. It is the gateway from the Indian Ocean to the South China Sea and Pacific Ocean. It is probably the busiest shipping lane in the world, and in the tight spots, a nightmare of navigation in the dark.

In not so many years past, the strait was home to pirates. The narrow strait made it easy for the native pirates to run out from nearby hiding places in the jungles and quickly board the commercial ships at night. Unfortunately, the owners of various shipping companies decided the best strategy to end the problem was to pay off the pirates for not attacking their ships. This simply confirmed that "crime pays," and it set the precedent for piracy that was now taking place offshore the Horn of Africa.

Tracking all the targets on radar was intense. With a standing, continuous, sundown-to-sun-up wheel watch with no breaks, I was very happy to see the sunrise. There are all kinds of boats, mostly heading north and south, but many fishing boats, smugglers, and locals cross the strait on goofy angles, at different speeds, and many without proper (or any) navigation lights, all sharing space with huge commercial ships. With such chaos in a restricted space, the norms of navigation are almost forgotten. The large ships loom out of the wind, rain, and darkness like black, silent monsters. Unstoppable, mindless, and without remorse, consuming all water and space before them and scattering smaller vessels like a tuna blasting through a bait ball, this was the "big boat rule." *Moana* and all other boats in Malacca Strait obeyed.

Captain's log, December 14

Anchor dn in 9ft, "Ranger Flat," Port Blair, Andaman Islands

As he stepped aboard, the customs officer sneered at Joubert and demanded, "I'm hungry. Tell your cook to make me breakfast!" Joubert, never to be outsmarted by anyone, schooled

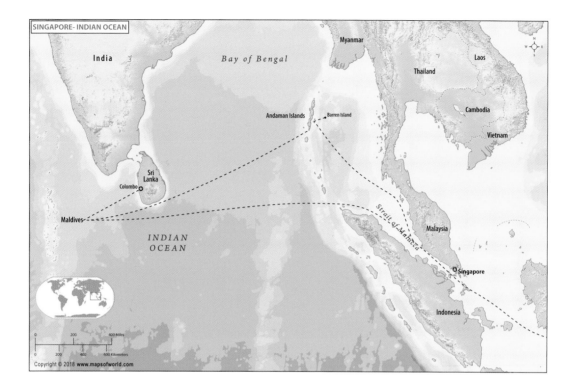

him with a look of apology, raised his hands in fake submission and said, "No English. No speak English." The customs officer was the last in a day-long parade of officials, and he was easily the worst.

After my experience at the Indian Embassy in Singapore, I hired an agent long before arriving in Port Blair, the capital of the Andaman Islands. Even so, I was astonished when he told us it would take over 100 pages of documents and many bottles of expensive whiskey to clear into the country. This was beyond anything I had ever experienced while clearing into even the most backward countries, and I was sure there must be some kind of mistake. No. One after another, over fifteen officials were shuttled to "Ranger Flat," where *Moana* was anchored, and they did indeed demand all the documents and all the whiskey, just as our agent said they would.

From the upper aft deck, I was amused to hear Joubert's response to the customs officer and quickly went to the galley to tell Fiona to hide out in her cabin. He got his two bottles of whiskey, but not breakfast; and when being helped back into the shore boat, Joubert gave him his famous smile and told him in perfect English, "A pleasure to meet you! Have a nice day, sir." This was day one of many days in a strange country and culture.

Fortunately, we arrived a week ahead of Michel and the family. We needed it. Port Blair was not exactly a sought-after, trendy tourist destination, confirmed by our first trip into town

Riding with Vejay, missed the bus by inches

Colorful sari

Port Blair laundromat

with Vejay, in his very old taxi. Snapping photos out of the windows, it was a combination thrill ride and trip in a time machine.

Everything was old, dirty, and gray, the lone exception being the beautiful saris of the women. "Sacred" cows, wandering freely and crapping wherever they wanted, shared the roads with worn out trucks, cars, and tuk-tuks, all belching black smoke and careening all over the place. Approaching the city, giant earthen vats served as the local laundromat, with sheets and clothes drying at the side of the road on clotheslines stretching for over a mile. It seemed humorous to me that clean laundry was drying next to the passing cars and trucks, with dirt and exhaust fumes flying.

Goats wandered on the roadsides, foraging in the piles of trash. A large traffic circle with a statue of Ghandi marked the city center, but the local driving habits made it seem more like a continuous race track of lunatics bent on self-destruction. In the midst of the noise, smoke, and frenetic traffic, I spotted a businessman walking along, and like all the dated vehicles, his clothes were right out of a 1940s Hollywood movie. It was amazing! I half expected to see Humphrey Bogart stroll past at any moment!

For Fiona, shopping was pretty primitive as well, but Vejay knew where the best fresh produce could be found, and we were happily surprised at the good quality. We knew we could not purchase the dry goods we would need, or buy good, clean fuel, so we made those purchases in Singapore. Joubert cleaned up the boat and we thought we were ready to go, but typical of all our time in the Andamans, one surprise followed another.

"You must call the navy and give your position twice a day," Rathman (he used only one name), our agent, said. "And that position has to match the dates and locations of the places you list in the itinerary you give to the authorities before you leave Port Blair. And here is a list of the islands you cannot visit. And here is a list of the places where you cannot go ashore." And, and, and….

"But Rathman, we have never been here before. How can I tell anyone where we will go, or where we will be on any given date? Before coming all this way from Singapore, you told us we were going to be cruising in a paradise of wild islands. Now, it sounds like we will be sharing our experiences and be totally controlled by the Indian Navy."

"Sorry, but you must follow the regulations."

Of course, my being one of those notorious, lawless American captains, the regulations fell on deaf ears. (There were several islands of native tribes so primitive the government did not allow visitors due to the fear of disease being introduced. From the start of our trip planning, we intended to visit those islands, but we were never told they were off limits. This was a sad surprise, and we did not attempt to visit them after all.) After our first day, we were miles away from my listed position, and my official itinerary was a joke for the entire time. I simply emailed our position instead of calling in via radio, prompting two visits by navy gunships.

We did have a good time in the Andamans, but it was far from the sensational adventure we anticipated. We found good, calm anchorages at very scenic islands I will always remember for one unusual thing: Towering, giant hardwood trees growing at the forest edges, right behind the beautiful, white sand beaches. Unlike many of the island countries we visited, such as the Solomons and Papua New Guinea, where shadowy Chinese and their Malaysian front men bought off island chiefs and ravaged all the valuable trees, these stately sentinels of another era had somehow escaped the saw. I gave them a long and loving look while hoping they would survive for future generations. The mountainous, volcanic, and densely forested islands were always surrounded by extensive (and poorly charted) coral reefs, and the remnants of fishing nets explained the absence of all large fish. Still, the water was warm and very clear, and we found the coral reefs swarming with small, exotic, and beautiful fish.

Christmas Day found us at Barren Island, anchored at the base of the lava flow of an active volcano. It was one of the most spectacular places we visited. With a steep drop off near shore, it took a little exploring to find a high spot for the anchor, and with a stern line to a lava outcrop, we were anchored closely broadside to a rumbling, erupting volcano. Every twenty minutes, a cloud of smoke and ash blasted from the caldera into the clear blue sky. Rocks the size of cars flew high in the sky before bouncing down the flanks of the volcano, and making us wonder just how safe our front row seat was. As darkness fell, we were further entertained by a fireworks

Christmas Day, Barren Island

show that dwarfed the best of man's. Invisible by daylight, a giant plume of small, glowing lava rocks and fiery ash lit up the night sky. I awoke many times; it was the first time in my life my sleep was compromised by an erupting volcano.

Trip's end meant a very long trip home for the family. Reaching the Andamans from Europe was a nightmare of multiple flights and long layovers between connections, but Michel was always willing to pay the price to take his family to the wild places. For the crew and me, it was a few days to catch our breath and begin preparing for the run across the Indian Ocean to the Maldives. Rathman arranged for our fuel, which turned out to be a long comedy of errors by the time it was aboard. During the exercise, he invited the crew and me to a birthday party he was giving for his three-year-old daughter the following evening. Always interested to learn more about different cultures and customs, I gladly accepted. Vejay, our always-worried and serious driver, delivered us to the party, which turned out to be at an orphanage for young girls, on a hilltop overlooking the city.

For me, the orphanage was the most memorable experience in Port Blair. An unfinished concrete structure, it looked to be built by a bomb shelter expert. It lacked windows or even paint, but its thick walls would survive any natural disaster, so the thirty-one little girls and their single caretaker were no doubt safe. Most of the girls were nine to eleven years of age, but a few were

Orphanage birthday party

Captain Lew and the magic thumb

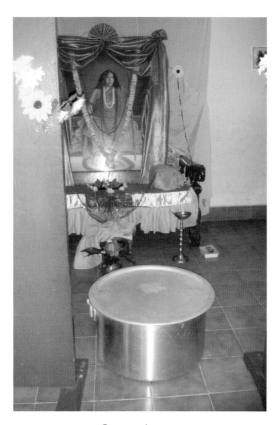

Giant cooking pot

a little older. They arrived at the orphanage for different reasons, but most were abandoned by parents who simply could not care for them. Two of the oldest lost their parents in a tsunami. All were automatically in the lowest social class in Indian society.

We arrived to see Rathman's little girl in traditional birthday dress (of the highest class in Indian society), cutting a huge, beautiful cake. All of the orphans, dressed in bright yellow, shiny dresses, crowded around and cheered as she gave the first piece of cake to her father.

I was sure the dresses were for special events, when four girls could not wait any longer and broke into song and dance with obvious pride and boundless energy. Gray cement floors, polished by bare feet that never saw shoes, reminded me of where I was as the precious orphans danced, sang, and entertained us with innocent enthusiasm. Several were curious about the American stranger, and I entertained them with my magic, removable thumb, just as I had done with my own two daughters, many years before.

We had one more day before departing, and I could not get the girls and their home out of my mind. I had seen the bedroom, with rows of three-high bunk beds, and the simple kitchen.

I had seen the little shrine in honor of the woman who petitioned the government and obtained the land grant in 1989. Construction began in 1992 and, while the building was still unfinished at the time of our visit, it was a good home for the girls. I wanted to do something worthwhile to help, and asked Vejay to drive me back up the mountain. With excited children all around us, the caretaker gave me a big smile and in the local language relayed her most important need. It was a simple request I could not wait to help with, and a few hours later, to the cheers of the girls, I carried in a huge cooking pot! The pot was so large it barely fit in the trunk of Vejay's taxi.

As a boat captain, I have always had a hard time with good-byes, and this time was especially so. When I asked the girls to give me a good-bye hug, they immediately formed a line and, one by one, stepped forward to hug. Each was wide eyed and smiled shyly, and it was a special moment. And the last, the oldest, looked deep in my eyes and held me tightly, reluctant to let me go. The slow going down the rough mountain road gave me time to reflect on such an emotional experience. Was it possible I was the first man to give the girls a hug?

But it seemed Port Blair and Rathman could not let us go. At the last moment, Rathman asked me if I would be willing to speak with the Port Captain and detail our experience in the Andamans, and perhaps make suggestions to improve tourism (and of course, help his business). This proved to be a very educational experience for me when I presented a sizable list of my biggest complaints, as well as some suggestions that would make a huge difference for visiting yachts.

"Very interesting, captain. We will look into your comments and suggestions."

"Great," I enthused. But having learned a little about the unbelievable bureaucracy in India, I asked, "In case we want to come back, how long will it take to make some changes?"

"Well, first I will select a committee to study the situation and your suggestions, and then, after careful consideration, recommendations will be made, blah, blah, blah…" and I started smiling.

With the formalities over, we were back on the seawall, waiting for Joubert to pick me up, and I looked out over the harbor and asked Rathman, "Why all the gunboats and naval sea power here in Port Blair?"

"It is understood that if another country invades India, it would start here, in Port Blair, so we have to be ready," he answered.

"Rathman, this sounds like the unfinished work of one of your committees. I'm not a military strategist, but I wonder if they considered that anyone taking your country would have to feed all your people?"

Rathman turned out to be a good man, and I wished him well.

Narcondam Island anchorage, Andaman Islands

Serious gunboats on patrol , Colombo, Sri Lanka

2010

INDIAN OCEAN, BAY OF BENGAL, MALAYSIA, MICRONESIA

Captain's log: February 27

0715 pos alongside commercial wharf, Colombo, Sri Lanka

Our cruising permit in the Maldives had expired, and their dated regulations demanded we go to another country, clear in, clear out with the authorities, and then return to get a new permit. Sri Lanka was the closest, so after 440 unwelcome extra miles, we rolled into Colombo. Idling into the harbor, passing under the watchful eyes of serious soldiers manning fortified gun emplacements on the breakwater, made it easy to understand why Sri Lanka was on the no-go list of our insurance company. The war with the Tamil Tigers had finally ended, but the government was taking no chances with any kind of resurgence.

I found a great, street-smart young man and made him our agent. Novada arranged the fuel truck and drove us to all the authorities so quickly, we finished everything that very day. So I hired him to give us a quick tour of the city the following morning. It was an interesting day, broken up with many inspections at sandbagged military checkpoints, but the armed soldiers let us pass with only a glance inside the car.

The long war had taken a toll. Tourists were not to be found anywhere. The streets, buildings, and everything else looked dirty and "tired." It was like everything just stopped while waiting for the war to end, and now the city was struggling to get going again. We visited a beautiful Hindu church, where street kids stole our shoes and sold them back to us later, and a park that was memorable because elephants, retired from logging work, lived out their days in the company of families having picnics. It was an interesting city and a nice break for the crew and me, but we were soon underway again.

Captain's log: February 16, Maldives

1403 pos 3°26'N, 73°35.3'E. Anchor down in 58ft, sand.

We found an interesting anchorage inside the lagoon of Vattarrurah Island, which was alive with breaking fish and diving birds. Soon after anchoring, we noticed something floating

Elephants and families on picnics

slowly into the pass of the lagoon, accompanied by many seabirds, diving all around what turned out to be a lost fishing net. Michel and the boys soon discovered an immense school of fish under the net and enjoyed a spectacular, underwater display of the entire ocean food chain. From the smallest plankton and tiny fish hiding under the huge tangle of netting, to large predator fish, including tuna, in the depths, it was everything a person could hope to see over years of diving, all together at the same time, in one place.

While anchored there, we observed two men moving around in the tall, dense bushes of the small island, next to the pass. It was a very small, low, sand island and the bushes could only provide shelter, but certainly not anything to sustain life. For sure, there was no water or food, so we could not understand why the men were there, sixty nautical miles from the nearest inhabited island. Without a word to me, Louis, and his buddy Quentin jumped into the dinghy and motored over to the island. The boys beached the small boat, and watching in the binoculars, I was stunned to see a very unkempt, bearded man emerge from the bushes, brandishing a very large knife that he held outstretched, in front of him. His crouching posture was menacing as he walked slowly towards Louis, who I was astonished to see, did not turn and run back to the boat. Instead, he walked directly toward the shirtless, dark-skinned, frightening man… and I held my breath. As they came together at the moment of violence

Sand island at Fettayoo Kandu

I feared was about to happen, Louis extended his hand like a man meeting an old friend on the street. It was an amazing scene. The man stopped in his tracks, stood upright, transferred the knife to his left hand, slowly extended his right, and with a look of surprise, shook hands!

I exhaled deeply and then smiled, remembering the funny twelve-year-old boy on our first trip with the family, ten years before. Now, as a twenty-two-year-old man, his big smile and clever personality had been molded by many positive experiences with the people of these remote island countries. He loved everyone, and they loved him back.

We were halfway around the world. In the middle of the Indian Ocean, the Maldives were on the bucket list of every professional diver, underwater photographer, honeymooner, or anyone wealthy enough to succumb to the spectacular photos and advertising of the beautiful low sand and coral islands.

It was our second trip in the Maldives, and the family was having a great time. It was exactly the kind of faraway place *Moana* was built to reach and explore in safety and comfort. With dazzling white sand islands and extensive coral reefs all around, the scuba diving and snorkeling in the transparent, warm water was fantastic. For the family and guests, it was paradise. They flew in, enjoyed several weeks of the most remote and beautiful islands, and flew out. For me and my crew it was something else.

Maldives is a Sunni Muslim country. We had visited many different countries in our travels, but this was our first experience in a country that was 100 percent Muslim. With the call to prayer emanating from the big mosque, it did not take long to learn what that meant. On our very first day, it was apparent our ship's agent, the very person we paid for assistance, held us in low regard. Ever optimistic, and confident the same respect we had shown all the people in so many remote countries would make us welcome, I thought my agent was simply having a bad day. I had no idea anyone could dislike my crew and me without even knowing our names, much less our political or religious views.

Male, the capital, is on one of the most densely populated islands in the world. Only 2.2 square miles, the first thing that underscored the population in our eyes was the thousands of motorbikes. At every intersection and traffic light change, the morning rush hour looked like the start of a road race as packs of motorbikes roared away in clouds of smoke. The second thing that caught my attention was how everyone calmly went about his or her life, despite the crowded conditions. Or, so it seemed. I had yet to notice the difference in the dress of the men.

Moana was anchored at the end of the airport runway, at Hulhumale Island, a short ferry trip from Male. I enjoyed the thirty-minute ferry ride across the channel, observing the different designs of all the various small boats, ferries, and commercial vessels that were going in every direction imaginable. The ferries were simple, practical wooden boats, about eighty feet long, housing rows of benches that could accommodate fifty to sixty people. They were fully enclosed to keep passengers dry during the many passing rain showers.

The most unusual part of the operation was the loading and unloading of motorbikes. After all the passengers were seated, motorbikes were ridden aboard, right down the center of the deck, until they filled all the space reserved for them aft, and all the aisle space between the benches. Of course, some of the riders were young, so they had to demonstrate their skill by riding a bit too fast and revving their engines as long as possible. As the noise and smoke of the motorbikes diminished, the noise and smoke of the worn-out ferry engines continued the frenetic scene as the ferry got underway.

It was always humorous to me to observe the passengers who sat quietly amidst the din and endured what was obviously another normal run across the channel. Aside from the headscarves and colorful dress of some of the women, I found nothing unusual about the people on the ferry. They seemed not very curious about my presence, as tourism is big business in the Maldives. To me, my fellow passengers were just normal people going about their lives with the usual concerns about family, health, etc.

My impressions were on a collision course with reality on a very hot Male morning. Struggling to carry a heavy bag of supplies to the ferry landing, and although only a football field distance away, I elected to take a taxi parked nearby. Asked if he was looking for a fare, the driver gave me a look of surprise, nodded his head and grunted something I took for a "yes."

Thousands of motorbikes

Runway anchorage

Loading motorbikes on ferry. Noise and smoke!

Unwilling to leave his seat, he popped the trunk, let me load my bag, and we pulled away from the curb. As I requested the short drive to the ferry landing, I was surprised to see raw anger in his eyes. My attempt at friendly conversation was ignored as he reached in front of me and turned off the air conditioning. Sweating profusely himself, he wanted only to show me what he thought of an American.

The taxi stopped in front of the ferry landing, amidst many people milling about, and I again went to the trunk to retrieve my bag. Standing next to his open window, I feigned courtesy, and asked how much I owed him. Like everyone, I knew every fare on the small island was twenty Rufiyaa, so my anger went off the scale when he sneered and loudly demanded thirty Rufiyaa. I was aware of a hush that came over the crowd of people close behind me as they watched the confrontation unfold. I handed him twenty Rufiyaa and stepped back.

"Thirty Rufiyaa!" he screamed.

"The other ten is in my pocket. Come and get it."

We were eye to eye for a long moment until, without another word, the taxi driver pulled away from the terminal. Immediately, the crowd burst into laughter and condemnation of the taxi driver. "Good for you, sir. Those guys are always trying to take advantage of people," was the loudest voice in the group.

Extreme emotion slowly drained as I made my way to the ticket counter. I was relieved with the outcome, but as I reflected on the whole event, a singular thought replayed in my mind, over and over. The entire crowd knew what the taxi driver was trying to do, and while they disapproved, they did nothing to help me.

There were other, unpleasant reminders of how the radicals intimidate and dominate through implied force, but this singular event was for me, the perfect example of how a small minority can ruin the lives of the many. Ignorant street thugs, ruling by fear.

Captain's log: March 30

Underway in Indian Ocean en route Sumatra. 2300 pos 4° 44.1' N, 84° 15.3' E. Full moon over glassy calm sea, clear sky. Beautiful!

Pirate activity around the Horn of Africa and reported recently, near the Seychelles, forced us to abandon our plans to travel further west and circle the globe. Michel let the kids vote for a return to their favorite place, so we were underway for a return to the fabulous atolls we had found in Micronesia, over 4,500 nautical miles away. The family did not travel with us on the long transits between the places we actually visited, so it was just Joubert and I, and Fiona, our English cook, grinding out the miles to Singapore and on to Palau.

The first leg of this run took us across the Indian Ocean in truly remarkable weather. In the winter months, the very same route we were traveling was rough to the extreme, but this time we experienced the longest run of calm seas I could ever remember. Day after day of a glassy, mirror-flat ocean, combined with the heat and humidity of the tropics, made it impossible to see where the sea ended and the sky began.

With only the hum of the engines to break the stillness, we ate and slept like travelers in the cosmos, with the endless stars for companions. On such runs, my thoughts invariably wound backwards to other times and places and, if I thought about it for long, returned me to where it all started, long ago….

Hornet was the pride of Pierpoint Landing, in Long Beach, California, a sport fishing landing where many boats tied up between one-day trips to the local banks and islands. Some of the boats were for charter only, but many were open "party" boats for individual fishermen who simply bought a ticket and got a day on the ocean, fishing or just escaping civilization. It was pretty basic in those days. For five bucks you could fish aboard one of the smaller, local boats that fished close to the harbor. For ten, you got a larger boat that fished farther offshore, maybe to Catalina Island. And for twelve bucks, you got a trip all the way to San Clemente Island, a primitive, wild, fisherman's paradise!

I knew all this when I was only ten years old because I watched Pierpoint Landing's weekly fishing show on TV. Every week I saw happy fishermen reeling in huge fish, one after the other, aboard these "modern" fishing boats. All the while, the sun shone brightly on a glassy,

Indian Ocean glass

calm ocean. Wow! And at the end of each show a fisherman held up a nice fat fish for viewers to identify and guess the exact weight in pounds and ounces. If you wrote in with the right answer, you got a free ticket. (Several years later I knew that if you wrote in, much less guessed the weight, the landing was happy to give out a ticket that no doubt would be matched by the fisherman's buddy.)

The thought of just missing the weight made me a little creative. Postcards were only 3 cents(!), so I sent off at least eight cards, naming all my family members and a few yet unborn, to cover the ounces spread. Calico bass, six pounds, seven ounces. My free ticket came in the mail a few days later, and I doubt I slept that night.

Of course, my choice was the *Hornet*. It was the only boat running all the way to San Clemente Island where the big ones were waiting. It was also the only boat that left the dock at two in the morning, a fact that my poor father must have dreaded. Many years later, I wondered why he did not come fishing with me that day, and the only thing I could think of was he did not want to encourage more middle-of-the-night adventures that kept him from a good night's sleep on a Saturday night. I'm sure he figured that a good thrashing at sea would cure me, so at some ungodly hour, he drove me and my fishing gear to the landing.

It was the stuff of dreams. The parking lot was already filling up with pickup trucks and veteran fishermen. Lugging their big tackle boxes and several rods and reels, and dressed in rough, real fishing clothes, they seemed like giants getting ready for battle. Fishing boats of all sizes floated lazily at their docks, awash in the lights of the landing and their own deck lights. Seagulls were squawking and fighting for scraps of yesterday's bait. The smell of salt water, diesel fuel, fish, beer, cigars, and everything else was the real deal! I have often wondered what my dad was thinking when he walked me down to the boat and made sure I was safely aboard. I was small, even for a ten-year-old, and I'm sure he must have wondered if this was such a good idea. Fortunately for me, I had wonderful parents who allowed me to go at life as hard as I dared.

As *Hornet* cleared the breakwater, the movie changed dramatically. It was early May and far different than the calm summer days of July, August, and September, when they filmed all those great TV scenes. A nasty breeze was up from the south, on mixed seas that snap-rolled the boat and sent spray flying everywhere. The veterans were drinking beer, smoking cigars, and playing cards at the small table in the bunkroom, all the while declaring the weather was "nothing compared to…." The pitching and rolling was bad, but the cigar smoke was worse. I fought the awful feeling in my stomach as long as I could and then took my place at the rail and launched my dinner into the blackness. To my surprise, many of the other passengers were already doing the same. It was terrible. In moments, I was soaking wet, cold, and completely miserable. Years later I would hear someone describe seasickness as "being afraid you are going to die, and then afraid you won't." I was in the movie from Hell, with all these people in the dark, lined up at the rail, retching and groaning with every big roll, staring down at the black sea and hanging on as the cold spray mercilessly soaked us to the skin, over and over. Interestingly, my strongest memory at the time was bewilderment. How could my big dream be like this?

Hornet approached the lee of the island as dawn broke, and the sea became very calm. As the sun began to rise, I felt for the first time, the feeling I would feel for many years to come on the ocean. With the coming of the sun and the light, the demons of the darkness are banished for another day. From that day to now, the dark is my enemy and the sunrise my forever friend. As the boat slowed and we approached the fishing spot, the deckhand emerged from the cabin. Twenty-something, in his rolled-down hip boots, blood-stained Levi's, long, blond hair, and stubble beard, he looked the tough, young deckhand type. He seemed a little bleary eyed as he nonchalantly walked aft to the large bait tank. Without hesitation, he plunged his whole head into the tank, amidst the anchovies and sardines, snapped it back and, with a loud gasp, shook it like some kind of Viking warrior! Standing close enough to feel the spray, I was paralyzed as the camera in my head captured a scene I would never forget. This was my hero. This was all I wanted to be, forever.

Captain's log, May 31

Underway in South China Sea. 2100 pos 1° 50' S, 108° 57' E, in calm sea, black sky, lightning over Kalimantan.

The night sky was clear, the ocean almost flat calm, but Joubert and I hated our wheel watches. Hour after hour winding our way through hundreds of squid boats offshore the south coast of Kalimantan (part of Borneo) was almost worse than taking a beating in heavy weather. The amount of bright lights employed by each boat to bring the squid up from the depths was amazing, and the combined light from the massive fishing fleet lit up the sky for over a hundred miles. Most of the boats were drifting, but some were slowly underway, and all were blinded to our approach by the glare of their lights. On many occasions, boats would get underway and drive right into our path. To make it worse, the boats did not use international navigation lights that help another boat know the direction they are moving. Instead, the entire fleet used an assortment of lights that seemed more like holiday decorations. Even at reduced speed, and intense concentration, it took almost the entire night to pass through the boats without a collision.

Captain's log, June 2

0600 pos 4° 22.6' N, 113° 32.6' E. Drop RPM to 1150 in very poor weather, intense rain squalls

Depth perception at night is a problem for the human eye. Judging distance to a light, in the black of night, is impossible, so the flashing buoy lights, low to the water and marking fishermen's nets, brought us to a stop, just as we were entering the Makassar Strait, between Kalimantan and Sulawesi, in Indonesia. Fishing nets are expensive, so fishermen are usually careful to keep them out of shipping lanes or areas of commercial traffic; but here, set right across the channel, I could see lights indicating net after net. An ex-fisherman, I did not want to damage the nets, but I also did not want the nets to get caught in my propellers and rudders. Tightly wound up in propellers, a net can actually stop a boat and create a dangerous situation when a diver must go underwater to cut it off. The intense, driving rain compromised my radar, making it impossible to see a path around the boats and nets, and I wondered if we would have to wait for sunrise.

Instead, a powerful tugboat, towing a huge barge, came plowing along. Passing by us and entering the channel, he was headed directly into the nets, and I fell in close behind him. "Hey guy, whatcha doing back there?" rang out in English from my radio. In that part of the world, few people are speaking English, so I was happy to reply, "Letting you chop our way through the nets."

"Don't worry, Cap. I run this channel all the time, and these guys know to set deep enough there is rarely a problem." All the same, I hugged the aft end of the barge for miles, letting my new friend give us a safe and very smooth ride.

Captain's log, July 18

Med-moored, Neco Marine, Palau

Four thousand nautical miles in open ocean, trade-winds–driven seas are not a walk in the park, but we had decent traveling weather, and Joubert, Fiona, and I were in pretty good shape when we finally arrived. It was *Moana's* fourth time back to Palau, so it was almost like coming home, and we enjoyed the familiar surroundings and good friends in the small community.

On Palau, we did one more trip to the famous dive sites of German Channel, Blue Corner, and Ulong Channel. They were indeed beautiful spots, and we hit them in great conditions; but knowing they did not compare to what we had experienced on Yap, Sorol, and Ngulu, we soon pushed on.

Like on Palau, it was great to renew friendships on Yap, especially with Ignathio Hapthey, the chief of the outer islands, and Bill Acker, the owner of Manta Ray Bay. I often wondered what we would have done without Bill's help, and the help of his daughter, Numie, to bring in our fresh food needs. Had I not met Bill, we probably would never have heard of Sorol.

We spent a few days diving with Bill's people, and as usual they took us to great manta ray encounters and photo opportunities. Bill had a big, wooden, authentic Indonesian sailing ship, anchored right behind his hotel, that served as his restaurant, so we could not resist a few dinners on such a unique vessel. All the divers staying at the hotel ate their meals on the ship, and in the evenings they watched videos of themselves diving that day, on the huge screen on the ship's mast. The camaraderie and atmosphere were as good as the food, so we stayed late into the night on several occasions.

Captain's log, July 31

0800 pos 8° 09.3' N, 140° 18.3' E, A/C to 130° to skirt edge of reef on W end, trolling to approach

As on our previous trips to Sorol, I was stunned by the postcard-perfect beauty of the atoll. It was paradise on every level except one.

For the family, it offered all the activities they loved: a calm anchorage in crystal clear, warm water, and swimming distance to the nearest white sand beach. Beachcombing and exploring on islands with diverse animal life such as coconut crabs, green turtles, monitor lizards, and many seabird species. Fishing in waters teeming with tuna and marlin, and diving in the many caves, canyons, and ledges swarming with grouper, snapper, and sharks. Or just the utter tranquility of the remote, primitive atoll, far from civilization.

For me, it was always about keeping the boat and everyone safe, and all the equipment up and running. A good pass into a clear (no coral heads) lagoon, with coral sand bottom for good anchor holding, was at the top of my list. There were no big swells rolling over the

Mnuw (Sea Hawk), Manta Ray Bay restaurant

reef at high tide, strong currents sweeping through the lagoon, or trade winds at the wrong angle, which meant calm nights with quality sleep. The tiny islands were not home to rats, or malarial mosquitos. Outside the reef, there were no dangers such as submerged rocks or detached reefs that the kids might hit with the dinghy. All the small islands could be visited by bringing the dinghy or kayak up on a sand beach. And from the lagoon anchorage, I could almost always watch over the kids going from island to island, or even when fishing outside the pass. Instead of nightmares, I probably dreamed of childhood visits to the corner candy store, where everything was wonderful!

Our visits to Sorol had not gone unnoticed, and an interesting rumor was circulating on Yap just before we left. The remote atoll was largely unknown to the outside world, and no one went there. But the owners were very aware of our visits, and the fact that we came back over and over confirmed what they were thinking: They know it is paradise. Our friendships with Chief Hapthey and Chief Mike were well known as well, so although we were outsiders,

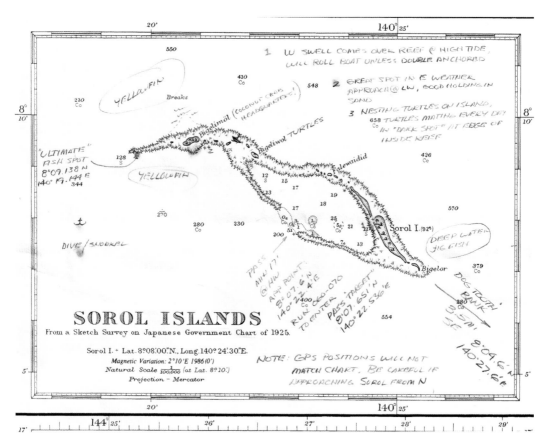

Reprinted, courtesy of United Kingdom Hydrographic Office

we had gained the respect of the local people. The rumor that reached me one day was that a chief who had lived with his family on the atoll over twenty years ago, was ready to ask us if we were interested in buying Sorol.

From Yap, a modern floatplane could reach the atoll. First circling and enthralling the wealthy passengers with their first sight of real paradise, it would land in the calm waters of the lagoon and idle up to the floating hotel where the guests would begin their stay at one of the most exclusive resorts in the world…. This was one of my thoughts on our first visit to Sorol. But it will probably (and happily) never happen because of the one thing: typhoons.

Typhoons are born not far from Sorol. The Japanese fishing boat, high on the reef, and the big steel buoy up in the trees on the lizard island were a daily reminder of the unbelievable power of the monster storms. This one thing would most likely ensure that the atoll to which we had become so attached would remain remote, pristine, and unscarred by man, for a very long time. Still, I felt honored the native landlords of this paradise considered us worthy to become the owners.

Inside the lagoon, Sorol

It was typhoon season in Micronesia, and every morning and every evening, I checked with our weather routing service in New York. Day after day, week after week, we had absolutely beautiful weather at both Sorol and Ngulu. Our last trip to these atolls in the middle of nowhere left indelible memories of true paradise. And being all alone.

Captain's log, August 2, 3, and 13
Birthdays in paradise

Over the years, several birthdays fell during trips with the family aboard. Now, ten years on, it was amazing to see how the kids had grown and matured. Joubert and I were always impressed by how close they were, and now it was clear the bond between them had grown even stronger.

Donald, Louis, cook Fiona, Michel, and Thomas. Team effort, and gourmet dinner by grown up kids

Louis getting haircut from big sister, Rachel

Normal and albino green turtles

2011

AUSTRALASIA, NORTH AMERICA

Captain's log, Dec 22

0951, anchor dn in 18ft, Art Island, Belep

Michel often had amazing luck with weather, and this trip would be the same. It was cold and rainy, day after day, on our run up the coast of New Caledonia, and it continued as we waited for the family to arrive at Belep. The crew and I celebrated Christmas in the rain, but two days later the family and guests landed at the dirt airstrip in sunshine and clear skies. It stayed that way for the entire trip back to Récifs d'Entrecasteaux.

It was still a wild place. Dangerous reefs and marginal anchorages were the norm, as before, but with the calm weather came very low swells and almost no current. This meant much easier access through the fringing, extensive coral reefs to reach the islands. Exploring the low islands, which were home to many bird species and turtles and were encircled by beautiful, white sand beaches, was probably the high point of the trip. The raw beauty of the remote reefs was breathtaking, from sunrise to sunset.

The fishing was not as spectacular, but the deck freezer filled as before. Huge Spanish mackerel filled in for yellowfin tuna, and the big dogtooth tuna were waiting for us at all the passes, especially at Huon.

Huon island, like Lacepede, offshore Western Australia, was a major nesting site for green turtles. Thousands of them returned year after year to mate and lay their eggs on the long, low, spaghetti-shaped sand island. And like Lacepede, they shared the island with many bird species, including boobies. Apparently, the International Boys/Boobies Peace Pact was still in force, but the boys were still not interested in spending a night on the island to watch the female turtles lay their eggs.

Instead, the boys were busy netting small tropical fish under our bright underwater fishing lights, off the starboard side, unaware of the sparkle of many little eyes, swimming directly for the stern of *Moana*. Hatchling turtles, about thirty in all, had made it past the predators on the shore and were making their life-or-death swim for the open ocean. Our big deck lights confused their celestial navigation and took the place of the moon or whatever star they were pre-programmed to use. Headed for bed, I had glanced around the boat and saw the little creatures approaching. I also saw the snappers rising behind them.

In less than one minute, I netted all of the hatchlings and put them in the bait tank. Staring down at the little turtles, happy to have saved them from the snappers, I noticed one of them was a stunningly beautiful albino.

"Boys, before you go to bed, please turn off all the lights, including the big deck lights. Have another beer (the days of Coca-Cola were long gone), and then release all the babies. Leave the albino in the tank."

In the wild, albino animals rarely survive to adulthood, and I guess I wanted to improve her chances. I was happily surprised the next morning when I discovered the boys had kept one of her siblings as well. My idea was to give the albino to a big public aquarium in Noumea, where children could see such a beautiful animal, but they were not interested. We kept her and her brother in the tank for several weeks, fattened them up, and released them in the open ocean, near some sea grass.

A sensational trip to the "Récifs" ended with another overnight stay at Surprise, and another incredible bird show at sunset. I reflected on how many thousands of years this amazing sight had existed, and how many thousands of years, unmolested, it will continue. To witness nature at its wildest is a sobering experience.

Captain's log, January 9

Underway, southbound on coast, outside barrier reef. 1451 pos abeam Passe de Koumac, .5 mi, in good traveling weather, breeze 10kts on swells SE @ 5–6ft.

Cyclone Vania, forecast to pass over the north end of New Caledonia, had suddenly turned and was bearing down on Noumea, the capital. A category-2 cyclone, packing winds of eighty knots and gusting higher, the city went on high alert. Cyclones were common to New Caledonia, and the city had a well-organized strategy to minimize damages. This included a cyclone-proof marina where we were moored.

Unfortunately, we were moored on the outside wall of a long dock, and as the eye of the cyclone passed nearby, the wind came around and began blowing directly into the cut of the breakwater. In moments, wind-driven seas began building and rolling right through the middle of the marina. The boats on the outside wall and those anchored were in serious danger.

In the ominous, moaning sound of the high winds, panic and chaos reigned throughout the marina. We had to leave and take refuge in a nearby part of the harbor where we would find protection, but as we got off the dock, it was impossible to get the bow around, into the wind. The ferocious wind and building seas were going to blow us broadside, down the marina channel, and onto the beach. My only option was to go forward, crash the dock, pin the bow, and let the wind drive the stern around. All of this took place in a matter of moments, and with the bows pointed into the wind and the breakwater entrance, we drove into the horizontal rain that raked the boat with the sound of gravel hitting glass.

The boat owners who waited too long or were too late arriving watched their boats pounded onto the beach and destroyed. Underway, we rounded a nearby point just west of the main harbor and watched a big sailing trimaran that did not have enough power, being driven onto the rocks, less than a hundred yards inside of us.

Inside the main harbor, we anchored in a nice lee and let the wind blow itself out. We had not escaped without a price, however. Joubert hurt his shoulder badly while positioning fenders, and the starboard bow was damaged when we rammed the dock. The boat was not damaged badly, but poor Joubert was in pain and spent a miserable, sleepless night before we could get him to a doctor the following morning.

Captain's log, January 25

Underway in Coral Sea for Sydney in very poor traveling weather. Mixed, large swells from S & SE, wind driven seas and steady breeze 20–25kts. 0300 pos 24° 58.3' S, 165° 12.5' E.

Another cyclone, this time passing right through the center of the Coral Sea. I was sure it would block our path to Sydney, Australia, where we had to meet a transport ship. The shipping company had a tight schedule and would not wait if we could not arrive on time.

"Lew, cyclone Yasi is going to be a monster, but it will stop tomorrow, turn around, and go all the way back to Australia. You can get underway any time after 0900 tomorrow."

WRI, my weather guys in New York, were the best, proven by all the years of great forecasting, but this forecast was "over the top," as my Aussie friends would say! We left at 1027 and got to Sydney just in time to clear in with customs and get *Moana* on the transport ship.

Cyclone Yasi was the most powerful cyclone to hit Australia in a century. Packing winds of 181mph, it did indeed turn around and go back to Australia, devastating the small town of Cardwell.

Captain's log, February 28

Underway for San Diego, 0833 pos clear harbor, A/C to 173°

We were the first boat off the *Super Servant 3* that carried *Moana* from Sydney, Australia, to Ensenada, Mexico. It was a strange, almost unreal feeling, to be underway for "home," where it all started twelve years before.

We went directly to the same boatyard where we built her, to find ourselves welcomed back by the few men who were still there. The yard had been sold, and most of the men we knew were gone, but Eddie and the Travel Lift crew were there and excited to hear of our travels.

Semi-submersible transport ship; after loading, the rear hatch is closed, water is pumped out of the loading bay, and the ship rises to normal configuration and steams off

For me, it was a bittersweet homecoming. I wanted to see all the people who were a part of the building process, invite them to the boat, and share our experiences in the faraway places we visited. I wanted to let them know what a great job they did, to build a boat that proved to be everything we hoped for. But they had all moved on. And now, instead of the wild places, my poor boat was in a yacht harbor, surrounded by boats that never went anywhere, owned by people who had no idea of what was out there. I felt like apologizing to *Moana*, to put her in the company of such imposters.

Eventually, with quite a list of repairs and upgrades behind us, *Moana* was like new again, and we got underway for the Pacific Northwest. It was a brutal trip.

Captain's log, June 22

1500 pos 42° 49.9' N, 124° 44.6' W, abeam Cape Blanco, 8 mi A/C to 358° in terrible head seas weather

Roughly 1,300 nautical miles from San Diego to the Strait of Juan de Fuca, the border between Washington State and British Columbia, Canada, it was a run I had made many times in years long ago. Stretches of gusty winds are common in early summer, especially off northern California and the Oregon coast, guaranteeing nasty head seas for at least a day or two. In our case, miserable weather hammered us day after day, forcing us to take shelter in several anchorages or harbors along the way. To add to our torment, we fouled some discarded poly rope in the starboard propeller and had to go into Crescent City to have it cut off. I had made the run in four to five days in the past, but this time *Moana* had to endure a non-stop beating for two weeks.

Captain's log, June 27
  0233 pos abeam Cape Flattery light, 1.7 mi

Rounding Cape Flattery and entering the Strait of Juan de Fuca was always cause for celebration because it meant the end of rough weather and the beginning of hundreds and hundreds of calm cruising miles in the Inside Passage, all the way to Juneau, the capital of Alaska. It also meant an entire summer of calm anchorages, breathtaking vistas, wildlife, rugged exploring, great fishing, crabbing, and wonderful seafood barbecues!

For many years, on other boats, the northwest was my favorite cruising area. I could not wait to show Michel and the family my favorite spots, and some places I had my eye on for years. From Juneau to Ketchikan, the wildness of Southeast Alaska was fully matched by the thirst for adventure of the entire family. The kids were all grown up now, and at fifty-eight degrees north latitude, the days are long. We filled them with priceless memories.

Everyone has seen TV shows and photos of Alaska, but to appreciate the size and scope, the wild beauty and how it affects the senses, you must experience it! Summer months in southeast Alaska are not about ice and cold. The nights can get cold, but the days are all about blue skies, glassy calm waters, and warm sunshine. The wildlife is prolific, especially on islands like Baranof and Admiralty, where deer and bear can be seen every morning. And when the salmon arrive, the predators are everywhere, including the majestic bald eagle.

I knew the family and their guests, so it was easy to show everyone a great time. It was impossible to take them to a place where they might be intimidated by the wildness factor, so we went to some places I suspected would be great but had never had the chance to visit previously. On several occasions, our explorers returned in the small boat with vivid stories of wildlife encounters. This included stumbling onto a family of wolves, including pups, where they had never been known to live before. It was a summer that exceeded all my expectations.

Riding icebergs

Panoramic Southeast Alaska

Tracy Arm Fjord

Chatterbox Falls, Princess Louisa Inlet

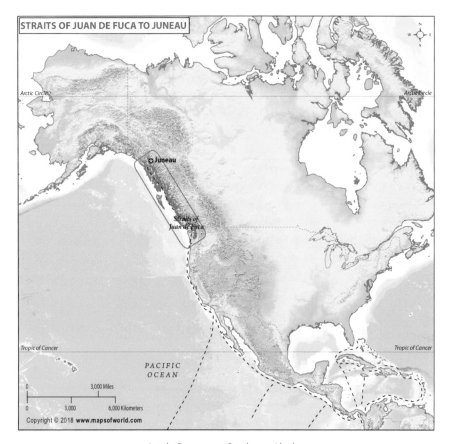

Inside Passage to Southeast Alaska

Captain's log, December 11

Underway off N coast of Baja Mexico in good traveling weather. 0100 pos 30° 02.9' N, 116° 17.5' W.

Bahia Tenacatita is a beautiful bay on the central coast of Mexico. I had visited the bay several times, years ago, when needing a calm anchorage, and found large schools of the green jacks and caballitos we were now fishing for.

After our sensational summer season in Alaska, we were now on our way to Clipperton Island, one of the most remote islands offshore all of North America. The French island, located 670 nautical miles off Acapulco, had an incredible history that included a Mexican outpost that was abandoned by the government, resulting in starvation and murder. The last survivors, a group of women and children, lived for years on the island, waiting for rescue. Guano miners had a go of it, and even the US had a temporary presence on the island

Rachel and Donald with world class king salmon

during WWII. To this day, abandoned machinery and shipwrecks can be found on the island, but no one lives there. It is simply too remote. Hurricanes are common; thundering, powerful surf sweeps all the beaches, and there are no good anchorages. But the lure of such a wild island and the world-class tuna fishing was irresistible for the true adventurers aboard *Moana*.

But to fish for the giant tuna at Clipperton, live bait was an absolute must, and I was prepared to spend several days, if necessary, to fill our tank. As it turned out, a little bit of luck made it very easy. As the anchor went down, a large school of green jacks, being chased by dolphins, hid under the boat. It was like fishing in a fish bowl! We filled the tank on that very first night and were underway for Acapulco at sunrise.

Little Bat Islands

2012

NORTH AMERICA

Captain's log, December 18

0913, A/C to various inbound courses to round Pta. Grifo, enter Acapulco Bay

Acapulco, the famous Mexican resort harbor known worldwide in the tourist industry as the "Pearl of the Pacific," was no longer a pearl. I had visited many times in years past, but on this return, ten years later, I was shocked.

For years, I had watched the harbor slowly fill with trash from a hillside slum in one corner of the bay. The floating debris and trash bags became such a problem, the water skiing boats were put out of business. Boat generators sucked the bags into their cooling systems and overheated, and the government did nothing. Finally, after a massive storm created a giant mudslide, washing the shacks and even coffins of the dead off the hillside, the government funded a half dozen basura (trash) boats to patrol the bay and skim off the trash. But a bigger problem came to Acapulco, and we had a front row seat.

A drug war broke out, and the cartels were locked in brutal warfare. Gunfire could be heard nightly on the outskirts of the city. The magazines and newspapers sold at the sidewalk kiosks were full of horrific photos of the murdered. Cruise ships stopped calling, and the normally safe Club de Yates marina had a full-time Special Forces unit living above the office. Kidnapping was big business, and members of the club arrived in bulletproof cars, driven by professional drivers. Hotels were largely empty, and foreign tourists deserted the beaches. This was our reality when we anchored off the Club de Yates marina.

From the smallest towns to the largest cities in Mexico, there are people who know everything that is going on. If you are friends with those people, it can be a good thing. In our case, the crew and I became very popular with the basura boats, waving one over on our first morning. After giving the three-man crew cash (not required) for picking up our single bag of trash and, more importantly, some good food, the word went out that Capitán Luís, on *Moana*, was a friend. The poor men were paid a pitiful daily wage that could not support their families, so the boats took turns visiting us every day. These were the men who knew everything that was going on in the harbor. They also knew who the bad guys were. We were never paid a visit in the night by anyone who might do us harm.

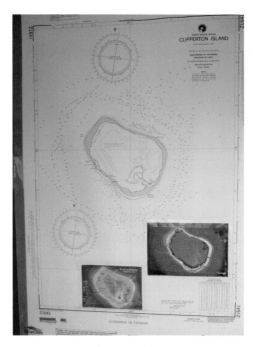

Clipperton charts

I hired a safe driver and picked up the family and guests at the airport on Christmas Eve. It was a different but happy celebration, and we were underway at first light the next day.

Captain's log, December 28

Underway for Clipperton Island. 0000 pos 11° 16.4' N, 108° 06.6' W, in light rain.

We timed our arrival for sunrise, and the moment I dropped our speed for trolling, we had a strike on every lure in the water.

Named after a British pirate, Clipperton Island was a forbidding wind- and surf-swept ring of coral around a large, brackish-water lagoon. Actually an atoll, the only remaining part of the volcano that sank eons ago was a big chunk of ragged volcanic rock, aptly known as simply "the rock." The ugly gray-and-black rock that once housed a crude lighthouse stood twenty-nine meters above the sea, and it was so different from the rest of the island, it looked totally unnatural. Only a few feet above the sea, the narrow, circular strip of "land" was a strange mix of a broken coral crust over sand, and including the lagoon, only a little over two square miles. Dotted with only a few groves of coconut palms, it was home to many sea birds, crabs, and rats. Close offshore, we circled the island, looking for an anchorage, and quickly understood our research was correct: 670 nautical miles offshore, Clipperton was not for amateurs.

Baby booby and crab

As expected, the bottom dropped off steeply, close to the island, so there was not a single, real anchorage. This was not unlike many of the places we had visited in our travels, so our solution was the same. We dropped anchor on the lee side of the island, on a ledge just outside the surf, and used a bridle off the starboard side to keep the boat broadside to the strong trade winds. This kept us close enough to hold anchor, and with our bows into the swell that wrapped the island, we were very comfortable. The risk in using this technique was the chance that the trade winds could stop, and the boat could swing into the surf, so a watch and daily weather predictions were the norm. The winds that fueled the powerful surf all around the island never slowed.

Of course, the adventurers aboard *Moana* were ready to explore the island, but the unrelenting waves were a serious obstacle. From a distance, surf never looks as big and powerful as it is, so a realistic strategy, based on experience, is essential to avoiding someone's getting hurt. It was too big to risk using the small boat all the way to the beach, so we found a channel where the surf was not quite as big, motored halfway in, and the landing crew bailed out as the small boat raced out and over the next set of waves. This still meant the landing crew, including Martine, had to swim past a thick, powerful, shore break. With backpacks carrying cameras, water, clothes, etc., this was not for the faint of heart and was a testament to the courage, confidence, and physical ability of our adventurers.

Our anchorage

Nesting boobies and WWII machinery

Once they were ashore, photo opportunities lay in every direction. Boobies, terns, shearwaters, petrels, and other bird species were nesting all over the crusty "ground," while frigates occupied the coconut palms. Hungry orange crabs patrolled and cruelly attacked newborn birds.

The ragged "rock" was full of holes and caves and was home to the reclusive red-tailed tropic bird and others. At the same time, it was like something out of a Hollywood sci-fi movie, where the script explains the demise of a prior civilization, and one finds, here and there, grave markers, machinery, sacks of rock hard cement, a rough shack with "Go Chargers" painted on it, and even an old WWII Jeep. A couple of wrecked steel fishing boats add to the drama, and, chillingly, the script includes wooden ladder rungs, sturdily fastened very high into a coconut palm, to scan the horizon for a rescue vessel.

To add an unusual twist to the movie, the following day a Frenchman is brought, via chartered Mexican boat, to the island; once a year, the French government sends someone to replace its flag, which flies at an official-looking concrete marker and steel flagpole.

The boat was chartered for only an overnight stay, so the Frenchman had to get onto the island, replace the flag, and be back on the boat before it departed the next day. After a frightening experience in their small boat and the wild surf, the Frenchman replaced the flag, but he was so unnerved he refused to return to the boat for the night. The Mexican captain

"The Rock"

radioed and, while laughing, told me they had named the Frenchman "Rat Man" because he told the Mexican crew, "I would rather sleep with rats than swim with sharks!" And indeed, we saw him rig a hammock between two coconut palms, where he slept for the night.

But the stars of the comedy show were the brown boobies. Juveniles, who were actually adult size but not yet able to fend for themselves, came to the boat en masse. They loved the hand-rails that ran around the forward deck, where they perched, looked brainless, and crapped. Joubert and I took turns with a water hose or whatever we could think of to drive them off, but they would instantly return. Finally, Joubert rubbed a bar of soap over the railing, and the "flipping and slipping show" was on! As they landed on the smooth, metal railing, their wet feet slipped on the soap and the resulting dance to gain balance was hilarious. After a while, however, they would manage to get erect and at times, a dozen or more would be lined up next to each other on the rail. But after a few moments, boobies being boobies, one would reach over and peck his neighbor, throw them both off balance and, like dominoes, bird after bird would go over backwards. I laughed myself silly.

We came for the big yellowfin tuna, and it was everything we hoped for. The Clipperton experience was hard core, but the fishing made it all worthwhile. It was so good, in fact, our deck freezer could not freeze the big fillets quickly enough, and we had to enact a one-fish-per-day limit on the giant fish. Numerous tuna in the 100–200-pound range got a "Get Out of

Jail Free" card, but even so, both the deck freezer and galley freezer were full to the maximum when we hauled the anchor on the last day.

Captain's log, January 8

Pos 18° 01.3' N, 103° 44.1' W, about 30 mi SW Pta San Telmo, Mexico

Sometimes sharing our ocean with dangerous people was a reality for us. Sooner or later, boats like *Moana*, that really travel long range, will be confronted with that reality, as we were, offshore Mexico. Almost directly on our course line, I saw the open boat from quite a distance in the bright sunshine and calm seas. As we approached, I kept the panga-style Mexican fishing boat in my binoculars and saw no sign of life aboard. Indeed, there was no one aboard the new, twenty-two-foot fiberglass open boat.

Alongside, it was not difficult to understand the boat was part of a drug- and/or people-smuggling operation. The boat was brand new, fresh out of the mold, with no bottom paint, or any hardware attached. A very nice, 200HP, Yanmar outboard engine was fitted on the transom, controlled at a nice, aft console; five full athwartship benches could easily seat twenty-five people, with enough room left for the eighteen plastic ten-gallon fuel drums and several bags of food and water we saw aboard. Only one fuel drum had been partially used, which told us the operation was prepared to travel far but had apparently found the pickup vessel early on. Floating along, abandoned in the open ocean, it was hard to believe that a brand new boat, representing so much money, could be trash. A one-time, throwaway item. We took a couple of photos and left her where we found her.

Captain's log, April 7

Anchor aboard, 0251, dep Club de Yates anchorage, idling outbound, CC E, underway for Clipperton

For Michel, Clipperton was so exciting it deserved another trip. But landing in a drug war zone, the long run out, and the hard-core fishing were a bit too much for the ladies. Martine and friends stayed home, and a boys' trip was organized. This included Charles, one of Michel's nephews, who was my assistant surgeon from the Osprey Reef trip. Charles was afflicted with some kind of strange fishing disease and was foaming at the mouth before the island was in sight.

A return to Clipperton was no small thing for the crew and me. It was not planned and necessitated a return trip to San Diego and another run down the coast to Bahia Tenacatita. For once, luck was really with us, and we had very good weather for almost all those 4,000 miles. We filled the bait tank with both green jacks and caballitos and rolled into Acapulco to the wide grins of our basura boat friends.

Fishing boat wreck

The drug war had evolved to the point the government felt compelled to do something, and everywhere we saw oversized pickup trucks seating six black-masked special forces and a mounted fifty-caliber machine gun. The idea was to make the citizens feel safe, but the war had become so deadly, with so many innocents caught in the mix, everyday people trusted no one. With reports of problems going out, there were few visiting yachts, and no one staying for long. At night, I could see small unlit boats moving around the harbor, but none approached *Moana*. Before leaving Acapulco on our previous trip, we had given the trash boat men and their families enough fish to feed them for some time....

Michel and the boys were late arriving at the airport. With my approved driver and big van, I was relieved when their plane finally arrived. The late-night trip to the yacht club, through empty streets and past numerous pickup-truck commandos, must have been a real eye-opener for them. A strange way to start a trip, and we left at first light the next day.

Castaways lookout palm

Young brown boobies

Smuggling *panga*, abandoned far offshore

Captain's log, April 9

1700 pos 10° 18.1' N, 109° 10.9' W, approaching anchorage

I was not surprised to see another boat fishing at Clipperton. Royal Polaris, a big, impressive sport-fishing boat that ran out of San Diego, was owned and operated by Frank LoPreste, almost a living legend on the waterfront. Frank was one of very few captains in the long-range fleet who ranged so far south, and he was the pioneer of sport fishing at Clipperton. Our meeting was extraordinary because he and I were teenage deckhands together, fifty years previous. He had no idea I was the captain on *Moana* when I called on the radio.

"That you, Frank?"

(pause)… "Yeah. You that big cat?"

"Yeah. How long you been here?"

(pause)… "Just got here today. Who am I talking to?"

"Voice from your past, Frank. Think *Sea Raider*."

"Impossible."

"Yeah. Lew Maurer, Frank."

French flag and official marker

This was our opening conversation, and our daily talks were a high point in the trip for me. As the days went by, we shared all the stuff fishing captains talk about, plus our personal histories. It was simply wonderful to have such an exchange with another captain who, like me, had spent a lifetime on the water and was still loving every moment.

We dropped anchor on the same ledge as before and set up the side bridle. As before, we were just outside the surf, with the bow into the swells wrapping the island, and very comfortable. The difference this time was immediately obvious. No one would be going ashore. The surf was so big, it was out of the question. Huge, dark blue breakers rose from the deep and pounded the entire island with jaw-dropping power. Met by the ever-present trade winds, plumes of spray, sparkling in the bright sunshine, blew off the tops and landed far behind the swells. The wildness of this remote atoll was on full display, and we would be fishing only.

Trade winds meeting big surf

"Fishing only" was fine with the wild bunch aboard on this trip. Michel was always the leader of the pack, but the rest of the group needed no motivational speeches. From the big boat at anchor, while trolling, or from the small boat, day or night, the energy and enthusiasm was never ending. Trolling from the big boat became almost too easy, so our anglers began using the small boat.

Set up perfectly for fishing and diving, including high-tech electronics, our small boat was quite the "war wagon," in fisherman's jargon. Low to the water, fighting and landing big tuna in such a small boat, on light tackle, was like hand-to-hand combat. Bouncing around in the choppy seas, fights were long and the big fish showed no mercy with our lightweight tackle. After two carbon-fiber reel seats exploded, we switched to medium gear.

But when we stopped trolling and began using live bait from the small boat, the real adrenalin pumping action evolved. This required much more skill than dragging artificial lures around, and it was far more exciting. With six to ten live baits in a bucket, we would run high speed to where we saw birds diving over a school of feeding tuna. Judging the direction of the school, we would run in front of the advancing fish and drop back a live bait. What made this so exciting was the wild scene all around. With the remote island and black rock for a backdrop, the now-drifting dinghy was bouncing around in the choppy seas as the noise from the screaming, diving birds increased. Both birds and tuna, wildly chasing a school of bait, turned the sea all around into a mass of churning white water. Floating directly in the path of

Boobies diving on feeding tuna

the chaos, anticipating the powerful strike and sound of the screaming reel, we were totally spellbound every time!

This was no sure deal every time. Judging the direction of the school and positioning the small boat required perfect timing. Many times, the school would turn or go down, the birds would fly off, and Michel would soon be looking for another school. But for sheer excitement in such a wild place, it was heart-stopping action!

Captain's log, April 19

1200 pos 14° 21.7' N, 103° 22' W, in very good traveling weather with light breeze NNE @ 10kts, wind driven seas 3–4ft, long swell S @ 7–8ft. Hazy & hot.

Unlike our previous return trip to the mainland, we had beautiful, calm seas almost all the way back to Acapulco. At one point, the sea went glassy smooth, which allowed me to glance a small head, rising and falling in the distance. Changing course, we soon came alongside a huge mass of lost longline fishing gear. It was made of polypropylene, which was why it was floating. It was a death trap to turtles and whales, and a very real danger to boats. A young Olive Ridley turtle, hopelessly

Hookup! Louis on rod, Captain Michel at controls   Battle won

entangled by its front flippers, fought a losing battle to free himself. Carefully keeping the endless coils of line out of our propellers, Joubert hauled the mass into the cockpit while Michel and Jean-Pierre dove in and cut the poor animal free. But the turtle was totally exhausted and they feared he would sink out and drown, so they brought him back to the boat. Resting without any struggle, we could plainly see the abraded skin on his flippers and wondered how long he had fought for his life. Rescuing and releasing such a beautiful creature seemed the perfect end to the Clipperton sci-fi movie, where the viewer is left to contemplate the past and future effects of man on nature.

Captain's log, April 24

1800 pos abeam Punta Ventosa light, .25 mi, A/C to 070° to parallel coast, .5 mi off

For once, the screaming winds and flying sand offshore Salina Cruz, in the Gulf of Tehuantepec, were still. It was eerie to make the close-in run, along the beach, in bright sunshine and flat calm sea. In these rare conditions, we enjoyed clearly seeing a coastline that was notorious for many tragedies.

Jean-Pierre to the rescue

Captain's log, April 27

1556 pos entering Los Sueños Marina @ idle

We were here eleven years before, when Bill Royster, an American, began construction of Los Sueños (the dream). Years before, on a fishing trip with his buddies, they anchored in Herradura Bay, looked around at the incredible setting, and the idea for a marina was conceived. It was no small undertaking, however. Millions of dollars were spent on the project, which also included development of the land around the marina. Many unexpected obstacles had to be overcome, but Bill had the resources, the imagination, and the stamina to see it through. The finished marina was really a masterpiece in every way and presently enjoyed worldwide fame. After all the miles recently behind us, Joubert, our current cook, Nadine, and I were happy to have such a beautiful place to catch up on rest and maintenance.

A fifteen-minute walk from the marina took me to a beautiful golf course behind a five-star hotel. Located just above a nearby beach, the golf course flanked a lovely creek that snaked out of a deep canyon and emptied into a stunning lagoon. The steep sides of the canyon were densely forested and included several varieties of giant trees. I discovered the golf course one day and, after finding it was seldom used due to the hot weather, decided it would be a great way to get my daily exercise away from the boat. After only two or three walks on the footpath, my walks turned from exercise to wildlife photography. The rainforest on each side of the golf course was home to wildlife I had never seen before, and in numbers that amazed me. The wildlife was so prolific, I discovered something new almost every day. Unless it was raining hard, I explored my jungle paradise every afternoon. But there was a surprising learning curve. The early part of my walk took me past some bushes that were home to birds I came to know were brown jays. They would immediately make quite a lot of noise as soon as they saw me. But as the days went by, and I quietly passed by at about the same time, they seemed to accept my presence and stopped their loud protesting.

It was like the keys to the kingdom! The brown jays were the sentries, and their silence signaled all was well in the forest. Magically, it was as if I was somehow accepted into another world. Birds and animals were suddenly everywhere, allowing me to come close for spectacular encounters and wonderful photo opportunities. Day after day, I returned to the boat, opened my books, and identified new species of animal life.

Captain's log, July 15

1900 pos entering Chatham Bay, Isla Coco, in light rain

After all it took to get the permits and make the tough grind out to Isla Coco, our return to the wild, remote island was a disappointment. The weather was simply awful, with wind and constant rain every day. The anchorage was rolly, the fishing was poor, and with the dark skies, the diving was not spectacular. Never discouraged by anything, however, the kids turned to exploring and wound up having a lot of fun. As usual, pushing the limits of everything sane, I was happy they survived things like hiking vertical mountain trails, or taking a shower high in a waterfall, where a misstep could have been a tragedy. All grown up, they were definitely the fearless offspring of parents who led by example.

Captain's log, July 25

0820 pos off Murcielagos Ranger station. Ranger off, anchor down in 30ft, sand and rock.

After the dreary, rainy weather of Isla Coco, the arid landscape of the northern, Guanacaste coast of Costa Rica was a welcome change, and a great place to finish our summer trip. Ruggedly beautiful with long, white beaches, the low land was indented with pristine bays, sometimes backed

Donald, Thomas, and Rachel; Isla Coco shower time

by rivers and lagoons. The bays provided calm anchorages, and the lagoons fantastic exploring in the kayak. Very different animal life lived there, including caimans, a type of crocodile.

Small rock islands that we fished so many years before again held big cubera snapper, and this time it was Donald catching dinner. Because this part of Costa Rica was well known for the strong, offshore winds known as "Papagayos," few yachts cruised here. This was always a puzzle to me because it meant ocean swells flattened by the winds, which meant calm anchorages if one knew where to go. We did not see another boat.

We could not resist another trip offshore to the Bat Islands and, as before, had a great time diving in the warm, blue-purple water around the unique rocks. The area was a National Park, and swarming with big snappers and amberjack. Our old ranger buddy, Freddie, now the head ranger, tried to be strict with all visitors. He was not completely successful with us, but when their government boat broke down and we brought one of his rangers out to the station, we were "okay."

Donald, kayaking in the lagoon

Costa Rica caiman; unlike saltwater crocodiles, very shy

Above: Graceful flight of zopilote; one of my favorite photos   Below: Los Sueños lagoon

Above: Brown jays, the rain forest sentries   Below: Tiger heron   Following page: Jesus Christ lizard, so named because it can run on top of the water

Above: Pizote, member of the raccoon family Below left: Zopilote (turkey vulture), feeding on dead pizote Below right: Iguana we saw daily and named Oscar

Above: Crested guan, a large, beautiful bird hunted and eaten by locals   Below: Green iguana   Right: Capuchin monkey, curious and unafraid

Above: Rainforest beehive   Below left: Broad-shouldered hawk at moment of landing   Below right: Scarlet macaw, always found near ripening fruit or berries

Above: White egret and roseate spoonbill   Below: Tent-making bats; they spent five days in this tree

Left: Green spiny lizard   Above: Collared anteater; note size of claw, for ripping open ant nests   Below: Chestnut-mandibled toucans

Above: Turquoise-browed motmot   Below: Pygmy owl; allowed me to come very close and never blinked

Above: Juvenile heron   Below left: Two-toed sloth   Below right: Leaf-dwelling crab

Darien girls in typical canoe

2013

NORTH AMERICA, CARIBBEAN

Captain's log, December 30

1658, anchor dn in 24ft, sand, Bahia Caracoles. Stunning anchorage with small river, detached rocks, beautiful old growth rain forest all around. Low swell, calm anchorage.

All our pre-trip research said it was safe, but as it got darker and the open boat off our stern remained stationary, it looked anything but. In my binoculars, I stared into the binoculars of one of the four heavily armed men. The old olive-green open boat and the camouflage clothes made me wonder why we were there, only a few miles from the Panama-Columbia border. Worse, I had dropped anchor behind a small island, and with the mainland to port and a rock reef to starboard, the gunboat sat blocking our only way out.

When it became completely dark, the radio finally came alive in Spanish.

"You cannot stay here. Raise your anchor and follow us."

This was our introduction to the Panamanian government's anti-smuggling unit. These were serious people who, it was explained to me later, dealt with drug-running killers on a regular basis. We silently followed their boat around the nearby point and into a small bay. In the total blackness, we had no idea of what was around us, or what this place was. Our only clue was the occasional crowing of roosters and the smell of smoke from a dying fire. It was a very calm anchorage, but I doubt anyone slept well.

The children of Guayabito, a small settlement at the edge of the jungle, were the morning greeters, paddling out in their beautiful canoes and making us feel safe and welcome. This was the Darien, home to the mysterious jungle people who had lived here for centuries. I knew this because, many years ago, I fell in love with their exquisite, handcrafted canoes that they sometimes sold in Balboa. I tried on two occasions to purchase one but was unsuccessful.

The officer in charge of the patrol boat came by to casually greet us and tell us what was safe and unsafe in the area. He then told Michel of a nearby river that was interesting, and after breakfast a group of *Moana* explorers were off to travel further into the jungle of the Darien. Many hours later, our adventurers came back with different versions of their experience. It must have been a tense day, as sandbagged military outposts and automatic weapons seemed to outweigh the wildlife experience!

This, the southern coast near the Colombian border, proved to be as remote and pristine as other places, thousands of miles away. One day, when the drug wars are done, this stretch of coastline will be a cruiser's paradise. Mile after mile, we enjoyed scenic, calm anchorages, empty beaches, and dense rain forest. With no human footprints on the sand, the sounds of the many birds and animals in our ears, and steam rising off the jungle every morning, we were again in a wild place.

Captain's log, January 6

0807 pos drifting and waiting for high slack off Boca de San Pedro

Running the most dangerous entrance to the river running up to Pedregal, Panama's third largest city, was probably the best test of my surfing knowledge in all my years aboard. The entrance shortened the trip up the river by many miles, but it was necessary to run through extremely shallow water, tight between surf and sand bars in the narrow channel. With absolutely no room for error, the passage was visually intense. The rest of the run up the river, difficult due to the muddy water and many shallows, was almost boring by comparison. Several of our guests flew out of Pedregal, and we followed a fishing boat back down the river. He did not attempt my shortcut, but the tide was wrong anyway, and we followed him through narrow, serpentine channels for several hours before reaching the sea.

Captain's log, January 16

0944, ar Shelter Bay Marina, secure boat stbd side-to

A last trip to Cuba was on the schedule. We had an uneventful transit of the canal and found ourselves waiting for weather at Shelter Bay Marina, on the Cristobal, or Caribbean, side. Day after day, we hoped and prayed for a cold front to shut off the strong winds in the Caribbean, but it never happened. Our weather guys told us we would not get a decent window for weeks, so we prepared for serious weather and shoved off. It was one of the worst beatings in all our years. I tried every tactic I had learned over the years, but there was no way to lessen our misery. It went on for over ninety-six non-stop, rotten hours before we reached the Caymans. I would not have blamed Joubert or Nadine if they took the first flight out of Georgetown, but I doubt it even crossed their minds. We were a team, and we took care of each other. The boat was fine and none of us were hurt, but we had been on the losing end of a real street fight. Besides the rest we needed, the best thing about Grand Cayman was the great stores for supplies, all near the marina at Governor's Quay. With supplies flown in daily, the outrageous prices were apparently no problem for those hiding their black money in numbered accounts. We caught up on sleep, Nadine stocked the boat with the best supplies and produce on the planet, and we were off for Cuba.

Anti-smuggling outpost

Wanted poster, Panama style

Poisonous frog

Captain's log, February 23

Underway on Grand Cayman–Cuba run in very good weather, low seas, light breeze. 0000 pos 20° 35' N, 81° 28.5' W.

We were last in Cuba in 2002, eleven years before. I had stayed in touch with Pire all that time, but seeing him again, in Cayo Largo, was a special reunion. As our agent, he had helped us in ways we could not expect from anyone else. I reminded him of his letter that kept me out of serious trouble, and we had a good laugh. Like so many Cubans, he had worked hard to survive and hoped change would finally come. Our meeting turned to what the changes in Cuba might mean for our current visit. He knew we would go straight to Jardines de la Reina, the Gardens of the Queen, and came right to the point.

"Avalon is still the only game in the gardens, and Pepe is running the show even more strict than before. You will be remembered and watched constantly. Because of what happened before, you can expect to be boarded by the military."

After eleven years' absence, this surprised me, but the Cuban government was well known to have a long memory, and somewhere out there was a naval officer who would probably like to even the score. We would have to be careful.

Captain's log, March 13

0700 pos 21° 08.2' N, 79° 31.2' W, A/C to enter channel

In a word, I was embarrassed. I somehow missed the channel and coasted right up on a sand bar at the entrance to Cayo Breton, a very good anchorage we had used before. The fishermen's sticks were no longer there, but I had my GPS numbers and knew where the channel was, so I was astonished to run out of water before getting into the lagoon anchorage. With the clever design of *Moana*, which kept our propellers and rudders out of danger in shallow water situations, I knew we were okay, but it was still embarrassing. The tide was rising, and after an hour or so, I was able to power off the sand. But something was wrong. No matter how perfectly I positioned the boat, I could not find the channel. The shallow water was clear, but all we could see was sand.

Three days later, we could not locate the channel into Cinco Balas, one of the prettiest lagoon anchorages in the gardens. Once again, the sticks fishermen place on the channel sides were missing. Michel was so frustrated, he explored with the small boat for some time, but even with the great electronics aboard our little sea truck, he could not find the channel either. While this was going on and I was idling offshore, the Avalon supply boat passed by and a familiar voice called out. It was "Elvis." He remembered us, saw what we were doing, and called on the radio.

"Luís, all the south-facing channels are full of sand, so you cannot use a single one anymore. In 2004, a hurricane swept over the gardens and the giant waves pushed sand into all the channels. If you want to use those anchorages I showed you before, you will have to go all the way around the cayos and come in from the other side."

This was not good news. There were other anchorages, but the ones we liked were so beautiful and calm, we knew the trip would not be the same. The kids were not with us on this trip, and instead we had several couples who had never seen Cuba. For them, the Gardens of the Queen, even in the other anchorages, were paradise, so the trip was still a good one. And I am sure they were impressed by the patrol boat and serious attitude of the officer in charge!

At the edge of a cayo, behind the mangroves, a small patrol boat appeared in my binoculars. Michel and Jean-Pierre were scuba diving, a prohibited activity, but the patrol did not see them going into the water. When they came to the surface, I was able to tell Michel about the coming inspection, and they swam to the side of the boat where they could not be seen. By the time the patrol boat figured out what was going on and got underway, we had all the scuba gear hidden in an engine room. It was a bit ridiculous, because Michel never used scuba gear for spearfishing, and they were just enjoying the underwater beauty of the coral reef. The inspection was over quickly, but the message was clear: "We remember. We are watching."

That old saying, "You can't go back," seemed to apply to this trip. I had hoped to see our fishermen friends again, but the hurricane had changed the bottom so much, their turtle grass fishing grounds had been destroyed and they had moved on. Even the delicious jutías, the tree

Swimming in the Gardens of the Queen

rats of the mangroves, had been wiped out. Fortunately, the unbelievably clear, warm water, the spectacular coral reefs, and swarms of all kinds of fish were there. But for us, the magic of the Jardines de la Reina would never be the same.

Michel, Martine, and guests departed in Santiago. I looked forward to coming back to the beautiful city and nice marina, but the hurricane did not spare this part of Cuba either. The damage to the concrete docks at the marina told the story of the storm's fury. It was hard to imagine winds powerful enough to cause such damage, but nine years after, the evidence was still everywhere. Palm trees uprooted or with their trunks snapped in half still lined the roads. It was awful and, for people already so poor, so unfair.

Political change had come as well. My marina manager friend was gone, as were almost all of the typewriter-pounding employees. No one could tell me what happened to the manager, but I was told the "employees" were security and with the economy in shambles, they were downsized by a failing system. The dusty video screen no longer played marching children. After all the Cuban people's years of suffering, they would have to endure more.

Captain's log, March 25
1502, anchor dn in 37ft, mud, "The Flats," Colon

Change was coming to Panama. Construction had finally begun on the very ambitious project of building a new route through the canal. It was to be much larger, to allow the big

Underwater beauty of "Jardines de la Reina"

Panamax ships to transit. This project had been a very big discussion for many years, but it had many potential downsides. Finally, the engineering challenges were thought solved and construction was underway. The earthmoving equipment and the scale of the cut were larger than anything I had ever seen. On a beautiful, sunny day, we got a great pilot and went alone and center chamber all the way through the locks on the Cristobal side, and alongside a tug on the Balboa side. Pete was there to greet us; he took care of our papers, and we were off for Costa Rica.

Captain's log, April 2

0900, ar Los Sueños Marina, Costa Rica

This was to be the last trip on *Moana* with all the family aboard, and since the marriage of Thomas, the eldest son, to Marie Christine, and the arrival of "Prince Henri," the family now numbered eight. For a grand finale, to cap all our years and thousands of miles, we planned to visit Nicaragua, Costa Rica, and Panama over a six-week period.

The logistics of this trip were daunting for both owners and crew. Michel had to find a way to get his kids away from their jobs or schools all at the same time, and arrange all the flights from Europe. For myself, I had to find agents in advance who could clear us in and out of the different countries, and arrange payments for cruising permits and permits to visit national parks such as Islas Murcielagos (Bat Islands). The usual logistics, such as fuel, food, and maintenance supplies, were a challenge because, aside from produce we knew we could purchase at farmers markets, we knew we would not be able to purchase anything in Nicaragua. We would have to have everything imaginable aboard before leaving Costa Rica.

Moana was moored in Los Sueños and would start the trip from there, clearing out with Customs and Immigration on July 5, 2013. The plan was to arrive in Nicaragua several days before Michel and Martine, to make sure the boat was ready and Nadine had time to top off the provisions with fresh produce. Our destination was Puesta del Sol, a resort on a big river system on the northwest coast of Nicaragua. We had never visited any port in Nicaragua, so I was lucky to find a boat in Los Sueños that frequently visited the resort. Joe Crawford, the captain of *Rum Runner*, was a great source of information. He gave me all the usual local knowledge stuff, but most importantly he told me about the river entrance that could be dangerous on a big swell and/or ebbing tide.

We got underway at 1800 and ran up the coast of Costa Rica in good weather. Live bait was always important for us, so we ran to Bahia Santa Elena, just south of the Nicaragua border, and anchored up over a sand bottom in sixty feet, pretty much in the center of the beautiful bay. The area was previously owned by the ex-dictator of Nicaragua but now was part of a big national park of Costa Rica. It is one of the most pristine, beautiful bays in Central America, so it's nice to know there won't be any fast food outlets built on the shores anytime soon. All alone, we got a beautiful sunset over the bay.

The bait fish did not show for several hours, but around 2100 they began to bite well and we had all we could use in the tank by 2300. A nice mix of green jacks and small jack crevalle—perfect for fishing marlin or tuna, or on the down rigger for big snapper. At 2330, we had the anchor aboard and departed Bahia Santa Elena. As soon as we cleared the bay we were greeted by a screaming offshore breeze and steep, wind-driven seas, and we had to run tight to the coast to get out of the snap rolling we really disliked in beam seas.

We arrived offshore Puesta del Sol the next day and, per Joe's suggestion, called the marina on VHF 16 to ask for a guide to bring us in. It was a Sunday, and apparently no one was listening or working, so we were on our own. The privately maintained buoys were well done, so the approach through the surf was easy to see. I had timed our arrival for high slack and, being a lifelong surfer, I picked a lull and ran the channel with no problems. A good-sized swell was running, and I was impressed by the big surf on both sides of the channel. I knew immediately this was a popular spot for international surfers. I also knew I would not be running the channel during an ebb tide and/or during a huge swell.

Up a rock strewn, serpentine channel, Marina Puesta del Sol was a beautiful resort on the bank of Estero Asseradores. The pristine setting was absolutely stunning, with untouched mangrove-lined shores of the estuary stretching to the eastern horizon, and a towering volcano in the distance. We were greeted by some friendly workers as we tied up the boat at the small marina and began settling in.

It was July 10, around 1720, and all our careful planning for this last trip with all the family aboard was changed in a heartbeat. *Chipolopolo*, a hot, go-fast sport fisher we knew from Los Sueños, had just returned from fishing offshore. They were hooking up their shore power when a bolt of lightning cracked nearby, lighting up the sky from horizon to horizon. The flash and deafening "crack" were simultaneous, with concussion I could feel inside the boat. When smoke rolled out of the salon air conditioning, we knew we had been hit.

Chipolopolo was two slips away and we saw the crew scrambling immediately, so we knew they were hit as well. This was a different situation than I had ever experienced in the past, when I was hit by lightning on at least three different occasions on three different boats. On those occasions, the boat was struck high on the superstructure, on an air terminal or antenna, with little or no damage at all. This time, there was damage. A lot of it.

Like an invisible knife with a blade the thickness of a human hair, the shock wave of electric energy passed through the boat in a microsecond, taking out every small-diameter electrical wire. In literally the blink of an eye, all of our sophisticated electronics were destroyed. This included the electronic interfaces for the main engines and steering. Even my pilothouse computer was fried, which took out satellite communication and email. *Moana* was dead in the water.

Because Puesta del Sol was located in such a remote area of Nicaragua, with no marine services available, our plan was to repair the important items that would allow us to run the boat back to Los Sueños, where parts and services for yachts were available. To make the boat seaworthy in the most minimal condition, we needed to replace the damaged navigation electronics, repair the steering system, and repair the electronics on the main engines. The main engines were a worry because Caterpillar had no way to know if the engines would run long enough to reach Costa Rica. They feared the port engine, which could be throttled up, would suddenly "derate" to idle RPM. Then, with both engines at idle, running anywhere in the open ocean, especially in weather, would be a problem.

Back at my office, Debbie purchased all the electronics and circuit boards that failed our test procedures to get the boat in a reasonable condition for the run to Los Sueños. We knew there could be more damaged components, or even weakened ones that could fail soon, but we had to take our chances. We flew the parts and my nephew, Bill, to Managua. Bill had installed all of the new navigation electronics the year before, and he also worked for us during the original construction of *Moana*. He was a good choice for the jobs at hand.

Bill and the electronics arrived in Managua on July 18, eight days after the lightning strike. We were excited to know he would come to the boat and hopefully get the electronics and steering systems up and running right away. We had no way to know we would not get our hands on our precious parts. Nicaragua Customs seized the parts at the airport. Nadine, who had gone to the airport to pick Bill up and knew all about corrupt customs officials, offered a huge amount of mordida ("the bite," a bribe). In any other Central American country, this would have gotten us our parts immediately, but this was Nicaragua. We hired Ratón Shipping, a customs brokerage company used by the owner of Puesta del Sol, to handle the release of our parts. They gave us a list of requirements that had to be met to obtain a release, and we gave them each and every detail asked for. Days dragged by as our agents promised us our parts and we made the three-plus-hour taxi trip from Puesta del Sol to Managua, day after day, only to hear customs make new demands.

Our agents knew that we needed the parts, especially the steering parts, in order to depart Nicaragua. It is common for customs brokers to know the government customs agents and work together to obtain the maximum bribe possible from desperate clients. Our agent told us of one client who had to wait six months for their goods, so I was sure they were playing the game with us too.

Captain's log, July 30

0922, underway in reverse, in Estero Aserradores, outbound at idle, various courses

We had no reason to believe Nicaragua Customs would release our parts, short of a massive bribe, so I decided to run for Costa Rica. We ordered a new, second set of all the electronics and related parts and had them shipped to Los Sueños, along with new ECMs and sensors for the main engines. After leaving the dock, we idled down the river in reverse, the only way I could steer the boat safely. Michel escorted us down the estuary in the dinghy, in case we needed tugboat assistance. It was the longest run of my life in reverse. Navigating the serpentine channel was not that difficult, but the surf at the entrance had my full attention. I was careful to time our departure to high slack, so there were no breaking waves in the middle of the entrance channel, but the channel was so narrow, I could not turn the boat around. I had to continue in reverse, coasting slowly over the swells to prevent swamping or rolling the boat. One of the most unnatural things I have ever done, it was an exciting experience to say the least!

Once outside the river, we were able to use the back-up steering system and start the long run to Los Sueños. With only paper charts and a compass, it was like being on one of the fishing boats I worked on as a young deckhand so many years ago. Three hundred and twenty four nautical miles later, we dropped anchor in Herradura Bay. It was 2014 on July 31, and as darkness fell I was glad I had paid attention to my old captains.

Our second set of electronics, main engines' controls, and steering parts were waiting for us in Los Sueños, and Bill worked his magic getting all of it up and running right away. As it turned out, however, he needed more than magic. We lacked engine and steering parts that could not reach us in time to save our trip.

Our original plan was to spend about a week with Michel and Martine aboard in Puesta del Sol and the northwest coast of Nicaragua, and then run south to Papagayo, on the northwest coast of Costa Rica. There, we would pick up guests for diving, exploring, and fishing around the Bat Islands before running south to Los Sueños. After the lightning strike disabled the boat, our guests flew to Managua, Nicaragua, and came to Marina Puesta del Sol, instead of Costa Rica. They had a great time in spite of the change, but now in Los Sueños, they departed for their homes in Europe. Louis stayed aboard.

The next part of the original plan was to run south from Los Sueños to Panama, where Thomas, Marie Christine, Prince Henri, Rachel, and Donald would join us for another three weeks. The plan was to run *Moana* to a beautiful resort on Isla Boca Brava, where they would come to the boat by a high-speed river boat down the jungle river from Pedregal. Michel had booked a charter fishing boat from the resort for three days. All of this was in question due to a lightning strike and repairs that hit a dead end.

A library-like silence descended. Like a black cloud hovering over the boat, it was a very unusual situation for a family that thrived on optimism and challenges. Especially for Michel. It was hard for Joubert and me to see them like this, so I made a decision not unlike the one I made to cross the Pacific in '03. I decided to lock off the starboard rudder dead ahead, and run with the port rudder only, at 1250 RPMs on port, and idle on starboard. We would run the trip at trolling speed, but if it all held together, we would run the trip! The mood on the boat changed from gray clouds to sunshine, and Nadine provisioned for another three weeks.

Captain's log, August 7
1113, dep Los Sueños Marina, idling outbound

In a marina full of high-end sport fishers that regularly cruise twenty-five to thirty knots, we must have looked strange as we slowly departed Herradura Bay, but we were on our way. I checked the autopilot one more time, to be sure, but it was still down. *Moana* steers exceptionally well on just one rudder, however, so hand steering for this trip would not be a big deal.

The weather was good, but by 2100, we were in rain squalls and lightning, offshore Punta Salsipuedes. We had run in lightning storms in many countries for many years, but now I was acutely aware of how destructive and dangerous it could be. After a very anxious night, we dropped anchor at 0736 off the old banana pier of Puerto Armuelles, Panama. The Customs and Immigration officials there are efficient and friendly, so we were cleared into Panama and on our way quickly. By 1539 on August 8, we dropped anchor off the Panama Big Game Fishing Club, on Isla Boca Brava. The small resort was well done, with a central lodge and surrounding cabins at the top of a steep jungle climb, with the reward of stunning, panoramic views all around. We were only one day late from our original schedule.

The resort had several good charter fishing boats, and Michel chartered a nice Bertram for three days. The captain and deckhand were local and knowledgeable fishermen and were a lot of fun. Each day was memorable: Louis caught a 500-pound blue marlin on day one, I caught a 140-pound yellowfin tuna on day two, and the final and most fantastic day was the best, with Joubert catching a beautiful big blue marlin while Louis took many great photos of the epic event! (For years, Joubert would seldom fish when the family was aboard, and never for marlin. He somehow considered it disrespectful to be having fun when he felt he should be working. On this trip Michel and I found a way to "insist" he share in the fun, so when he caught his big marlin it was truly a wonderful day!) We caught several other nice fish, including cubera snapper and amberjack. All in all, a great three days of fishing on an offshore, uncharted bank.

On the 12th, we ran out to Isla Montuosa. We had visited this wild, beautiful island several times many years before, and we were familiar with the rolly, often miserable anchorage. Having learned from those previous trips, we double-anchored with the technique that was invented there. In spite of the swell rolling through and the breezy weather, we were quite comfortable inside *Moana*. The fishing was not the same as in previous years, but we still managed to add to the freezer, including a really big amberjack.

We departed Montuosa on the 14th, running out to the Hannibal Bank. The Hannibal Bank is a well known seamount that sometimes produces fantastic fishing, but on this day the water was off color and there was no life on the bank. We ran on to Isla Coiba, anchoring in Bahia Hermosa, a beautiful, large bay with a long, smooth sand beach and small river. The river mouth is home to caimans, and also schools of snook, one of our favorite game fish. The bay was also home to interesting history, when it housed a prison and airstrip in the jungle on the north end. Years ago, a small sailboat anchored in the bay, and prisoners swam off the island, killed the husband, and forced his wife to sail them to the mainland. No such drama for us, thankfully; but after a beautiful first day, the weather turned poor, and we raised our double anchors and departed on the 16th.

Captain's log, August 18
   1700 pos 7° 23.8' N, 81° 37.7' W. Anchor dn in 34ft, off Pta Fea.

I had long wanted to explore the southwest end of Isla Coiba. Passing offshore on boats many years ago, I could see a pristine coast in my binoculars, with beautiful river mouths fronting dense rain forest. In those days, Isla Coiba was an island prison, with dangerous people freely wandering about. (It was well known that the government jailers locked themselves inside the prisons at night, for their own safety.) Now, the island was a national park and safe to visit, but the few rangers all lived on the north end of the island. On the south end of the island, charts and cruising guides listed many dangers to navigation and suggested more that remained uncharted, so no one went there. It proved to be everything I hoped for.

The surf at Rio Colorado and shallows inside the estuary at Boca Grande were perfect challenges for our adventurers. After all our years and travels, they loved the excitement and rewards found in such untouched places. We spent several sunny days there, exploring the rivers, beaches, and rain forests.

On August 22, we raised anchor off Boca Grande, Isla Coiba, and departed our last Panama island. It was a beautiful morning, and we idled off with the sounds of the monkeys and

Nicaragua swimming hole

parrots in the nearby jungle. We took one last look at this pristine island paradise and began the run back to Panama City.

Captain's log, August 23

1000 pos close abeam yellow "Y1," inbound at idle in heavy ship traffic

Moana arrived outside Marina Playita at 1029 on Saturday, the 23rd, and anchored in the small anchorage just off the entrance to the Panama Canal ship channel. Ironically, the sky went black and heavy rain pummeled the boat. But after all the challenges created by a bolt of lightning, after all the team efforts to make this last, wonderful, trip happen, a little rain could not dampen our spirits. Or keep me from deep sleep!

Our old friend, Taxi Billy, arrived with a nice van the next morning. Smiles, hugs, and tears all around, it was an emotional moment for all of us: the end of the *Moana* story; the end of the last chapter in a long book of epic adventures and unforgettable memories across so many oceans. The children, no longer little kids running around on deck, were keenly aware that this was probably the last time they would see *Moana* and their second-family crew. It showed.

Excited Joubert, the moment before release

Captain's log, September 30
San Diego, pos 32° 42' N, 117° 14' W, 118,100 nautical miles

Caribbean, Pacific, Tasman, Coral, Indian, South China, Arafura, Australasia, Micronesia. All names we knew intimately. Venezuela to the Maldives, Alaska to New Zealand. I like to think the ancient Polynesians, the finest navigators the world has ever known, would have been proud to know a catamaran, like their double hulled sailing canoes, and named *Moana*, had followed in their footsteps and, like those master mariners, understood they were like a tiny star in the vast night sky, carrying their family, hopes, and dreams to new lands.

River mouth, Rio Colorado

En route to the next horizon

Juan and paint crew longboarding forward cabin top

1998–2000

BACKSTORY, THE MAKING OF *MOANA*

Building large, expensive, custom yachts is a tough business. It requires enormous trust between builder and client, and even the best projects can turn sour and wind up in lawsuits. Sometimes a builder who has more than one boat under construction at the same time falls behind schedule with "boat A" and takes progress-payment money from "boat B" to finish the first vessel. This house of cards invariably collapses when there is then not enough money to finish boats B or C to the satisfaction of the clients. This was the scenario I found when I visited the boatyard.

In this case, boat B was Michel's boat. He was the owner of what was only an empty skeleton and had to retain the lawyers that I was now working for, to get clear title to his boat so he could find a way to finish his project. He had paid hundreds of thousands of dollars to fund his dreamboat, only to find out he was financing the completion of boat "A," while his project was barely inching along.

The focus of my report was to determine the quality of construction and how far along the project actually was. Fortunately for my client, the actual construction, thus far, was very good. But at this point, Michel had little confidence in either the seller or the boat builder and wanted to know what alternative actions could be taken to build the yacht. In short, he wanted to know who and where. What reputable boat builder, in San Diego or elsewhere, would be the best to finish the yacht?

Boats were my life. As a young boy, I grew up on fishing boats, beginning as the wash-down boy, the lowest rung on the ladder. By age twenty, I started my first business, a yacht maintenance company. In the ensuing years, I built and operated commercial fishing boats and yachts in all the current construction materials, and all of them to sophisticated designs. In 1980, I launched Compass Rose, a marine services company that came to specialize in representing owners with the construction of large, expensive, custom yachts. This was interesting work, and it took me to some of the finest boatyards in the world. Indeed, I was an expert, but the situation at hand had no easy solution.

For me, the easiest solution was to suggest the boatyard continue, with my company closely watching over all aspects of the construction, and I tried hard to do this. I met with the yard owners and their engineers on several occasions, and every time I came away knowing it would be a disaster for my client. We were simply worlds apart in our approach to boatbuilding. The sophisticated systems, particularly the backup systems that would be absolutely necessary in a long-range operation, would never happen.

Suggesting my company finish the yacht was a possibility I considered, but not without a lot of soul searching. I had the experience and knowledge to do it, and I personally knew the best craftsmen on the waterfront who would be happy to take on such a project with me. I understood the complex construction specified by the designers, and I even knew the shortcomings of one of the seller's previous boats, which would enable me to correct design problems and build an even better boat.

I also knew that building this boat would take at least a year and a half. That much time would take me out of contact with all the boatyards, yacht brokers, and insurance companies that were the source of my business. When the project was finished, I would have a difficult time getting current with emerging technology and regulations, and reconnecting with all my contacts who, in my absence, would have done business with someone else.

On top of all this, I knew that a custom, one-off project would not have the luxury of the manpower found in a typical, established boatbuilding company. I would organize a small but excellent group of craftsmen, but I would personally have to wear a lot of hats, including selecting all the equipment and engineering all the systems. It would take gut-wrenching determination and long hours to build the boat to a high standard. No one could appreciate how difficult in many ways this project would be for my little company, so when I presented this option to the lawyers, I told them I would only consider it after meeting with the client. I will always remember their unanimous and immediate response. "When you meet him, you will do it."

I finally met Michel and, over a nice, long dinner, he asked the questions I expected. A lot of questions. Finally, after relating just about everything in my life story, I had the opportunity to ask him some questions as well. After all, a project such as we were discussing would require knowing each other intimately. Communication and trust would have to be as perfect as human nature could allow. And that old devil, money, would have to be spent in huge amounts.

His response to my question of his business was direct and humorous. "I'm in the retail business," end of subject! This was my introduction to a very successful European businessman. English was not his native language, so it was much later before I learned it was modesty, and not a language issue, that motivated him to keep it so simple.

As we talked further, I was pleasantly surprised to learn he had owned a custom-built boat before. It was a sixty-five-foot cockpit motor yacht, built in Hong Kong. He had owned the boat for ten years, while cruising all over Indonesia with his wife and young children. I was glad to hear this for several reasons. Most of those boats were a maintenance nightmare and unreliable for offshore, long-range cruising. I guessed that after ten years of frustration and problems, my client would have clearly defined and sensible objectives in his new boat, and that proved to be the case. Finally, I knew that since he had been through the process before, he would understand

Master cabin laugh with Martine and Michel, the owners, and Jay and Sebastian, major players in the construction

the difficult nature of custom boatbuilding and be a good partner. His experience would be extremely valuable in making all the endless decisions in a quest to build a boat that, done right, would ultimately be an extension of him and would be the boat of his dreams.

By the time we finished dinner and the last glass of Chardonnay, Michel and I knew the chemistry was right. Our personalities were a great match, and our honest, straightforward way of communicating would serve us well in the long and difficult road ahead. The lawyers were right. I would do it. It was September 24, 1998.

My company set out to build a very special boat for Michel and his family. It would be a long-range boat that could visit the faraway, remote, and beautiful places of his dreams in comfort, safety, and complete reliability for extended periods. This required great equipment, well-engineered systems, and backup systems.

Fortunately for me, Michel visited the project at least once a month, and we were able to go over all my plans of the various equipment and especially the sophisticated systems I intended to build into the boat. I liked to describe systems that were typical of current boat builders, and how they differed from what I wanted to build, and especially the difference in costs. Michel was a great client because he knew from experience that he wanted first-class equipment and systems that would be dependable and reliable over the long term in primitive locales. In every case, he approved the best of the best.

Joubert

Shortly after one of their visits, I received a fax from Michel and his wife Martine. It was a letter that would change my life: They offered me the job to be the captain on their new boat. This came as a bit of a surprise because Michel well knew how serious I was about my company. He knew I had worked very hard to develop a thriving surveying and consulting business, taking advantage of many years of experience fishing, building, repairing, and operating boats. It was a lifetime and thousands of miles at sea, and with my present company, I was happy to be closer to home, occasionally running a boat for a delivery from one port to another to satisfy my lifelong love affair with the ocean.

Michel was clever. On a previous visit to the yard, I invited him to my apartment for dinner. Typically, Michel would take me to dinner at a very nice restaurant after a long day at the yard, where we would further discuss the boat project. I discovered Michel loved seafood as much as I did and thought I would impress him with a dinner of black cod, one of my favorites and a fish I was sure he had never eaten before.

My apartment was a bit of a maritime museum, with boat stuff from my life all over the place. Michel took it all in quickly and asked if I had a world atlas, which I did not. He wanted to show me where they had cruised in his previous boat, mostly in Indonesia. I had no experience in that part of the world but shared with him how, as a boy, I had spent many hours looking at world atlases, imagining how exciting it would be to visit all those faraway places, all those little islands that were just specks in the vast South Pacific.

The next day, he presented me with a huge world atlas. Beautifully done, it contained fantastic photos and was full of up-to-date information. And to plant the seed, Michel told me he wanted to visit those wild, faraway places. In fact, I well remember him saying, "If you can read about them, it is usually too late. We want to visit the really remote, primitive places before they are discovered and changed forever."

Although I initially did not consider accepting Michel's offer, the seed grew in my mind. After all, I thought, what could be more exciting than to visit such wonderful places with a great family, on the perfect boat?

Michel explained in his offer he considered me a very positive influence on his children, something he and Martine valued a lot. He also wanted me to consider the job on a long-term basis, providing continuity of what he saw as a lasting, valuable relationship with his family. For a man in love with the sea, my decision turned out to be easy. I was excited to accept Michel's offer, excited about the prospect of traveling to those little specks on the pages of my world atlas. Even with many years and thousands of miles of experience behind me, I could not guess how fantastic our adventures would prove to be.

Halfway into a marathon effort by my crew of very talented professionals, our project was blessed to have Joubert. He was an Indonesian man who had been the engineer aboard Michel's previous boat for four years. He was an amazing engineer and the family loved him, so Michel kept him on the payroll until we could use him on our project. I well remember picking him up at the airport, shaking his hand, and seeing for the first time the smile that endeared him to all who would meet him over the years.

Joubert's impact on the project was everywhere and not to be seen, all at the same time. He would help anyone with anything, all the while completing his own tasks. Without being in anyone's way, and largely unnoticed, he singlehandedly, and all by hand, prepared all of the interior teak-wood cabinetry, moldings, and wall panels and applied three coats of a special finish I had been using for many years. But the real value of bringing Joubert to the project was enabling him to help with the installations of all the equipment and systems. By the time the boat was launched, he knew every nut and bolt of everything aboard. This would prove to be immensely valuable in the years to come.

The final weeks and days before launch were a blur for me. On top of my project manager role, where I was required to be at least three people, I was now overwhelmed with endless details related to documentation, insurance, offshore delivery, boat movers, lease agreement, work-dock electrical considerations, etc. It was mid-morning, January 24, 2000, and my secretary, Debbie, cracked a bottle of Chardonnay over the bow of the boat, and christened her *Moana*, the Polynesian word for sea. We had already celebrated the launching on Michel's last visit, with a nice party for the crew, so the "official" christening turned out to be just

Ready for launch; big day for captain and crew

Debbie and me, while the crew worked feverishly on all the pre-launch details. It had been exactly sixteen months since I met Michel and told him I would do it.

The endless details, including all those on my captain's list, were finally coming to an end, and we had a firm departure date for our first trip. Next, we had to shut down our address and cancel all accounts with Compass Rose International, vacate our office, and dispose of leftover parts and supplies. Last on the list was to sell the boat to our customer, and put aboard the delivery crew, fuel, spare parts, food, and supplies.

The last payment to Compass Rose International was tendered and documented 4.7 nautical miles offshore, and Michel took official delivery of the boat of his dreams. We immediately got underway to return to the harbor and our work dock at the boatyard. Our project was officially over, and our feelings of accomplishment to have built such a beautiful boat were tangible, with congratulations, handshakes, and smiles all around. All those long, hard months were finally at an end, and we were proud of our individual and team achievements.

I paused at the top of the boatyard work-dock ramp and looked back at *Moana*. It was late afternoon, and Joubert was washing down our future home. No one will know, I thought, just how hard this was. She was truly a beautiful boat, and I allowed myself to feel quite proud. It was March 11, 2000.

GLOSSARY

Captain's log:

- » We used a 24-hour clock, so 0000 is midnight, 1300 is 1:00 p.m., etc.
- » **pos** is position, expressed in latitude & longitude, or distance off land
- » **kts** is knots, or nautical miles per hour
- » **seas** are usually wind-driven waves that can change at any time
- » **swells** are dominant ocean swells, can come from more than one direction at any given time, and usually last for long periods of time
- » **ft** is height of swells or seas, or depth of water, in feet
- » **RPM** is revolutions per minute, a measure of engine speed
- » **SOG** is speed over ground
- » **CC** is compass course
- » **A/C** is alter course, to new direction

Text:

- » **beam**: the width of the boat
- » **beam-to**: sideways to (the seas…)
- » **bilges**: interior spaces at very bottom of boat
- » **bow thruster**: small, power driven propeller unit to provide sideways thrust, usually mounted in an underwater tunnel, on the bow
- » **Ciguatera**: poisonous toxins found in some fish, usually those near coral reefs
- » **downhill traveling weather**: running with the ocean swells
- » **fenders**: soft, protective devices, usually rubber, hung between a boat and dock, seawall, or anything that could damage the yacht; in the Panama Canal, car tires are sometimes used
- » **high slack**: when the tide rises to its highest point of that tidal cycle and is neither rising or falling, usually the calmest time to enter or depart a harbor entrance prone to dangerous waves and/or current
- » **lee**: calm area, behind island or land mass that blocks the wind & current
- » **med-moored**: secured stern-to a seawall or marina dock, with anchor/s off bow
- » **range**: nautical miles a vessel can safely run on full load of fuel
- » **range (markers)**: lights or structures, which, when in alignment, mark the center of a channel
- » **slog**: physically difficult, usually long passage
- » **spindrift**: blowing foam, running down faces of swells, which begins to occur when wind velocity reaches 40 knots
- » **Tico**: local, friendly term for Costa Rica native
- » **uphill traveling weather**: running against the ocean swells

ACKNOWLEDGMENTS

As one would expect, the fifteen-year adventure of *Moana* that included the building project and endless travels was touched by the lives of many people not included in the text. Some contributed large amounts of time, energy, and dedication, while others gave only brief friendship, but all are a part of this wonderful story. Unfortunately, not all of these people are still with us, but I have listed them to place their names in the book and give appreciation for their contribution, however small or large. All the rest, you know who you are, and I will be forever grateful for your friendship and all you gave.

Building crew: Debs, Bill Sr., Bill Jr., Jay, Tom, Gary, Greg, Juan, Seb, Michael, John C, Chris, Harry S

Yard crew: Howard B, Shakey, Eddie

Deckhands: Jose, Cliff, Tomminator, Mike H, Steven T

Cooks: Kari, Pascale, Ali, Susie, Emma, Mandy, Fiona, Gaelle, Ogi, Nicole, Nadine

Agents: Pete S, Etienne & Pascal, Pire, Carrie, Rathman

Shippers and suppliers: Gary T, Mark W, Kobelt, Tom J, Dale D

Outside workers: Alistair, Gilley, Wayne, Xenek, Tonga David

Captains: Rey "Elvis," Craig D, Conrad B, Frank L, Rocka

Marinas: Bill Royster, Bill Kirby, Bill Acker, Shallum E

Taxi drivers: Billy, Ronny, Sancho, Tina, Jack M

Friends: Chief Hapthey, Chief Mike, Tokapae Moses, Nicole, Jesse E, "Pepe La Poo" Charlie, Jason K, Michael Selter

Readers/critics: Brenda Scott, Angie M, Azzura M ("Official Italian Reader"), Meike, Don C, Sandy

Legal counsel: Cris Wenthur

Consultants: Jeniffer Thompson and Chad Thompson at Monkey C Media, who taught me how to deliver a professional product

Copyeditor and proofreader: Lynette Smith at All My Best

HAME: A very distinguished title I gave my mentor and dear friend, Otto Lehrack. Famous author and ex-Marine, who believed in me when when I did not believe in myself. My HardAssMarineEditor!

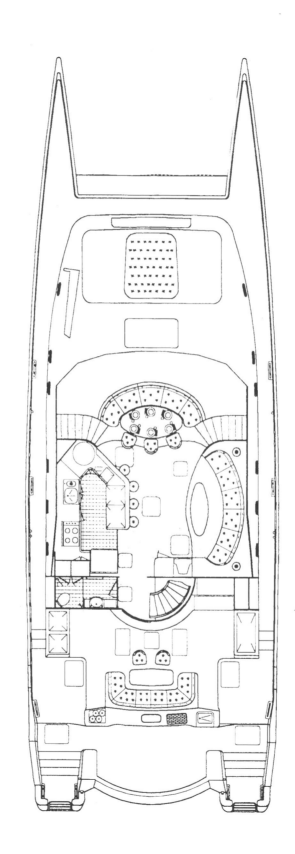